For
Brian

[signature]

TRUMPETS AND TUMULTS

Trumpets and Tumults

THE MEMOIRS OF A PEACEKEEPER

Major General Indar Jit Rikhye

MANOHAR
2002

First published 2002

© Major General Indar Jit Rikhye, 2002

All rights reserved. No part of this publication may be
reproduced or transmitted, in any form or by any means, without
prior permission of the author and the publisher

ISBN 81-7304-409-0

Published by
Ajay Kumar Jain for
Manohar Publishers & Distributors
4753/23 Ansari Road, Daryaganj
New Delhi 110 002

Typeset by
FineCurve Computers
1, Prahalaad Nagar
Meerut City 250 002

Printed at
Lordson Publishers Pvt. Ltd.
C-5/19 Rana Pratap Bagh
Delhi 110 007

In memory of
my Mother

Contents

Illustrations

Preface

On a short vacation in India in 1965, I made my usual stop at New Delhi to meet friends and to visit various officials, including some at Army Headquarters. I had by then completed five years of service seconded from the Indian Army to the United Nations. When I visited the headquarters I learned, as I had feared, that after my long separation from regular army service I could no longer expect to return to a normal army career in India. I asked the Government of India for permission to retire in 1967; permission was granted. I left the United Nations two years later.

Although I have published several works on UN peacekeeping, including an account of the withdrawal of UNEF I from Gaza and Sinai in 1967 and of the UN operations in the Congo in 1960-64, I have hesitated until now to write my memoirs. The reason for my hesitation has been simple: I left the two services content with my work and felt that I had little to explain or expound. Furthermore, my peers in the Indian Army and the United Nations, as well as numerous scholars and pundits, have published their own accounts of events in which I was involved. I may not always have agreed with their interpretations, but they have undoubtedly provided a rich source of description and analysis for the interested reader.

Recently, however, I was persuaded to reconsider the matter of writing my memoirs. The remarkable growth in the number and complexity of peacekeeping operations during the 1990s, and the many obstacles and setbacks that the peacekeepers encountered, generated an increasing demand for first-hand accounts of previous peacekeeping missions. Many former military commanders responded to this demand, publishing memoirs that included recollections of their peacekeeping experiences. I was reluctant to add to this literature until it was pointed out to me that my experience with peacekeeping— and with conflict resolution more generally—is unusual, if not unique, insofar as I have had the experience of working on three different yet parallel tracks of conflict resolution. First, I have had a broad and long experience of soldiering during both war and peace in India, where the military has often assisted the civilian government in maintaining law and order and rendering humanitarian assistance. Second, I have participated in UN peacekeeping at many different levels and in many different places. I have commanded a national contingent of peacekeepers, served as chief of staff and commander of a UN force, and been military adviser to two UN Secretary-Generals. In the latter capacity, I had a view of peacekeeping from the top. I assisted both the political leadership at the United Nations and the individual peacekeeping missions in organizing and managing operations. I was often called on by the Secretary-General to undertake various special assignments. On occasion, I was called on to assume the duties of the head of a peacekeeping mission. Third, after leaving the United Nations, I embarked on a career as a peace educator, a role that I played for twenty years and that included founding a peacekeeping institute.

I was tempted to name my memoirs *Soldier, Peacekeeper,* and *Peace Educator.* I am, however, more content with *Trumpets and Tumults.* I have always loved the sound of trumpets that called me to duty, and I am very happy to have escaped safely from the many tumults I was exposed to.

My memoirs are in five parts. Together, they not only chronicle my life but also throw light on some of the most momentous events of the twentieth century: the decline of the British Empire; the Middle Eastern and Italian campaigns of the Second World War; the Independence and Partition of India; the first clashes between India and Pakistan; the advent of UN peacekeeping; the Cuban missile crisis; the Congo peacekeeping mission; and the Six Days War. I do not wish for a moment to suggest that I was a key player in these events—even though I was a good deal more than a bystander in many of them—but I was well positioned to see events unfold both at the highest political levels and down in the trenches. In a tribute published in the memoirs of General Lord Ismay, Winston Churchill's chief of staff, Churchill wrote, "For many years he has held positions of high importance at the center of affairs, and he has an intimate command of events of the war." My responsibilities during my career were not directly comparable to "Pug" Ismay's in magnitude, but they ranged across the world.

Part I of this book is about my birth in an Indian family which was at the Sikh court when the British annexed the Punjab, and which remained aloof from the British for the next half century. It is about growing up as a Hindu with a British education and Muslim friends and neighbors. The struggle for Indian Independence had reached a formative stage when I decided to join the Indian Army. But for Mahatma Gandhi's intervention with my father, my parents would have stopped me from choosing the army as a career, because the British were increasingly using the army to suppress India's struggle for freedom. I was among the few hundred pre-War Indian officers to receive a regular commission from King George VI, and I joined a regiment with its origins in the Bengal Lancers.

Part II describes my experience as the first Indian officer in my regiment to set-off with British officers for the Second World War. Our regiment played a reconnaissance role and was often the lead unit in the defense of oilfields in northern Iraq, in operations in Iran, and in guarding the northern frontier of Syria. During the Italian campaign, I spent a year as a junior operations officer. I was the only Indian officer on the divisional staff. After that, I was given command of a lancer squadron in the Apennines in the winter of 1944-45 and later of the headquarters (support) squadron for the advance through north Italy. On my return to India at the end of the war, my regiment spent two years guarding the North West Frontier. At the time of the Partition of India, I was acting commandant of my regiment and remained with it for six weeks, serving under the flag of Pakistan.

Part III is about my service with the army in India. Within a week of my return from Pakistan, I headed an armored squadron to fight Pakistan's frontier tribal incursion into Kashmir. I returned to peacetime duties only after the force that I was with had driven the raiders out of the Kashmir Valley. Although Lt. Col. Leslie Sawhney preceded me by four months as the first Indian commandant of the Deccan Horse, a renowned tank regiment, I was the first to remain in command for a full, three-year tenure. Soon after that, I took the regiment to secure the Indian troops' southern flank in Jammu and Kashmir from Pakistani armor and other raiders.

Part IV is about my service as a United Nations peacekeeper. It began with my appointment as commander of the Indian contingent of UNEF, the UN operation charged with keeping the peace between Egypt and Israel. After six months with the force, I became the first person from the Third World to be appointed chief of staff of a UN force; I was later acting commander for a few months. At the end of two years in Gaza, I returned to India to command an infantry brigade group. After a short spell of airlifting troops to Ladakh, I was appointed military adviser to UN Secretary-General Dag Hammarskjöld. I served the next nearly ten years with the United Nations. I was commander of UNEF in 1967, when the force was caught up in the Six Days War. The subsequent reduction in UN peacekeeping operations obviated the need for a military adviser for the Secretary-General.

The last part of the book describes my role as a peace educator, the conception and foundation of the International Peace Academy, and my association with academia. During this period, I had a number of off-the-record conversations with key actors in contemporary conflicts. One of these encounters, with General Zia ul-Haq, president of Pakistan, is described in Chapter 17. As the reader will soon appreciate, the conflict between India and Pakistan touches me very deeply.

I wish to offer my thanks to three staff members (past and present) of the International Peace Academy—Dolores Fenn, Linda Margraff, and Florence Musaffi—for their help with research and word processing of the early drafts of this book; to my wife, Cynthia, for her advice and encouragement throughout my writing; to Ruth Forbes Young, the founder of the International Peace Academy, whose faith in my efforts and whose support remained constant; and to my esteemed friend, William N. Bancroft, who, since Ruth Forbes's death, has managed her trust and given me continued support. I am also grateful to Anthony Verrier, professor in the Department of Government at the University of Essex, United Kingdom, for his guidance in writing this book. Furthermore, I learnt more about writing memoirs after Charles Nelson, then vice president, the United Institute of Peace, Washington, D.C., arranged with the help of his wife Judy, also a biographer, for me to join a biography writing group of which she was the convener. I am grateful not only for the pains they took to facilitate my attendance but also for their gracious hospitality.

My search for editorial help started and happily ended with Nigel Quinney. He was familiar with my writing, having edited early chapters of my manuscript on UN peacekeeping while I was a fellow at the United States Institute of Peace in Washington, D.C. Born and educated in Britain, he has an understanding of the world I come from and where I spent most of my adult life. He has been generous in accepting this assignment, for which I will be ever thankful.

I sought advice in finding a suitable publisher for these memoirs from Pushpinder Singh Chopra, a respected Indian commentator on defense affairs and a friend of my son, Ravi, himself an established writer and commentator on defense and political affairs. I wish to convey my sincere appreciation to Ravi for his assistance and to Pushpinder for his helpful advice. Pushpinder, a son of the soldier-diplomat General Mohinder Singh Chopra (my brigade commander in 1948) and a son-in-law of Brigadier Gurbux Singh, an army associate and friend of mine, showed the manuscript to the latter.

At an enjoyable evening in Delhi in October 1999 with Gurbux Singh and his charming wife, Gurbux raised the kind of questions that only a friend of many years could have asked. What was new in the manuscript that was not already known? Why should anyone want to buy a book on the life of an army officer who had spent his life doing what he was expected to do?

In searching for an answer, I reflected on India's varied experiences since gaining independence. It fought a war with China, three wars with Pakistan, and several battles over lines of control in Jammu and Kashmir. It continues to deal with insurgency within and along its border states. Although India and Pakistan have now gained missile and nuclear capabilities, their armed forces are only just leaving behind post-Second World War weapons and equipment systems and adopting high-tech materiel. However, Indian defense forces are the fourth largest in the world, increasingly self-reliant in defense production and easily the most powerful in the region.

At the diplomatic level, India has maintained its strident leadership of the Third World, but its international prestige was severely dented by its defeat by China and by the death of Jawaharlal Nehru in 1964. In South Asia, it has long been an unpopular regional power. This began to change under the able leadership of Inder Kumar Gujral in the mid-1990s and the trend has continued over the past two years under Atal Behari Vajpayee. Although India has still far to go in eradicating poverty and providing essential services to its population of more than a billion people, it has matured as a democracy, improved its industry, and established a free market economy. Given that it also ranks among the world leaders in information technology, and that almost one-fifth of its population enjoys middle-class status, India can rightfully expect to become a world power in this millennium.

Indian leaders have much to learn from the experiences of other democracies and world powers. This book describes the behavior of nations, including the great powers, in dealing with complex issues of peace and security. The book also recounts episodes of high-level, high-stakes decision-making, some of which were crowned with success, others led to disaster. It is my hope that this book will provide some insights to Indian leaders and the Indian public as our nation strives to regain its status as a world power.

I asked Walter Hauser, Professor Emeritus of History at the University of Virginia, to review my manuscript and advise on a publisher. With his great understanding of India and his experience with his own publications there, he recommended my manuscript to Ramesh Jain of Manohar Publishers & Distributors, New Delhi. Walter also recommended my manuscript for review to Dr. Mushirul Hasan, Professor of History at Jamia Millia University, New Delhi, who is currently a visiting professor at the University of Virginia, Charlottesville. I am most grateful to Walter Hauser for his recommendations and to Professor Hasan for his suggestions. I met Mr. Jain on a visit to New Delhi in late 1999. Within a week of looking at my manuscript, he agreed to publish it. I am honored to join the list of his authors, a list that includes Walter Hauser and Mushirul Hasan. I greatly appreciate his many considerations and understanding in completing our common venture.

RIKHYE   MISAR-SUDAN

Godanya Rishi → s. Rattan Chand

s. Kanahya Lal — s. Mokham Chand

- s. Mohan Lal
- s. Sham Lal
- s. Nand Lal
- s. Dharam Chand — s. Sham Lal, s. Ram Chand
- s. Sukhdes Lal
- s. Madan Lal — m. Dayawanti

Two ds.

Bhagwan Das

three ds. incl. d. Thakro — m. Misar Kesho Das

m. 1 Durga Devi Bhardwaj   m. 2 Raj Rani Sudan

Basti Ram, Beli Ram — s. Megh Chand
s. Lachman Dass
d. Dhan Devi — m. Bindra Ban Sudan
s. Manmohan Nath, s. Raj Kumar, s. Raj Krishan

- s. Hira Lal
- d. Vidya Rani
- s. Satinder Lal
- s. Indar Jit Lal
- s. Sodarshan Lal
- d. Indra Rani
- s. Rajeshwar Lal
- s. Hemwant Lal

m. 1 Usha Erry   m. 2 Cynthia de Haan

s. Ravi Inder Lal   s. Bhalinder Lal

1m. Pamela Bunbury   2. Christian Komp   3. Rachna Gandotra

s. Evan   s. Kartikay

m. Anna-Lisa Johanson

m. Doris Catherine Hall

d. Kiran   d. Gaia

Family Tree

PART I

Growing Up in the Punjab

Khazanchi (Treasurer) Kanhaya Lal Rikhye, Maharaja Ranjit Singh's Sukerchukia *Khazana* (Treasury), Gujranwala, Punjab.

1

My Parents

I grew up in a happy and traditional Punjabi Hindu home. My parents were scions of two prominent Brahmin families that had gained fame and wealth during the Sikh rule in the Punjab in the nineteenth century. The records of the family, like the old history of India, were largely oral. On religious occasions, generations of Rikhyes were reminded that they descended from Godanya Rishi, who came to India in 1500 BC with the Aryans, an Indo-European tribe who had earlier crossed into Asia over the Caucasus. Presumably, his descendants answered the call to become Brahmins when Manu, the first traditional king of India, introduced the caste system. The earliest written records concerning the Rikhye family were found from the 1760s with the *pandays*, or priests, in Varanasi, a premier Hindu holy city.

My mother's family, the Misar-Sudans, must have gained prestige and wealth earlier than my father's. An ancestor of the Misar line was royal treasurer to the Sukerchukia Sikh chiefs from about 1780, and was followed by his son and his grandson, Misar Beli Ram, in the same position at Ranjit Singh's court. Ranjit Singh was the Sikh maharaja who unified the Sikh chiefs and gained control of north India. My paternal great-grandfather, Kanhaya Lal, when barely sixteen and from a poor Brahmin family of an obscure village near Sialkot, went to Lahore to seek work and a better life at the Sikh court. One day, while staying at a free *serai* (inn) of a Sikh *gurdwara* (temple) next to the fort, he sang in yearning for his home and family, and his melodious voice drew the attention of the court. The maharaja sent for the lad the next morning and was impressed. On learning that the boy was a Brahmin, an idea came to the maharaja's mind. His minister royal, Misar Beli Ram, was without a male heir and the boy would make a perfect son for him.

I learned of my family background from my elders through stories which they often related to me. I recall conversations with my mother's grandmother at a wedding at Dalwal, District Jhelum, my mother's maternal ancestral home. Beji, as my great-grandmother was addressed by everyone in the family, was barely twelve years old when she was married to Lachman Das, the only grandson of Misar Beli Ram. Lachman Das died at a young age. Beji had a son who too died and her surviving daughter became my maternal grandmother. Beji assumed responsibility for managing the vast family estates, the tenants of which were loyal and mostly Muslim. At harvest time she would go to her villages to collect her share from the sale of the crop. In those days, Pathan tribes would often raid across the Indus. She had heard that during Maharaja Ranjit Singh's rule the tribes were too afraid to come anywhere near the Indus. She added in admiration, "The famous Sikh general Hari Singh Nalwah had subdued the tribesmen and frightened them to such a level that the Pathans quieted their wailing children by invoking Nalwah's name." The British now ruled, and they had not yet succeeded in dealing with the Pathans; the villages between the Indus and Jhelum suffered annual raids. Beji was caught in one of such raids. The tenants saved her life, but only after a Pathan raider had charged at her, torn her earrings from her ears, and ridden away.

On a visit to my father's ancestral home at Gujranwala, forty miles north of Lahore, we drove through the crowded market, or *mandi*, to reach our *haveli*, or mansion. We left the car in a street just off the square in front of the municipality building, the birthplace of Maharaja Ranjit Singh, and walked a short distance to the alley behind our *haveli*. At one end of the alley, behind Ranjit Singh's old *haveli*, a few steps led to a wide terrace with a wide, heavy wooden gate. Father's uncle, Sham Lal, occupied the rooms above the entrance. A small courtyard with a well in a corner had a large reception room on one side and entrance to the residence on the other. A dark staircase, lit with oil lamps, led to the four living floors. The women shared all the household chores. The men, with the exception of Sham Lal, were joyfully devoted to cricket and hockey. The men were also enthusiastic supporters of an *akhara*, a wrestling club where the traditional Indian form of the sport was practiced.

Pandit Sham Lal, retired from a lucrative law practice at Lahore, had educated my father. When he was growing up, my father saw little of his wandering father, and so regarded Sham Lal more like a father than an uncle. Addressed affectionately as Bare Lalaji, Sham Lal lived in a suite a short flight of steps up from the entrance hall. I recognized him immediately from his photographs when I walked into his book-lined parlor. He sat in a wooden chair with a cane seat and back. The room smelled of pipe tobacco smoke, a scent different from that of my father's *hookah*, or water pipe. He looked old, with bent shoulders, gray moustache, and a wisp of hair behind the ears on his otherwise bald head. He was fair skinned with a flush of pink in his cheeks. As I bent down to touch his feet in obeisance, he patted my head with his right hand. I noticed that it was shaking. He asked me to sit in a nearby chair, then picked up his pipe. His hand shook the whole time he held it. My father had told me that this debilitation, caused by Parkinson's disease, had forced Sham Lal to give up his practice.

He asked me about school. Did I have any plans for the future? I said that I intended to go to college. Had I thought of becoming a barrister? I replied that I knew that he was among the few barristers in the Punjab and that my maternal grandfather was a lawyer, but I had not thought yet of life after college. Then he spoke at length about how lawyers help people and the country. He said, "Your father chose the medical profession under the influence of Colonel Sutherland, the principal of King Edward Medical College, Lahore, and husband of my Princess Bamba. Although I had brought up your father as my son, I did not wish to interfere because the Princess was also keen that Madan Lal become a doctor. Later, when my own son, Sukhdes Lal, was born, he wanted to follow the example of his older brother."

Turning toward me he added, "Now you are the first of my grandchildren. I would like you to think of joining the legal profession. You will have my library and I am sure Bindra Ban [my mother's father] would be pleased to leave his to you as well. All our client families will seek your legal counsel. I can read in your face that you will do well."

Bare Lalaji's reference to Princess Bamba had excited my curiosity.

I had only a vague knowledge of our families' connections to the Sikh rulers. It was only now, while I was staying in a house next to where Maharaja Ranjit Singh was born and on a street whose houses had been owned by famous Sikh generals of the past, that my interest was raised. So I asked my uncle why Princess Bamba was so important in his life. I must have touched a chord: for the next hour or so Bare Lalaji spoke of family history, as I sat enthralled. At 1 p.m. a maid brought his lunch and told me that my mother had called for me to return to the main house for my meal. I never had another opportunity to talk to Bare Lalalji, as he soon departed from this Earth. Many years later, when I began to collect bits of information about my family from various archives, including the India Office Library in London, I was able to put the memory of my conversation with my grand uncle and my father's benefactor into the coherent picture that I describe below.

On his adoption by Misar Beli Ram, my paternal ancestor Kanhaya Lal served his apprenticeship at the royal treasury in the Lahore fort and on occasions of state was called upon to display the Koh-i-Noor. The largest known diamond at that time, the Koh-i-Noor was acquired from Shah Shuja, the exiled king of Afghanistan, in return for safe refuge. When a son was born to Misar Beli Ram's new wife, the maharaja appointed Kanhaya Lal to Sukerchukia misal treasury at Gujranwala. Kanhaya Lal bought a *haveli* next to the maharaja's in an alley full of homes of the great Sikh generals: the Nalwahs, the Chimnis, and Mokham Chand, younger brother of Kanhaya Lal and commander of the Sikh army sent to capture Multan.

When Ranjit Singh died on 27 June 1839, he left several claimants to the throne. His youngest son, Dalip Singh, a minor, emerged to become the ruler. But confusion continued, when quarrels and jealousies between Ranjit's widows led to the assassination of the prime minister, Dhian Singh, and Sindhianwala chiefs murdered Dhian Singh's favored ruler, Sher Singh. These events not only tore apart the Sikh state but also led to war with the British East India Company. The British annexed the Punjab and sold Jammu and Kashmir to the late prime minister's brother, Gulab Singh.

Misar Beli Ram had refused to accede to the demands of both the royal widows and the prime minister that he hand over the royal treasury, including the precious diamond Koh-i-Noor, to them. After Dhian Singh's death, his son Hira Singh, on assuming the prime minister's office, put to death the enemies of his father. He also ordered the killing of Misar Beli Ram, who had stood in the favor of the great maharaja and was strongly opposed to the aggrandizement of the Jammu family. Beli Ram's widow escaped with her young son to Dalwal, near Jhelum, and withdrew behind the walls of the Misar ancestral estate there. Before his arrest, Beli Ram had entrusted the diamond to a member of his family, Misar Megh Raj. When the British-appointed 'resident' (the term used for British representatives to Indian princes) arrived in Lahore, Megh Raj handed over the diamond to him. Misar Beli Ram and his family had thus complied with the wish of Ranjit Singh, that the diamond should belong only to the ruler of the Punjab. Later, the stone was passed on to Queen Victoria and, after cutting, was mounted in the crown of the Queen Mother. When I first viewed the diamond at the Crown Jewels exhibit at the Tower of London, I was overwhelmed with emotion. My two sons were with me and looked at me in amazement, as they had never seen me in such a state.

While the Misars took refuge in their ancestral home, Kanhaya Lal withdrew from public office to look after his acquired estate and his family. My ancestors, declining service with their British rulers, built on their estates and passed on to their successors a strong work ethic and a commitment to serving the community. Kanhaya Lal's elder son, Sham Lal, whom I met so many years later in the family *haveli*, was appointed as a Persian translator at Dalip Singh's court. Shortly after the British takeover of the Punjab, Dalip was exiled, first, beyond Delhi and, later, to England. Sham Lal managed to abscond from his family and join the prince in England. When Dalip became involved in plots for his return to the Punjab, his relationship with Queen Victoria and her government deteriorated severely. As the situation worsened, Sham Lal took up legal studies on the side. He was called to the bar at Lincoln's Inn, coincidentally at the same time as Mohandas Karamchand Gandhi, who was destined to lead India to its Independence. After Dalip Singh died, Sham Lal returned to the Punjab and started his practice at the Lahore High Court. Gandhi went to South Africa. After the First World War, Gandhi became increasingly involved in India's Independence struggle and saw Sham Lal on his visits to Lahore. But Sham Lal, although sympathetic to Gandhi's course, refrained from participating in politics, in keeping with the family tradition.

After the end of Sikh rule there was little contact between the Misars and Rikhyes. However, the coming decades were to witness dramatic developments for the two families. Sham Lal had no male heir and sent for his nephew Madan Lal, the eldest Rikhye male child, from Gujranwala. Madan Lal was placed in the best day-school in Lahore, Central Model School. It was near the end of his schooling that Colonel Sutherland, married to Princess Bamba, the daughter of Maharaja Dalip Singh, was appointed principal of King Edward Medical College. Under Sutherland's influence Father joined his college. Father graduated during the First World War and again, on Sutherland's advice, joined the Indian Medical Service (IMS) of the Indian Army.

Father was first married when he was eighteen years old, after he had begun his medical studies. His wife, a Bhardwaj from Hafizabad, near Gujranwala, remained with his mother. His wife gave birth to two sons, Hira Lal and Satinder Lal, and a daughter, Vidya Rani. What with his studies and military duties, Father saw little of his family. He was soon posted to the Imperial Expeditionary Force in Mesopotamia and was appointed regimental medical officer to an Indian cavalry regiment that was part of the Bengal Lancers group.

On his return to India, Father was devastated to learn that his wife had broken her hip and had died soon after that. An uncle of my father arranged his marriage to Raj Rani, the only child of Dhan Devi, the heiress to Misar estates scattered from Lahore to Jhelum, and Bindra Ban Sudan, a brilliant and rising Lahore lawyer. Raj was fourteen, very pretty and petite, and had attended the local convent school for a year. She was withdrawn from the school after relatives protested that she was being sent to a "foreign school". She had private tutors, who educated her in Hindi and Urdu. As the only child for the first eight years of her life, she was spoiled but had a great sense of humor, loved music, and had an enchanting voice. It proved to be a great marriage and it was my good fortune to be born as their first child a year later in 1920.

The Afghans, seeking their independence and taking advantage of Britain's military fatigue at the end of the First World War, launched what came to be known as the Third Afghan War in 1919. My father, promoted to acting major, was appointed to the Chitral Expeditionary Force and was away when I was born at the home of my maternal grandparents at the entrance to Anarkali bazaar in Lahore. I was a few months old when Father was posted to Sialkot Cantonment and moved into a bungalow with his new bride and child. Since the IMS was a mounted corps, trumpets could be heard throughout the day. I was told later that the sound of the nearby hospital lines' trumpeters invariably stopped my wailing. I have always loved the sound of trumpets and I was to answer their call as an adult.

On his demobilization, Father joined his old medical college to complete his doctorate and thereafter was appointed house physician. He specialized in tuberculosis, a killer at that time. My parents rented a town house between Anarkali and the Mall and gathered the family, including my half-brothers and sister, together for the first time. Father's subsequent postings out of Lahore were mostly to districts in West Punjab that also provided easy access to the provincial capital and to the family estates of both my parents. Father retired from service (though he did do charitable consultation thereafter) about the time that India was hurtling toward the Partition and Independence. My parents divided their time between their house in Lahore and a bungalow they rented for the summer in Dalhousie, about two hundred miles north in the lower ranges of the Himalayas.

After the Partition and the Independence of India, my parents, like millions of others, lost their homes. They subsisted on Father's government pension and moved around India. During the summer of 1948, Father, among a small group of senior retired Punjabi doctors, was invited by Lady Edwina Mountbatten, the vicereine and head of the British Red Cross, to establish medical facilities for refugees. He was offered a post at Faridabad, a planned industrial center just beyond Delhi, on the road to Agra. He gladly accepted the offer. My parents roughed it out, living in a tent for nearly two years. When the Punjab government decided to build an industrial city for refugees at Rajpura, fifteen miles north of Ambala on the Grand Trunk Road, Father was transferred there at the request of the state government. One day, after his morning rounds, he came home and complained of a headache. Within minutes he died of a cerebral hemorrhage. My mother moved to a farm near Ambala, Haryana, gifted to her by her mother. It took a few more months for settlement of the compensation claims for my paternal family estate left in Pakistan. This made it possible for mother to buy a house in Shimla, Himachal Pradesh.

I had always spent my annual vacation with my parents, except during the Second World War. After my father's death, I visited my mother more often until I was satisfied that she had settled down comfortably. I continued to visit her after I had moved to the United States. My Shimla visits became an annual ritual.

My last visit to Mother was in May and June 1995. On a beautiful morning, after breakfast, I stood by her side as she leaned on the wrought-iron fence on the edge of the terrace that ran the length of the family house. Like other houses in our town, our house is constructed on the side of a sloping hill. There is an untended footpath below the stone foundation walls of the house, dividing our estate from other properties below. Further down, the hill slopes toward a group of derelict houses that are a perpetual eyesore. Happily, the wall is covered with wild rose bushes that are often laden with bunches of white flowers. The owners of the houses have let the buildings deteriorate because they get little rent, even though the state capital is afflicted with an acute shortage of housing. The tenants are lower-grade state office workers who do not earn enough to afford better rented accommodation. The Tenancy Acts protect both the tenants from eviction and the landlords from an obligation to make many repairs. The house owners have to wait and pray for the early collapse of the walls and for the roofs to fall, forcing the tenants to abandon the houses. Once free of their tenants, the owners will make a killing by selling the land at the current inflated real estate values and throw in the rubble as a bonus.

On this early June 1995 morning, with a few wisps of clouds high up in the blue sky, the bright sun brought out many hues of the abundant forest in Annandale, the verdant valley below us. When the British ruled India, the valley was a favorite of theirs for picnics, fetes, outdoor excursions, cricket, and pony races. After Independence, there appeared an Army Physical Training Camp. An old nine-hole golf course on the fringe of the grounds was revived by the army staff when they returned to Shimla after India's Independence. The crescent-shaped valley of Annandale is formed by two parallel spurs. The main Shimla spur is covered with old, towering deodar trees. The spur to the south of our house, the original site of the British camp in the Shimla hills, has a number of historic houses. The Kennedy House is the site of the first house built by Captain Charles Pratt Kennedy, the first British superintendent of the hill states to receive tribute from the local hill chiefs after the Gurkha wars of 1815-16. With an increase in demand for housing, Kennedy negotiated with the raja of Keonthal, ruler of much of the area required for expansion, and with the raja of Patiala, who too owned some of the land in the vicinity. By early 1824 a few private cottages and a sanitarium were built for British civilians and officers escaping from the dusty, hot, and mosquito-infested plains of the Punjab. Now Vigyan Bhavan, the Himachal Pradesh State Assembly, stands on this spur. On the neighboring hill is the residence of the commander-in-chief of the newly established Army Training Command, which has its headquarters in the old army headquarters on the Mall, closer to the center of the town. Lord Roberts conducted the Afghan wars of 1878 and 1880 from here. Beyond the army commander's house is the tall mast of the recently erected TV relay station, and on the adjoining hill is the majestic Viceregal Lodge, built with granite stone and last occupied by Lord Louis Mountbatten of Burma. The Indian Institute of Advanced Studies is housed there now. All the furnishings vanished from the house when the British left, just as it was emptied of its authority and influence. This is where Lord Mountbatten brought Pandit Jawaharlal Nehru and Mohammed Ali Jinnah to sign the agreement that divided India into the separate independent states of India and Pakistan.

To the north of our house are the mountains of Kulu and Spiti, covered with pine, deodar, wild fruit, and rhododendrons as large as apple trees. Kulu and Spiti rise gradually from Shimla's altitude of about 7,100 feet to form the curving, snowy line of the peaks of the Greater Himalayas. The nearby range carries the road to the Sutlej River some thirty miles from our town. Popular picnic areas and the

Naldera golf course are halfway along the route, by which our water is also brought to town. The north and south ranges join to the west, with a narrow entrance that provides a clear view of the plains below on most days. This entrance is also an easy helicopter approach that makes Annandale a natural helipad. With an unhindered view of the valley from our house, we can see with ease the comings and goings of visiting VIPs. The arrival and departure of helicopters has ceased to be a novelty for our household, including our two family dogs, who generally ignore the noisy whirring birds. But sometimes, knowing that the rest of us are not paying attention to the visitors, they vent their anger at the noise-making machines with lusty barks.

The cool climate of Shimla attracted not only the invalid and retired British officers but also the British viceroy to spend part of the hot months away from steamy Calcutta. Shortly after Shimla hills opened to British visitors early in the nineteenth century, up-country tours by the governor-general of the East India Company gradually lengthened to the entire summer. It was not long after the first viceroy visited Shimla in 1821 that it became the summer capital of the British in India. After the annexation of the Punjab, the British built a provincial capital here for the summer as well. From then until the Second World War, Shimla bustled with activity: people who came to conduct business with the British Indian and Punjab governments; officials and petitioners; merchants and tradesmen; and British families escaping the heat. During the Second World War, a greatly enlarged British Indian Government and a vast army headquarters, supporting some two million men under arms, made New Delhi the eastern hub of the war effort. This shift of the administration to New Delhi and away from Shimla was reinforced by the availability of electric power and the advent of air-conditioning, which made it easier to cope with the hot weather.

Many of the houses in the town exhibit the Victorian and the Edwardian architecture of the period. Parts of Shimla—for example, the Mall, which extends from the former Imperial Secretariat for about 2 miles to the former Punjab Secretariat in East Shimla, now our state secretariat—still retain a look of a small English town. Luckily, the municipality has introduced measures to preserve some of the town's most handsome buildings.

Spring had already arrived when I reached Shimla in 1995. From spring until the advent of the monsoons in July is a good time to come up here. The sky is usually clear and the air is crisp and fresh. The distant mountain peaks of the Himalayas can be easily identified. The flowers in the valleys and on the mountainsides are abundant, beautiful, and fragrant. It warms up by June and a hot day invites a sudden shower to cool temperatures. With schools on vacation in the plains, the town is full of tourists and there is barely room to walk on the Mall. The onset of the monsoon only adds to the tourist population. But the residents find this time trying because of the heavy rains that soak everything. I have often been obliged to come in the rainy season, though I like it the least.

The two seasons before and after the monsoons are also convenient for other members of the family to visit Shimla. In fact, we three brothers who live away from home try to coordinate our visits. The youngest brother, Hemi, and his wife, Nimmi, as well as our only sister, Indra, with her son Sonny and his family, reside in their separate homes, all within the Rikhye Niwas compound. I am the only member of my immediate family who lives abroad. I have been in the United States for more than forty years. I have lived with Cynthia—my American wife of twenty-seven years and before that my companion of twelve years—in Manhattan and Bronxville, New York, and now in Virginia, where we have a house in the Piedmont between Charlottesville and the Blue Ridge Mountains.

We children addressed our mother as Bhabiji, but our children and grandchildren called her Biji. On my visit in 1995, she was frailer than when I had seen her last in Shimla, and the arthritis in her left knee had made walking difficult and painful. She carried a heavy, formidable-looking stick to lean on, though it seemed to me to be of little help. Biji always enjoyed her walks. Some ten years earlier, she could walk most days up a very stiff climb to the Mall to shop or visit her club for a chat with her old friends and a hand or two of rummy. In her advanced age she would walk down the road to Annandale through the narrow winding Kaithu bazaar, crowded by Himalayan-style low wooden houses with ornate woodwork and murals of Hindu gods on the walls, and by small but cozy general stores selling everything from commodities, spices, and sweets to electronic goods. Further down, the blacktop footpath wound to the Krishna and Shiva temples. Here, amid the loud incantations of the priest and ringing of the temple bell by devotees as they entered the temple, Biji would offer a short prayer. She would always put some rupees in my hand and ask me to make the offering while she invoked the blessing of our gods for me. Though the difference in age between us was comparatively small, I would always feel like the toddler that I once was.

Both Biji and I relished these walks together. She opened up to talk about her concerns, usually matters dealing with Rikhye Niwas, our family house, named after the villa my parents left behind in Lahore, and the temple I had built for her near her farm in Haryana. She, like her mother before her, was a respected leader at religious services and was adored for her recital of *bhajans*, sung in her enchanting voice in praise of Lord Krishna. And she was always called on to resolve conflicts and issues within her extended family, among her children (or rather their spouses) and their progeny and her remaining vast network of *sudan* (paternal) and *missar* (maternal) relatives. Usually, people came to her for advice and help. On occasions, when she felt it was necessary, she did not hesitate to intervene of her own accord.

Biji liked to talk to me and felt comforted by our conversations. After my father died in 1951, although I had an older stepbrother, it was always assumed that I was the next in line to accept family responsibilities. Besides, I was my mother's first born. It was not possible for me to fill the void in the life of my mother, widowed at age forty-five, but I always tried. This is not only because I was close to my mother but also because of the responsibility imparted to me by custom and upbringing.

In the aftermath of the tragedy of the Partition of India, our family, like many others from West Punjab, was unprepared and became refugees with few personal possessions and only the money left in our pockets. Now, Biji and I could look back over the last nearly fifty years with the satisfaction that together we had been able, with the help of judicious compensatory arrangements established by the Indian Government, to recover a good part of the family estate left in Pakistan and build a new life for ourselves and our family. Our mutually supportive relationship and affection had survived the test of time.

This day, as I stood with Biji on the terrace, we observed at least three forest fires. Biji's attention turned from the fires in the woods toward the dust-haze covered plains of the Punjab. Pointing at the TV tower she commented, in the witty style typical of her Sudan ancestry, on the uneven quality of Indian TV programs, and she regretted that the signal from this relay tower had obliterated Lahore TV, "which we could pick up easily at our high altitude. I enjoyed their plays and Punjabi humor". We chitchatted on TV programming for a while. I find it hard to understand the Hindi as spoken on the Indian airwaves because the language's Sanskrit component has been emphasized at the expense of its Persian element. Similarly, in Pakistan the Urdu language now makes greater use of its Arabic component than of its Persian element. The evolution of a common language for the subcontinent so carefully nurtured since the Mughal emperor Akbar has been reversed. Not only are India and Pakistan divided but they seem to be relentless in their efforts to become ever more different. Biji, like most of us, missed the old plain, unsubtle humor of the Punjab.

After a pause she lifted her face toward the west to get a better look at the plains in the distance. Then she turned to me and said, "I sometimes think of Lahore and our past in the West Punjab. I think of your father who was taken away from me too soon after the Partition. He was a good husband and father and I have missed him terribly all these forty-five years that I have been widowed. God has been very kind to me and my children and I have fulfilled all that your father had wanted to do. I performed his *sradh* (an annual memorial service performed in a period prescribed by the priests) and fed the poor and the pundits, and made offerings at the temple below us. I don't know if any of my children will remember to offer *sradh* for your father, but I have done my part."

I was about to say something, anything, not knowing what to say, but her poor hearing saved me from uttering some nonsense. She continued, "I have completed all my religious ceremonies for my departure from this world. I have dictated to Indra and Hemi my last wishes. I want to go over it with you when we meet for tea." Just then, there was loud barking from Raja, one of our dogs, and heavy thumps on the corrugated roof of our house, which shook like in a minor earthquake. A huge langur, a monkey almost the size of an adult human and with a black face and gray coat, leapt from the roof on to the upper terrace, raced across it, and jumped for the pine tree that was once partly burned by lightening, behind Indra's house, and Raja in a full chase that ended abruptly at the edge of the upper terrace. All of a sudden there was total pandemonium, with the servants running around, trying to control Raja and Victor, the other dog, who had been awakened from his midmorning slumber. Nimmi came tearing down the awkward, winding high brick steps from her house, loudly complaining that the langur had messed up the only pear tree, which for once had a good crop. One of the Gurkhas on Hemi's staff cleared the mess under the pear tree and, after much bemoaning by Nimmi over the loss of the fruit, it was quiet again. Through all this chaos Biji had obviously forgotten what she had said to me. I preferred to shelve the discussion on Biji's last rites until I was better prepared for it.

Najko, Biji's graceful hill woman caretaker, came to Biji from the house. As we turned to enter the parlor, Biji turned to Najko and me and said, "What was there to get so upset about by the damage to the pear crop. They are not fit to eat and it is hard to make anything out of them. The langurs come every year to loot the pears just as they ripen. They chew a few and throw them away, as they find them tasteless. Fancy relishing the pears that langurs reject." Najko reminded us that it was time for tea.

When my sons, nephews, and nieces were attending schools in Shimla, they enjoyed high tea with Biji on the weekends. The school food was bare of taste and rather inadequate. So, the children depended on extras that were called "tuck". Biji had an occasional tea party for her friends and visitors but preferred to give lunches. Since the use of automobiles is restricted, most people walk in our town. As the weather is unpredictable, social life is mostly limited to the daytime.

Never shy to say what was on her mind, Biji looked forward to the late morning teatime, when she could discuss her agenda and express her views. Often, Biji's mind would pick up a thread, leading her back several years. She was a great storyteller and we, having grown up in times of silent pictures, hand-cranked gramophones, and wireless radios, had relied on her storytelling or book reading to quench our increasing thirst for entertainment and knowledge. As adults, we were still entranced by her family anecdotes and vignettes, which she wove with her incredible capacity with words and humor. I know of my family, my ancestors, and our past mostly from Biji, for virtually all papers, photographs, and indeed everything else that the family possessed connecting us with our past was left in Pakistan and from all accounts destroyed. Only some family photographs and documents relating to the family estates in Pakistan survived, and they were in possession of my eldest brother, Hira, and my father's first cousin, Sukhdes. Hira and Sukhdes were posted to army stations in what remained of free India, and therefore they escaped the loss of personal belongings suffered by those of us who came from Pakistan.

Mother had become quite weak over the past year. She was sleeping longer and resting often during the day. I realized that she could go any day, so I spent most of my remaining time in India at home. My brothers who also lived away from Shimla had always tried to come during my visits. I was glad that they came again, making it possible for all Biji's children to be together with her and share a happy week.

This was the last time I saw her: she died peacefully in October 1995 at the age of ninety-one. In accordance with her wishes, her ashes were immersed in the Ganges at Hardwar. On the first anniversary of her death, a religious fete was held at her temple in Semla village near Ambala, Haryana. A prominent priest presided over the ceremonies, which were attended by five hundred villagers. Biji's women relatives and friends sang her favorite *bhajans* and my sister Indra's son-in-law, Purushotam Dutt Sharma, a retired rear admiral of the Indian Navy, delivered the eulogy in fluent Hindi. Then, all Biji's children served lunch to the blind, the handicapped, and the poor, some three hundred in all. The fete concluded with a meal for everyone else. The large attendance of the fete on a working day demonstrated Biji's popularity as a devotee of Krishna. Although she did not reach sainthood as her mother had before her, she had established a reputation for generosity and sagacity.

Her passing has ended an era. Biji managed to continue traditions of the two families who had reunited after the advent of the British in the Punjab. She led the rehabilitation of our immediate family after Father's sudden death in early 1951. I supported her efforts, but as I was busy serving first India and later the United Nations, her personal watch over the future of the family was crucial. After her mother's death, she took over the social and religious responsibilities of the *sudans* and *missars*. Her aristocratic style, generosity, wisdom, and selfless affection are sorely missed.

My annual ritual has come to an end.

2

My Youth

I started school in 1925 at Shahpur, where Father was appointed superintendent of a jail for prisoners afflicted with tuberculosis (or "TB" as it was commonly called). Shahpur was about three miles from the east bank of the Jhelum River. It lay along the historic route that led from central Asia, through the North West Frontier, across the narrows of the Indus, and after traversing the Mianwali desert reached Khushab, where it crossed the ford at the Chenab River entering the rich irrigated lands of the Punjab. From the Punjab, the route continued east to Lahore and beyond to the Ganges Valley. The British had provided links to the frontier with railways, and had built railroad bridges across the rivers. Shahpur and the surrounding area had prospered under the British, who had overseen the conversion of the desert into rich agricultural lands. Famous Muslim clans, the Ghakhars, Noons, and Tiwanas, populated the region, filling the ranks of the Indian cavalry and displaying fierce loyalty to their benefactors. Their tribal chiefs as well as landlords and the few professionals in the area frequently called on my father for medical advice or for company. Relatives and friends came more often for treatment than for social visits. My parents were only too pleased to have company in an otherwise lonely post.

Shahpur, with its fertile agricultural and grazing lands, had attracted many Muslim clan chiefs and over the centuries had become an important town and an administrative center. The advent of irrigation caused the administrative center to be switched in the early twentieth century to Sargodha, a new town built by British architects with the help of two young Sikh landlords-turned-contractors, Sobha Singh and Uttam Singh Duggal, who were later to build New Delhi and prosper.

The new towns in the region were well designed and their development strictly controlled. Shahpur was built around two crossroads, with shops, produce market, and municipal buildings in the center. The police station was at the edge of town and the jail was just beyond the town limits, where cultivated fields spread out, surrounded by planted trees. Our rented house belonged to a wealthy landowner who preferred the night life of Lahore to country living. The house, placed on the road to Sargodha, was large to accommodate our growing brood, and had separate rooms for guests and an enclosed yard at the back for *zenana*, or women's quarters. A spacious verandah ran the length of the house, parallel to the road. There was a privet hedge, flower beds, and lawns where we could play, sit out in the summer evenings, or bask in the winter sun. Another enclosed area included servant quarters, cowsheds, a poultry and goat enclosure, and a carriage house for the horse and the two-wheeled *tonga* that it drew. Daily, a gang of volunteer prisoners, on parole and free of TB, came by. They not only provided labor but also became playmates to us children. Mother served them the same food she served to our household staff, who mostly ate what we did. Our breakfast and the afternoon tea were different, for my parents had taken to English-style food for these meals, whereas the staff and many of our house-guests preferred purely Indian menus. Duty at the superintendent's residence was popular with prisoners, for Father gave them maximum remission for good behavior.

At Shahpur, Mother assumed full responsibility for the house. Aunt Dayawanti kept Hira, the eldest son from Father's former marriage, at Gujranwala. Hira was a year older than Mother and proved too obdurate for Father, so Aunt Dayawanti took him back to his school. My sister Vidya, like Mother, was married early, to a tutor of a small princely state in the Shimla hills. Only Satinder, who became the eldest child at Shahpur, came with us. We were brought up as one family and no one would dare to even hint that Satinder and I were born of different mothers.

The local school was basic, with Urdu as the medium of instruction. Satinder and I had tutors at home to bring us up to standard for our future education. Attending school in a small town in rural surroundings provided us an opportunity to spend our early lives in the grassroots society of India. Life in Lahore would perhaps have made it easier for us to advance in our studies and at sports, but our understanding of India at large would have been scanty. More importantly, growing up with village and small-town children and later being educated at the best schools in India certainly made me comfortable in any social group. I grew up in the belief that all men are equal. Some of us had a few advantages, but that did not make us superior.

Shahpur was mostly Muslim. Friends of my parents and the people they dealt with were generally Muslim, as was our household staff. From childhood, I have never been bothered by people of different faiths, although I do want to know their beliefs, because the cultural and social dimensions of religion do influence personal attitudes. We children did not want for religious and spiritual instruction, because every morning and at dusk my parents prayed in a corner of the living-room made into a miniature temple. On religious festivals, we went to the local temple. My parents supported the annual celebrations of Janmastami (Krishna's birthday) and Ramlila (the staging of *Ramayana* legends). In time, my music lessons advanced sufficiently to enable me to sing the role of Sita in *Ramayana*, for which I was rewarded with a gold medal, the first of many that I was destined to win for music.

Shahpur had many other attractions. On festive days or visits by the governor of the Punjab, there were sports in a large field set aside for this purpose. People came from surrounding villages in their best clothes, their horses bridled and saddled in polished brass and leather, coats groomed, and manes and tails well dressed. The colorful horse carriages were polished and shining and the array of automobiles on these occasions was a rarity for our sleepy town. The sons of the rich would bring a galaxy of cars from the playgrounds of Europe, which they normally showed off at the racecourses of Bombay, Delhi, and Lahore.

The popular sport was *kabaddi*—which was then quite a popular game all over the Indian subcontinent. There were blood sports too. Cock-fighting was common in most villages. But these special occasions included exhibition fights between bulldogs and wild boar. Dogs were often torn apart in the fights, but occasionally a boar would rather try for freedom than fight. In these cases, the drum beats would grow louder, as horsemen with lances were let loose. Many would no doubt now call this sport cruel and primitive, but it should be viewed in the perspective of those times.

It was shortly after Father had bought a 1928 Dodge convertible and engaged our big mustachioed driver, Ghulam Mohammed, that we woke up one morning amid a lot of activity. A telegram had arrived during the night from Lahore that my sister Vidya, after the birth of her second child, was very ill and was arriving at Sargodha by the morning train. Mother had taken the car to fetch her from the station seventeen miles from our house. When they arrived, Vidya was indeed very ill. She never recovered, and died a few days later. The household went into Punjabi-style mourning, where women must cry and wail aloud every time someone comes to offer their condolences. Never having witnessed mourning before, we children, unable to control ourselves, joined in the crying until we fell asleep of utter exhaustion.

In the early 1930s, the Punjab government decided to centralize treatment of infectious diseases under the Health Department and the special jail at Shahpur for prisoners suffering from TB was closed. We, the children, were ready to go to a proper school and our parents looked forward to their return to Lahore. Meanwhile, Father was given temporary charge of the medical services of Sargodha district.

A memorable experience at Sargodha was Satinder's and my introduction to airplanes. One day we were stealthily sucking ripe mangoes dangling from the branches of a tree when we heard a noisy machine coming over the tops of the trees. It looked like an ugly version of a European roadster that we saw occasionally and that was owned by the wealthy children of the clan leaders. We jumped off the trees and raced to the end of the orchard to see the machine land in the field. We recognized it as an airplane. As we climbed over the fence and approached the machine, a red face with a large blond mustache, cocooned in dark brown leather, frantically waved us back. Then the engine roared and the airplane took off. Later, Father told us that the RAF at Chaklala, Rawalpindi, used the field to practice emergency landings. Satinder and I really took to the airplane and the exciting prospect of aviation. Years later, we both ended up flying airplanes.

In the early 1930s Father was posted back to Lahore, where Satinder, Sodarshan, and I joined Central Model School and started regular studies. Cricket was compulsory and each class spent half a day each week in turn at the pitch for practice. I also played soccer, joined the Boy Scouts, and was persuaded by the Gurkha band master to play the flute in the fife-and-drum band.

After a year, we moved to a new housing development, Chauburji Colony, built for the staff of the Punjab secretariat. The community's interest in the arts was manifested by an amateur dramatic club, which we joined with enthusiasm. My ability to sing made me an immediate candidate for lead child roles in musical dramas. Since women generally were still not allowed to perform on stage, it fell to teenage boys to play their roles. This became my lot until my voice broke. Two members of our club were to achieve prominence later. Baldev Raj Chopra, a couple of years older than Satinder, became and remains a leading film producer in India; his younger brother Yash Raj Chopra, followed the same career.

On a summer vacation with the Sudans in the Murree hills, I contracted typhoid. In spite of good treatment, the fever persisted. On our return to Lahore a battery of tests showed that the fever had weakened the left ventricle of my heart, preventing it from fully closing when it should. Weakened by long illness as I already was, I was forbidden any exercise from then on. When I was able to return to school my parents got me enrolled in Mahila Mahavidyalaya, a leading north Indian-style classical music school, of which Pandit Janaradhan, a legendary singer, was the principal. At the end of the school day, instead of playing sports, I was taken in a car to the music school on the banks of Ravi River, not far from the fort. After a year or so, Pandit Janaradhan left and was replaced by the famous Indian violinist Dhondi Raj Apte. On finding me a serious student, Apte first thought of changing my major to violin, but after hearing me sing each day, he allowed me to continue as a vocalist. Unable to take part in sports, I was happy with music. I sang at concerts, winning prizes, and took part in religious plays, comfortable with the feeling that I could choose a career in music and drama. But my matriculation exam was looming ahead and I had to work hard to get good grades to enter Government College.

I had just turned fifteen when my maternal grandmother wrote to my mother to announce her decision to separate from Grandfather, because he had taken a mistress. She intended to move to Lahore for the higher education of her three sons. My parents found a house in Krishan Nagar, a growing suburb between Chauburji, where we had been living, and the city. Within a month, the Sudans were installed a couple of miles from our house.

Grandmother had for some time been growning increasingly religious. It was beyond us children to understand whether this piety was inspired by her stage of life or by the misdeeds of our grandfather. Whatever the reason, Grandmother earned a formidable reputation with women's groups for her hymnal writing, leading of prayers, and singing. We knew her to be strong willed, someone who demanded and usually got her own way. As we grew up and began to become acquainted with foibles of human nature, we started to perceive some discomfort in our grandfather. He liked his Scotch before dinner, but we never saw him inebriated. Yet there was no end to Grandmother's nagging about his drinking. He usually made his escape to his study immediately after dinner.

Only a few months after Grandmother moved to Lahore, Father was posted to Rawalpindi to take over the major hospital there. Grandmother insisted that we should have nothing to do with Grandfather. My father explained to her that as the leading doctor in town, a member of the same club as Grandfather's, and responsible for medico-legal work in the courts, it would be impossible for him to avoid Grandfather. But my mother had no choice but to comply with her mother's wishes. We children, backed by Father, were determined to make it easy for her.

We moved to Rawalpindi soon after my matriculation examination and the start of the summer holidays. I obtained a first division in matriculation, in spite of my having missed some important part of schooling, especially in mathematics. However, with my admittance assured because a generation of Rikhyes, including my father, were "Ravians" (graduates of Government College, Lahore), I joined the Faculty of Arts for a B.A. My older brother Satinder, already in college and residing at the hostel, had chosen to continue studying for a B.Sc., with the expectation of trying for medical studies.

During my second year at college, Father, on one of his visits to Lahore and after checking my heart, which he did frequently, decided to take me to the leading heart specialist in town. The specialist confirmed what Father had already found, that I had recovered. They agreed that I could start with tennis and swimming. I should, however, return later for a final check-up. Father took me to Anarkali bazaar for a celebration.

In 1936 Satinder and I were already boarders in college. Sodarshan and Indra were to join us in due course. My parents decided to build a house for the use of the children at college—a house that they could also use after their retirement. Satinder and I assumed the responsibility of keeping an eye on the contractor and paying the bills. In fact, I did most of the work with only occasional help from Satinder, who had to spend long hours in his laboratory.

When I entered college, my old school scouting colleagues introduced me to the Pioneer Troop, a private scout group organized and led by an extraordinary troop leader, Sher Singh Dhawan. Our troop participated in the All India Scout Jamboree in New Delhi in 1935, where we were chosen as the best troop in the country. This was my first travel outside the Punjab and was a thrilling experience, and made more so by a daylong visit to our camp by the founders of Scouting, Lord and Lady Baden-Powell. The following year, during the summer holidays, I accompanied the troop on a trek along River Lidder, one of the most beautiful valleys in Kashmir.

After the trek we boys were allowed a couple of days on our own. I took my pack and walked to the Bund in Srinagar and rented a small houseboat for Rs. 6.00 (about $2.00 then) per day. The boat owners, the Hanji family, were extraordinary hosts. As a teenage boy, I was immediately adopted by the Hanji family, and their twelve-year-old son became my companion. They poled the boat to Dal Lake for me to see the Shalimar garden. Here a Mughal emperor had left an inscription that read, "If there be heaven on this earth, it is here, it is here." I agreed with him and was to return to Kashmir often.

We continued our journey to Wular Lake, the largest lake in Kashmir. Not having seen the sea yet, Wular Lake seemed like one to me. Our boat made its way to the lake through the city, sprawled on both banks of the Jhelum River, and through cultivated saffron fields and fruit orchards. A bus appeared, bringing my attention to a road along the banks of the lake. My knowledge of this road turned out to be of great value when I fought the frontier tribal incursion into Kashmir following the Independence of India and its Partition. This beautiful land, with its gentle and hospitable people, was sadly fated to witness much fighting, death, and destruction, and it was my destiny to play a role in that drama.

Once, taking advantage of a break before the next phase of the house construction, Satinder and I went to visit our parents at Mianwali, where Father was posted at that time. This was a sleepy district town in the middle of a desert. The town had little to offer other than a cinema and an officer's club, where we had easy access to the tennis courts. For excitement, the family would drive to the Indus River at Attock for boat rides and picnics. Although there was little to do, Father enjoyed his work, especially dealing with serious bodily injuries. The population of the district was of mixed Pathan stock, tall, handsome, and wild.

Mother had become acquainted with the Brahmin family of a railway engineer in Mianwali. The Dutts had at least three daughters that I recall. Their two older children were teenage girls, shy but very pretty. We learned that their first daughter was betrothed. Satinder was nearly twenty years old and had shown an obvious interest in girls. After we returned home, he told me that he would like to go back to see the Dutts again. This was the beginning of a romance between Satinder and Sarla, the second daughter, which ended in their marriage some five years later.

While I was happy for Satinder, I was excited about my own future, which I talked about as often as I could with Satinder and our parents. I always enjoyed listening to Father, his cousins, and his friends talk of their war experiences. By now I had read a lot on war, both fiction and history. I loved to see military parades, my interest having been fired by the private mounted escorts of the big landlords at Shahpur on ceremonial occasions. Now that my heart was on the mend I wanted a career in the army. Mother reminded me that her father had promised me his library if I chose law and that there was also a room full of Father's uncle Sham Lal's books in storage at Gujranwala waiting for me. Father was more circumspect and simply said that we should wait for my final check-up at Lahore. I couldn't wait to get back.

3

On Joining the Army

Shortly after the spring of 1937 and the beginning of my studies for a bachelor of arts degree, Father arrived in Lahore for a visit. He took me for my physical check-up. The heart specialist confirmed that I was completely cured and could resume normal activities. I could not wait to join the University Training Corps (UTC) and Professor Allen Hett's army class, which coached candidates for the All India Competitive Examination for entrance to the service academies. Father agreed to the first but demurred on the second. He pointed out that my studies would by themselves prepare me for any government entrance examinations, so I had no need to declare my final choice of a career by joining the army class at this stage. He also cautioned that I should wait to see if my experience with the UTC confirmed my desire for a military life. I felt that I had crossed another bridge. Still, I would have to work on my mother.

Within a few days of Father's visit, his cousin Ram Chand ("RC") Rikhye from Gujranwala made a surprise visit and took Satinder and me along to spend the afternoon with him and meet his deceased sister's children, who lived in a bungalow in the nearby civil lines. RC was from Mokham Chand's branch of the family. He was a bachelor, and lived in a house down the street from our ancestral home. He spent a month each year, no doubt his happiest, as an army captain in the Army in India Reserve of Officers (AIRO) training camp at Lahore.

Uncle RC introduced us to his nephews, including Surendar Mohan Goswami, an army cadet working his way to an officer's commission through the ranks; a pretty niece, Kamla Goswami, my age and in the same class as I was at Kinnaird College; and her fiancé, Rajbir Chopra, freshly commissioned from the Indian Military Academy. Also present was RC's best friend, Captain Dewan Rameshwar Nath Puri, husband of Rajbir's only sister. Looking at RC and Dewan Sahib, I could not help thinking that the British Raj had made a very astute move by opening the AIRO to the Indian landed gentry and thereby keeping them happy in the pursuit of healthy and clean fun.

Meeting these four impressive men made me even more determined that the army would be my career, and I said so in my weekly letter to Father. He wrote in return to say that it was time for him and Mother to come to Lahore to see the progress on the house and begin to think of furnishings. On the day after their arrival, Father came into my room and said, "I heard from friends last evening that Mahatma Gandhi is in the city and there will be a prayer meeting in the grounds of the DAV College [a private Hindu college] a block away from your college. It has been quite a few years since I last met Gandhiji at Uncle Sham Lal's place, but I am sure that he will recognize me. I feel like going to pay my respects to him and hear him tell us what the future holds for our country. Would you like to come with me?"

I jumped at the invitation and was only sorry that Satinder was to miss it, as he had already returned to his college. By the time we reached the DAV College, the meeting had already started. Father held my hand and pushed his way through the crowd. Finally, he stopped on the edge of a path to the stand, saying that we might catch Gandhi's attention when he left. After the prayers, Gandhi spoke of the importance of maintaining religious unity in India's efforts to gain independence. At the end, the Mahatma rose from the dais and came down the path, just as Father had anticipated.

Surrounded as he was by admirers, I wondered if he would see us at all. However, volunteers were keeping a path open and as he approached us he beamed at Father with a toothless smile. When he came closer he said to Father, "Dr. Rikhye, I am so pleased that you kept your promise made to me in Sham Lal's house, that you will wear a turban. It was your turban that attracted my attention, and then I remembered you."

At their last meeting, Mahatma Gandhi had tried to persuade Father to join the Congress party. When that failed, he made Father promise that he would wear some item of national dress and Father offered to wear a turban. During the hot times of year in West Punjab, Father had reverted to wearing a solar hat when he had to go out in the sun, but normally he wore a turban.

Turning to me, Mahatma Gandhi put his hand on my head to bless me and asked Father, "And who is this boy?" Father introduced me. The Mahatma asked, "What do you plan to do with your life, child?" Overwhelmed as I already was at seeing the great man, and what with his hand on my head, I was tongue-tied. So Father came to my rescue and said in a witty manner, "The silly boy wants to join the army." Looking me in the eyes, Gandhiji said, "But that is good. We want good, educated young boys to become officers of the army of free India." Patting my head, he again said, "This is good." Then, waving at Father, he departed.

Father and I were quiet on our *tonga* ride back to Krishan Nagar. I was so overwhelmed at meeting the most respected Indian in the land that I did not fully realize the consequences of what he had said. When we reached our house Mother came out to the verandah to greet us. When she asked about the meeting Father told her, ending by saying, "Gandhiji gave Indar Jit permission to join the army."

Mother was visibly shaken, but she controlled herself. She gave me a hug without saying a word. It was only then that I understood that my parents would no longer oppose my trying for the IMA.

After the First World War, the Muslims had launched a campaign called Khilafat, or opposition, to force the British to undo the damage inflicted on Turkey and Arab lands by the 1920 Treaty of Sèvres. The Indian Congress joined the Muslim leaders in this effort, bringing the two major communities together.

The British declared martial law to deal with the campaign of passive resistance known as Satyagraha, but the situation was by no means tranquil. Two incidents closer to the Punjab greatly influenced the public. The first involved the Garhwal Rifles (Hindus), who, on their refusal to fire on a Pathan crowd in Peshawar, were disbanded and severely dealt with. The other was the tragic shooting of peaceful demonstrators at Jallianwala Bagh by Gurkha troops, under General Reginald Dyer's orders.

Among the many suggestions put forward by Indian political leaders at the time was that Indians should gradually replace British officers in the armed forces. However, most educated Indians were opposed to their children joining the armed forces because of their increasing use by the British to suppress the independence movement.

The East India Company had long since engaged Indians to lead native troops. As the company's forces expanded, it took in existing armed bodies or raised new units. The troops were under command of Indians who held Indian rank titles. The East India Company officers provided higher leadership and staff. This arrangement continued after Queen Victoria became the empress of India, except that company officers were replaced by officers from British regiments and officers directly commissioned for the British Indian Army. Indian officers were classified as viceroy's commissioned officers.

Initially, a handful of boys from princely or chief's families and well-connected families were trained at army schools at Banglore and Indore. Then in late 1920s, a few were sent to Sandhurst or Woolwich in England for training to become King's commissioned Indian officers (KCIOs). All KCIOs received the same emoluments, except for their overseas allowances. They formed the senior cadre and eventually led the Indian forces through transition to its independence. India owes them an enormous debt of gratitude. But KCIOs were too few to meet India's needs. So, after years of committee work and consultations to address this problem, the government established the Indian Military Academy (IMA) at Dehra Dun, an attractive spot in the beautiful Doon Valley in Uttar Pradesh.

The IMA opened in 1931 with forty gentlemen cadets. Thirty of these, fifteen each from the army and schools or colleges, were to be trained for the Indian Army, while ten were to undertake training for the Indian state forces. The course was for two and half years and consisted of five terms of four months each. The IMA broke in summer (during the monsoons) and winter (around Christmas and New Year). The IMA training was a year longer than training in England. The additional year provided extra education, to meet the British school standards, especially in English. To make up for some of the advantage British officers enjoyed by entering the army a year earlier, IMA graduates received ante-dated commissions.

I joined Professor Hett's army class the day after my meeting with

Mahatma Gandhi. I had almost a year and a half to prepare for the IMA entrance examination and I got down to my studies with determination. During this time, Satinder and I moved to our new house on Multan Road, where we enjoyed every moment of our lives. Sodarshan had joined us by now, and he was soon followed by Indra. Before the year was out, our house had become one of the best amateur music salons in the city on Sunday afternoons.

The arrival of the cool weather increased the pace of social activities and concerts. I received an invitation from a wealthy private banking family, patrons of Indian classical music from Kot Lakhpat, just south of Lahore, to meet Rabindranath Tagore, the first Indian Nobel Laureate for literature. Tagore had also received a knighthood from George V but had returned it protesting against the Jallianwala Bagh shooting. My meeting with Tagore was a memorable cultural and intellectual experience. On learning of my interest in music, he offered to help me to enter his school at Santiniketan. I demurred, but did not discuss my plans to join the army.

In the spring, Professor Mani Ram, my coach for my studies for the IMA entrance examination, stressed that the interview was as important as the written test. And he suggested, before my examination, that finding someone who knew a member of the selection board might help me in the interview. When I spoke about it to father, he was appalled at Mani Ram's suggestion. However, his British colleagues persuaded him that such introductions were not necessarily underhand, and that in fact they helped the board to obtain a better understanding of the background of candidates and their loyalty to the British. He soon learned that Sir Sher Mohammed, chief of Ghakhars of Jhelum and a close friend of a cousin, was a member of the IMA selection board.

I met my benefactor at the Marina Hotel in New Delhi after I had finished my written tests. He was a large man and wore a tall turban. We settled down at a corner sofa and he offered me a drink. I asked for a Vimto, then a popular imported drink, but my host exploded saying, "Come on, young man, if you want to join the army, you had better learn to drink!" I was flustered for a moment, then I said to myself, "What the hell! I will try it."

Sir Sher Mohammed and I chatted about the family, about my college, and about my studies and other activities. Although overpowering in his manner, he had charm and put me at ease. He rose after about twenty minutes to attend a dinner party. As he shook my hand, he said that he would see me in a couple of days, meaning the day of my interview. I was left with a comforting feeling that at least I had met a member of the board on my side, even though he was the only Indian.

Sir Sher Mohammed was the only one who asked me questions at the interview. When he asked me what new films I had seen, and I answered that I had seen *Marie Walewska*, a film about Napoleon's Polish mistress. This opened a dialogue in which other board members chipped in with their questions and brief comments about the film's star, Greta Garbo, Napoleon as a military leader, the wisdom of his campaign in Eastern Europe, and his defeat in Russia. As I was well prepared for these topics, it was almost as if someone knowing my studies and interests had planned the discussion. At a nod from the chairman the interview came to an end.

For Christmas holidays that year I went ot Mianwali with my brother Satinder. On the morning of 30 December a telegram arrived announcing that I had been selected for the IMA. I was to appear for a medical examination at the Military Hospital, Lahore Cantonments, where Father had served at one time. On being declared medically fit, I was scheduled to leave soon thereafter for Dehra Dun by rail, in a special coach.

The news of my selection for the IMA threw all of us into joyful turmoil. There was not enough time for celebrations or prayers. Satinder, who unhappily agreed to part from Sarla, accompanied me on the overnight train to Lahore. On the appointed day, I arrived at the railway station to depart. Jai Gopal Singh and one other classmate, Amrik Singh, had also made it to the IMA on their first try. Hett was surprised and pleased.

The IMA was set in idyllic surroundings, among well-kept tea estates. The Himalayas provided a backdrop to the north, while the Shivaliks were to the south. About four miles out of town, the academy was isolated enough to prevent us from slipping out for snacks and films, but close enough for us to cycle to town when we were permitted to visit. Mussoori, a jewel among hill stations, was a couple of hours away by car, but permission to go there was restricted because a visit required a long weekend and a pocketful of money for a hotel stay. The British had done the IMA proud. It had superb facilities, including well-furnished single rooms, sufficient common ablutions, comfortable anterooms, and a large dining hall. We were assigned to quarters according to which of four companies we belonged. Each company had a commander and another officer, while the remaining ranks were Gentlemen Cadets (GCs), from an under officer down to a plain GC. Except for some of the staff at the equitation school, the staff and instructors were all British. A viceroy's commissioned officer (VCO) and non-commissioned officers (NCOs) cared for the horses and managed the *syces* (stable hands). The food services were provided by an Indian contractor. On weekdays the menus were English, with lots of roast meat and Victoria puddings, except for Sunday lunches, when *parathas* (flat unleavened bread fried on a griddle) and potato curry could be bought. As if to round off our management education, the batmen were Gurkhas, mostly ex-servicemen of the Gurkha regiment based at Dehra Dun.

My maternal grandmother had relatives in Dehra Dun who had been exiled by the British after the annexation of the Punjab. They had joined the British during the Gurkha wars and the present head of the family was Colonel Jang Shamsher Singh Bahadur. My grandmother had written to her cousin about my joining the academy. It was not long after my class was allowed to go to town for an outing that Shamsher invited me to a *shikar*, or hunt. A car came to fetch me and drove me to a hunting lodge some thirty miles out of town, where Shamsher and his eldest son met me. Shamsher did not accompany us, so we would have room for guests on four elephants.

The party included the colorful Maharaja of Kapurthala, two of his family members, two British Gurkha officers, a beautiful Indian widow, Shamsher's son (who married the widow some years later), and me. A tiger had been seen in the area and the maharaja was to have the first shot at it. This was my first big *shikar* from the back of an elephant. My young host seated me with his lady friend, saying that since I was green at big game he had arranged for an experienced hunter to be my companion. I was amused at his gibe, but soon learned that the lady indeed knew the jungle and the techniques of *shikar*. We never sighted the tiger. On the way back I got a good head of a sambar (a large deer) and two jungle fowl to add to the pot.

When I look back at my time at the IMA, I am impressed that the British, once they had decided to train Indians for the officer ranks, went all out to give us the education we needed. Our British instructors were tough yet sensitive, highly disciplined, and an example to us in personal conduct. They helped us build character, did not demean any of us, and were fair and just. When a GC was removed, it was because he deserved it; when he failed, it was because he was not good enough to lead men in war. I enjoyed life at the IMA and felt comfortable with my decision to make the army my career.

In September 1939 Britain went to war with Germany. The commandant informed the assembly that the government had decided to reduce gradually the training period for regular army commissions. The government was determined to develop a cadre of properly trained Indian officers for the future. However, war would require a much larger army and more officers, who would receive shorter training. All the details had yet to be worked out and he would keep us informed. In the meantime, he enjoined: "Go back to work. This is time for you to learn. You will have your day in battle. Good luck."

When the senior GC under officer called the assembly to attention, as the commandant rose to leave, my eyes caught the IMA's motto, emboldened in gold letters on a board behind the speaker's dais. Based on an address given by Field Marshall Lord Chetwood, commander-in-chief, India, at the opening ceremonies of the IMA, it read:

> Your life and loyalty belongs to
> your country first, always and every time,
> your men come next, always and every time,
> you come last, always and every time.

During my last term, the commandant told us that the Indianization process for a selected few regiments had ended and that Indian commissioned officers (ICOs) and emergency Indian commissioned officers (EICOs) were to be posted throughout the army. We would have to submit new choices for postings.

Since I could no longer join 16th Cavalry, which had been my preference, I opted for the 6th Duke of Connaught's Own Lancers, then stationed at Delhi. My decision was based on two considerations: first, my father had served in Mesopotamia with a Bengal Lancer regiment during the First World War; second, 6th Lancers had a squadron of Punjabi Mussalman (Muslims), including men from my mother's ancestral home in Jhelum and Shahpur.

My choice turned out to be a good one. However, on learning later that 6th Lancers were on a slow track for conversion from horses to vehicles, I worried that I might miss the war, so I volunteered to take a wartime transfer to the Indian Air Force. On graduation from the IMA, I spent a month on ground training and then went to a flying school in Hyderabad. I was in the first batch of trainees to go solo. A few days later, I was shaken by the news that because of the planned expansion of the Indian Air Force (IAF), seconded army officers were required either to transfer to the air force or to return to the army. I had a few days to decide.

The Secunderabad Club was the meeting place of many former GCs from the IMA. The first Saturday evening at the club friends told me that 6th Lancers were now on an accelerated mechanization programme at Ahmednagar and were assigned to 8th Infantry Division to go abroad for war. The next morning I took a taxi to the post office and sent a telegram to the commandant of 6th Lancers, offering my services again to the regiment. A week later I received my posting order from the military secretary to return to my regiment. I was far too committed to the army to switch to the air force, and now that 6th Lancers were going to war, my proper place was with my regiment.

PART II

Serving with the Lancers

1. Maternal grandparents, Pandit Bindra Ban Sudan and Misarani Dhan Devi.

2. The author's parents, Madan Lal and Raj Rani Rikhye,
shortly after their wedding, with Vidya.

3. Rai Sahib Dr. Madan Lal Rikhye (*center*), the author's father, with Countess Edwina Mountbatten and a camp doctor, 1948.

4. Raj Rani Rikhye (*left*), the author's mother, with her caretaker, Najko Devi.

4

War in the Middle East

Preparation For War

I joined 6th Lancers at Camp Arangaon in the first week of May 1941. The regimental camp was some six miles south of Ahmadnagar. The commandant, Lt. Col. M.S. Bendle, in posting me to C Squadron said, "You know that is our Punjabi Muslim squadron. You don't see any problem there?"

I answered, "No sir. Punjabi is my mother tongue."

"All right then."

I was sent to Captain F.H.B. Ingall. In his late thirties, athletic and handsome, the captain looked suited for a role in film about life in Imperial India. After a warm welcome and exchange of first names, Bingle, as he liked to be called, took me to see the squadron tents and the men at vehicle maintenance. I was introduced to Risaldar (troop leader) Feroze Khan, the senior squadron VCO, the troop leaders, and the senior NCOs. I had an instant liking for Feroze Khan. Short, fair, blue-eyed, and with a ready smile, he proved to have a penchant for amusing stories. As the squadron officer, I was going to spend a lot of my time with him and I felt comfortable with the thought that it would never be dull.

On my way back to the squadron office I ran into a distinguished-looking VCO who stood not far from the commanding officer's (CO's) office, surrounded by two or three other VCOs. On seeing me, this officer left the group and approached me alone. He introduced himself as Risaldar Major Dadan Khan. I knew that he was the most senior VCO, an honorary captain, decorated, and the first adviser to the

CO. He was thin, with graying hair and a henna-colored mustache, and although he was about my height and bow-legged, he looked much taller because of his erect turban. He was effusive with his welcome and I in turn showed appreciation and respect to an elder gentleman. He knew of my connections with Jhelum, from where he too came, and expressed pleasure on my joining the regiment. He told me that the CO had expressed some hesitation to him over the posting of a Hindu officer to the Punjabi Muslims. The Risaldar Major said with some amusement that he told the CO, "Rikhye Sahib? *Woh to apna bachcha hai* [He is our own kid]." I knew that I was in good company.

At the end of the day's work, before going home and then to the club for sports, the CO and other married officers dropped in at the officers' mess to have a beer and chat with the single officers. The "English pub" habit was a great way for officers to become acquainted, and it fostered regimental spirit. This, combined with sports matches between units, helped to promote an *esprit de corps*. In another attempt to bring the new officers into the regimental family, Bingle took me to his home one Saturday to meet his wife, Susan, who was a reputable painter of horses. I spent an enjoyable evening with the Ingalls, viewing her paintings and getting acquainted.

The CO had arranged weekly assemblies at which he would deliver pep talks to all ranks. He turned to his new young officers, fresh from their schools, to take charge of these events. In doing so, he had a dual purpose: first, giving the officer an opportunity to demonstrate his military knowledge and ability as an instructor; second, providing an opportunity for the men to get to know the younger officers. I made my debut with a demonstration of a dismounted night reconnaissance patrol. In his closing remarks, the CO complimented me on a good demonstration, commenting on my properly spoken "Oxford Urdu." The troops clapped hard, in appreciation of the CO's wit as well as my presentation. At the end of the day, I was left with a feeling that my apprenticeship as a young green officer was over.

In July, the regiment was ordered to commence mobilization. In the main, this required a great deal of administration and staff preparation. Hardly a few days had gone by when, as I was getting ready for breakfast, after the daily routine of morning physical training, I was informed that Pat Williamson, the quartermaster (QM), had suffered a bad fall from his horse and had been removed to the hospital in the cantonment. The CO had appointed me acting QM, a job I was unprepared for.

First off, I went to the QM office and met the senior staff. Seeing that I was overwhelmed with the weight of my responsibilities, the QM Jemadar (troop officer) and his staff assured me that they were familiar with what Williamson Sahib wanted done. "Don't worry, Sahib," they said. "We will take care of the work and keep you informed and you can report to the CO on progress. On your part, please Sahib, keep us informed of the CO's wishes."

Taking only a few hours a day for sleep and meals, we still did not have enough hours in the day to complete our work as we prepared for mobilization. Sunday was our day off, when all single officers went to the club for beer and lunch. Here we met staff and students of the Armoured Corps Centre and School (ACC&S) from other regiments, including several KCIOs and ICOs. I was glad to become acquainted with two 6th Lancers officers at the ACC&S. Also, I was fortunate to be adopted by the family of a senior engineer of the Jammu and Kashmir state, who had volunteered for the war to serve with the Indian defense forces. Mr. Nanda was the garrison engineer, Ahmednagar. His gracious wife and attractive daughter, Kamla, were most hospitable and provided tremendous support at the time of my departure for service overseas.

Orders finally arrived in September for the regiment to move by train to Bombay and embark for overseas. Our destination was kept a secret. After a round of farewells, the regiment was seen off at the railway station with pomp and ceremony by the ACC&S and other units in the station. Within a week we were aboard a Haj Line ship which headed westward. I was greatly relieved when Pat Williamson rejoined us at Bombay before our departure, allowing me to return to C Squadron.

Our ship, packed with over two thousand troops and heavy with cargo, left port during the night. Early next morning, when I went on to the deck for exercise with my squadron, I saw that we were part of a large convoy escorted by British and Indian naval vessels. A Royal

Air Force long-range aircraft flew above us to keep watch. We were kept busy during the day at boat drill and refresher training, and there were daily talks for officers on the progress of the war.

We were all warned to refrain from rumor mongering. But once inside our cabins, we could not help but speculate where we were headed. Three possible destinations were East Africa, Egypt, and Iraq. Since the British Indian troops had secured Iraq, ousting its Axis-supported leader, and safeguarded Iranian oil fields, the odds seemed to favor Egypt as our destination.

At the end of a week, we all suspected that we were heading up the Persian Gulf. The next morning the CO confirmed Basra as our port of disembarkation. Fate had ordained me to follow in the footsteps of my father, who had served in Iraq years before.

One morning, while I was at work with the men, I was ordered over the ship's public address system to report immediately to the captain. On the bridge, our short, stocky, and now somewhat amused captain pointed to an Indian navy gunboat about the size of a tub. He gave me his binoculars and said, "That is your brother waving at you. He is a daredevil all right. Leaving his station and coming so close to the wake of my ship." And there was Sodarshan, wearing his cap with shorts but no shirt. We waved happily across the foaming waters of the gulf for a few minutes and then his gunboat pulled away. He was escorting me to my first war.

Protecting the Oil Fields in Iraq and Persia

Our ship was due to arrive in Basra in another two days. There was a lot to learn about Iraq, the progress of the operations, and the future role for the regiment. As the reconnaissance regiment, 6th Lancers was assigned to the 8th Indian Division, under command of Maj. Gen. C.O. Harvey, formerly of the Central India Horse.

Iraq was central to the British defense plans for Persian Gulf oil, because of the refinery at Abadan, and for maintaining the lines of communication to India. After the Allied victory over the Turks in the First World War, Britain had been awarded mandatory power over Iraq by the League of Nations. As we arrived in the gulf, the Germans had occupied all the states of western and central Europe, as well as Norway and Denmark. The assault on Britain had begun.

In Africa, however, General Sir Archibald Wavell had turned defeat into Allied victory. He had pushed the Italians out of Cyrenaica. He had conquered Eritrea and British Somaliland. And he had forced the Italians out of Abyssinia.

In Iraq, a clique of officers with the support of the army and air force had carried out a *coup d'état* and replaced Taha el Hashim with Rashid Ali. It soon became evident that Rashid Ali, supported by the Axis powers, was opposed to the British. With a paucity of troops from the Middle East Command, the British Government asked for help from India. British Imperial forces put down Rashid Ali's revolt, and shortly thereafter the 8th Infantry Division arrived in Iraq to join the operations and to secure the oilfields in Iran. The British Indian troops in Iraq, Iran, and Syria were now being positioned to defend Allied interests in this region from a possible attack by the Axis powers from the north.

6th Lancers, together with the entire 8th Indian Division, spent the winter of 1941-42 preparing the defenses of Mosul. The Germans had advanced deep into Russia and occupied parts of eastern Europe. If the Germans succeeded in seizing the Baku oilfields on the Caspian Sea and persuaded Turkey to join them, or if they chose to violate Turkish neutrality as they had done with western European nations, the German armies could pose a serious threat to the security of Middle East oil and the sea lanes to the British Indian empire, the colonies in the east and the dominions beyond. The British and their allies marshaled their scarce resources to defend northern Iraq. Our division was responsible for establishing a defensive line to protect Mosul and prevent entry into Iraq from Turkey or northern Syria. Other Indian forces had responsibility for the Kirkuk and Khanaqin oilfields.

In the spring of 1942 a new divisional commander was appointed. Maj. Gen. Douglas Russell came to us after two years of combat experience in East Africa and the Western Desert of Egypt. He had commanded a well-respected Indianized infantry battalion, 6th/13th Frontier Force Rifles, and had been popular with his officers and men. He and his wealthy American wife had no children, and she was known to dote on the young officers and was generous to the men and their families. The general was a legend in the army from his days of active service before the war on the North West Frontier and, more recently, in Africa. He injected a new spirit in the division, and we expected to see combat soon.

We were soon ordered to move into Iran as part of the Persia and Iraq Command. Persia's ruler, Shah Reza Pahlavi, was pro-German and resisted Allied attempts to open a route to supply the beleaguered Russian armies through the Persian Gulf and Iran. The infantry was involved in fighting to clear Paithak Pass, on the road from Khanaqin to Kermanshah. The 6th Lancers saw no action as the Iranians surrendered quickly, and the British replaced Shah Reza with his eighteen-year-old son. Our division was returned to Iraq, to be deployed to help protect the Kirkuk and Khanaqin oilfields.

One evening in August, the BBC news, after reporting on the progress of the war, including the Japanese invasion of India, which was of immediate concern for all of us, reported the mass arrest of Indian political leaders. The Japanese occupation of Burma and their campaign in Arakan had led to a renewal of talks between the British and Indian leaders on the future of India. Already, India had become a bastion of the Allied war effort. But as a major source of manpower, India could do a lot more.

The Indian National Congress called for independence as a condition for its support for the British war effort; the Churchill Government, however, was prepared to promise only dominion status at the end of the war, and insisted on immediate cooperation from the Indian leaders. When the talks broke down, the Congress leaders launched a non-cooperation movement against the British, resulting in mass demonstrations that interfered with the war effort. In a crackdown, the British authorities arrested the high command of the Indian National Congress, including Gandhi and Nehru. This left India divided and bereft of leadership and provoked in uncontrolled rioting and other acts of violence. With a major war in progress, the British had little patience for Indian aspirations and dealt with the near-revolt with a determination and ruthlessness that had not been witnessed in India for some decades.

The news of the arrest of the Indian leaders and the large-scale, anti-British demonstrations affected those persons, particularly officers, who had family members involved in politics. John Jacob, a young subaltern from Travancore (now Kerala), who had recently joined us, had several family members active in politics. Like the others, Jacob listened expressionlessly to the BBC broadcast. During the night a telegram from India addressed to Jacob was delivered to the duty officer, who on reading it woke the commandant. The telegram told Jacob that all his senior relatives were in jail and that he was urgently needed at home to take care of the family and their business.

The colonel gave the news to Jacob personally, asking how he could help him. Jacob, who had spent the night thinking of the possible consequences to his family of the arrest of Congress leaders, was ready with an answer. "Sir," he said, "I hereby resign my commission in the Indian army. You will understand that I cannot continue to serve the British and therefore cannot remain with the regiment that I have grown to love. I ask that I be permitted to return to India immediately to take care of the women and children of my family while my resignation is formally accepted."

The colonel allowed Jacob to leave for Basra by the morning train and arranged for him to get a berth on a ship to Bombay as early as possible. Jacob left with great regret. He wanted to be part of the war effort. As he left, he sadly told me that he would soon have to join the struggle for independence from the British. He was gone in a cloud of sand. No one in the regiment ever mentioned his sudden departure or even his name. Somehow, everyone knew what had happened but pretended as if Lt. John Jacob had never existed.

The development of radio communications was still in its infancy. There was radio communication between each troop and its squadron commander, but contact between squadrons and regimental head-quarters was poor. The shortcomings of radio equipment also made it hard to conduct mobile warfare; it was difficult to command large numbers of units spread over a vast area, particularly in a difficult terrain. In the days of horse cavalry warfare, the generals employed mounted orderly officers, who were young, intelligent, and good horsemen, to convey their orders and to bring reports. In the absence of a more satisfactory means of communication, the mechanized cavalry generals reverted to the old practice, except that the orderly officer now was mounted on a motorcycle.

I was selected for a monthlong course at Baghdad for mounted liaison officers. I took a Triumph 3.5-horsepower motorcycle with me from the regiment and for the next month we were inseparable. I learned junior-level staff work, and to navigate by day with a sun compass and at night by the stars. I rode for hours in the desert north and west of Baghdad and learned to negotiate difficult sands and irrigation ditches. I returned to the regiment more self-assured and was immediately appointed intelligence officer.

Internal Security Duty in Syria and Palestine

The British Government policy was to avoid entanglements in Syria, controlled by the French Vichy Government, but to resist occupation of that country by any hostile power. Following General Maitland Wilson's operation in the Levant, his entire force was reconstituted as the Ninth Army and was made responsible for the defense of Palestine, Trans-Jordan, and Syria. Lebanon was then a part of Syria. The British repatriated the Vichy military personnel to France and French North Africa, but retained sufficient former Vichy civil officials for the administration of Syria.

The Lancers were ordered to replace the Trans-Jordan Frontier Force (TJFF). Our task was to take over three frontier forts, at Al Qamichli, Tel Alo, and Tel Abiad, along the Baghdad–Istanbul railway, which ran along Syria's border with Turkey. We were to prevent any crossings in our sector and were especially to look out for German agents who might attempt to cross over to join sympathetic Arab tribal chiefs. Our new commandant, Lt. Col. Arthur Poole, located one squadron at each fort and placed his headquarters at Al Hasseche, further from the frontier and near the center of the Jazireh, the land between the Tigris and Euphrates Rivers. I was already an acting captain, not yet twenty-two, and to my delight was given command of B Squadron, the Jats. I was first sent to Tel Abiad, a small town with a Free French officer as its administrator. Tel Abiad was about three miles away from Ras al Ein, famous as the site of Rebecca's well. At Ras al Ein, a Free French Foreign Legion squadron, under the command of a French Canadian, was stationed.

This was my first command and I was determined to apply what I had learned and to do it well. There were minor violations by the sloppy Turkish frontier guards, and whenever I complained to my prearranged contact across the frontier, I was treated most kindly, assured that the incidents were unintentional, and obliged to accept gifts of French liqueurs. After my first visit to my Turkish contact, my vehicle was well stocked with Australian whiskey and Gordon's gin so that in future visits I could match the other side in gift giving.

Occasionally, we were asked by the French administrator to assist his gendarmes during their searches of tribal encampments for suspected German agents, but more often our presence was used to secure the release of young Assyrian women abducted by lusty tribesmen.

After a couple of such raids, and after the administrator and I had become better acquainted, I accompanied him on his meetings with the chiefs. On the first such occasion, we began with a lengthy exchange of courtesies while sipping coffee. Having read T.E. Lawrence's *Seven Pillars of Wisdom*, I was acquainted with the Bedouin coffee ceremony, and my French colleague had confirmed what I knew. The first cup was offered as an act of hospitality, the second was an offer of friendship or at least peaceful intent, but when the third cup was offered, it had to be refused, for to accept it would imply an abuse of hospitality and therefore would be an insult. The business at hand was never discussed early in a visit because it was discourteous to do so. Such a delay provided an opportunity to size one another up, which proved a useful negotiating technique when time was available, as was usually the case in the life of a Bedouin chief.

The routine of our lives in the desert was soon to be broken. Because of political unrest in Damascus, our regiment was relieved of its frontier duty at the end of the summer and moved to Mezze airport at Damascus to assist the Free French administration. During this time, the fighting between the Arabs and Jews in nearby Palestine (then governed by the British under a mandate from the League of Nations) had led the British to divert some of their resources there. Jewish extremist groups had bombed some important buildings, killing and injuring some British officers and personnel. While at Mezze, my regiment was given the secondary task of remaining on standby to assist in the maintenance of law and order in Palestine. Our new commandant, Steffy Robinson, who had replaced Arthur Poole, ordered the officers to visit Palestine to get acquainted with the lay of the land. Each group of officers was briefed by our British hosts and warned to look out for terrorists. Menachem Begin, who was later to become the prime minister of Israel, was at the top of this list. Within a month, most of us were well acquainted with Palestine and Syria.

Early in 1943 it became evident that major events were under way. Our regiment was first sent to Tripoli to practice mountain warfare, and a group of us attended a training course in this type of warfare at the Cedars in Lebanon. By this time, the Eighth Army, under General Bernard Law Montgomery, had broken through at El Alamein and was chasing German forces under Erwin Rommel along the coast of North Africa. Many of us were sent to the Bitter Lakes in the Suez to learn sea-assault landings. By now, we all believed that we were being readied for an assault on Crete or Rhodes.

The Allies had learned the importance of air power in land battles and had introduced special staff training at Aqir, an RAF air base near Lydda, Palestine, to teach air and army officers in these techniques. I was selected by the divisional headquarters to attend this course, probably because of my experience with the air force. After settling into my quarters at Aqir on the eve of my training, I walked to the officers' mess for a drink. I was sipping a tankard of fresh orange juice, a luxury made possible by the abundance of oranges in the area, when a well-decorated RAF officer approached me. He introduced himself as the commandant of our school, as well as the base commander. Looking at my bush shirt, which in the Indian Army at the time only the cavalry and a few rifle regiments wore, he remarked, "Cavalry, I see." Then, peering at my shoulder badges, he added, "Hmm, 6 Lancers, eh! Can you ride?" I replied somewhat indignantly that of course I could, but I admitted I was out of practice. I had not been in the saddle since my reconnaissance work in the Kurdish mountains in 1941-42. To my surprise, he invited me to ride with him the next morning. He explained that he had purchased two horses when a British cavalry regiment had mechanized in Palestine. He had not found another rider and could exercise only one horse each day. I reminded him that I was there to attend a course and my first class in flying began at five in the morning. He made me an offer that I could not refuse. I would ride with him every morning. Either he or his adjutant would be responsible for my flight training and I would rejoin the class later. He added, "You will miss some academic stuff. But you will get all that to read when you need to refer to it. Besides, you are here to learn about the air force. Damn it, if you can get along with me and ride with me while you are here, you should have learned all you need to know about the air force!"

The next three weeks turned out to be the best vacation I had until the war was over and I went on furlough in Kashmir. We would ride out at 5:00 a.m. and after an hour stop at a kibbutz. As a major employer of local laborers, the commandant was well known and popular. At breakfast we heard the local news from the Jewish farmers. The farmers talked about the fighting with the Arabs and wondered why the Arabs would not let them live in peace. They drew our attention to what the Jews had done with the land, building towns and the city of Tel Aviv. They had, they said, so much to offer, and, after all, it was their land just as it was the Arabs'. Since there was plenty of land, why couldn't they share it?

The Jews were sore at the British. They had joined the war effort, providing volunteers and organizing units in service with the Eighth Army. The Arabs, on the other hand, had refused to cooperate. We were told that in spite of this the British favored the Arabs. What with the fate of the Jews in Europe, the British must make good their promise to provide a Jewish homeland, a promise that had been made during the First World War but had yet to be fulfilled.

On our outings for swimming and dinghy practice at the British officers club in Jaffa, I had occasion to meet some of the well-to-do Arab families in the town. The Arab Palestinians were very anti-British. There was no question of their supporting the war effort when they were denied freedom. Palestine had been their land for three thousand years and now parts of it had been given away, and there was a danger of more Jewish immigration. The Europeans, the Arabs declared, didn't want the Jews and so they were to be dumped on the Arabs, who were under the thumbs of the British. In India, they reminded me, our own leaders in Congress had refused to cooperate and had preferred imprisonment. The Palestinian Arabs wanted an assurance of independence and of limits to Jewish immigration before they would agree to join the British war effort.

I had started the process of learning about the region and its peoples. Little did I know then that this was only the beginning of a relationship that would last many years. Too soon, our course came to an end, and I bade farewell to the horses and the friendly commandant. On the day of our departure, results of the course were posted on the notice board. I could hardly believe that I had passed first in the class. There was more good news waiting for me at the regiment in Damascus. I was selected by General Russell to join his staff in a new appointment, as general staff officer third grade for air operations (GSO3Air).

On joining the divisional headquarters, I learned that we were on alert to move the division to Alexandria, Egypt, and wait to hear of developments in the Mediterranean. At Alexandria, the division was to get ready for an assault landing either on Sicily or on mainland Italy.

5

The Campaign in Italy

Italy entered the Second World War at a time when the tide was
going against the Allies. Mussolini, failing to obtain any large territorial
gains in the Balkans or France, turned his attention to Africa. But
within two years the British Middle East Command, though smaller
in size than the Italian force, defeated the Italians and eliminated
Mussolini's forces as a threat. Thereafter, the Italian empire in Eritrea
and Ethiopia collapsed and British forces gained full control of East
Africa.

Germany's Afrika Korps, under Rommel, maintained the Axis
presence in North Africa, employing the remaining Italian troops on
the front lines to take the first onslaughts of the attacking Allies.
Eventually, Rommel was checked, at El Alamein, and forced to retreat.
The Eighth Army, under Montgomery, set out on the long march
across North Africa in pursuit of Rommel. Meanwhile, American
forces under General Dwight D. Eisenhower landed in Algeria and
Morocco. Caught between the two Allied armies, the Afrika Korps
was mostly destroyed or captured and the continent was rid of the
Axis forces. The defeat of the Axis powers in Africa coincided with
a check of Hitler's forces by the Russians at Stalingrad.

At the Casablanca meeting in January 1943, Prime Minister Winston
Churchill of Britain and President Franklin D. Roosevelt of the United
States agreed on a grand strategy to defeat Germany and Japan. While
an invasion of France was seen as a necessary course against Germany,
such an operation could not be carried out until 1944. But the situation
in Russia could not admit of inactivity. The British and Americans

agreed to drive the Axis forces out of Italy, liberate Rome, seize Corsica and Sardinia, and press hard against the Germans in north Italy to prevent troops there from joining the fight against the Russians or being sent to bolster German forces in France.

The Allied forces, under Eisenhower's command, invaded Sicily on 10 July 1943, within two months of the collapse of the Axis powers in Africa. The assault force was the Fifteenth Army Group, under the command of General Sir Harold Alexander and consisting of the Eighth Army under Montgomery and the U.S. Seventh Army under General George Patton. This force completed the capture of the island by 17 August. The quick and successful campaign led to the fall of Mussolini on 25 July and the formation of a new government, under Marshal Badoglio, which was friendly to the Allies.

The German forces, however, were ready to meet the Allied invasion of Italy when it was launched on 3 September. Alexander's plan was a double attack. The first attack, undertaken by troops of the Eighth Army, was launched across the Strait of Messina and directed against Calabria; the second, which followed later, was by the U.S. Fifth Army, which landed in the Bay of Salerno. British troops captured Potenza, fifty-five miles east of Salerno, as the Americans moved on Naples. Meanwhile, British paratroopers captured Taranto without opposition and secured Bari, Brindisi, and Foggia by the time the Americans captured Naples on 1 October. The first phase of the Italian campaign had been completed.

The 8th Indian Division landed on 19 September at Taranto, where it was posted to V Corps. We opened divisional headquarters at Ururi on midnight 19-20 October, at which time the division took command of the Larino sector.

Since 1939, when I joined the army, my training and service had conditioned me for battle. I spent the first year of the fighting in Italy on the staff of General Russell. In October 1944, I rejoined my regiment and served with them until the end of the war. I survived the campaign in Italy without a scar and had gained some stripes. At the end of the war I was more mature, having gained experience on the staff and in warfare. I had lived among Arabs, Iranians, Jews, and Italians. I had associated with the armed forces of the British dominions, the United States, France, and Brazil. These experiences laid the foundations for my later UN peacekeeping career. In writing about fighting in Italy, I do not intend to focus on the routine life of a staff or regimental officer, but to touch upon the influence of these experiences on my personal and professional development.

I do not remember much of the first year of operations. We joined battle at the Trigno River and later at the Biferno and Sangro Rivers. Early in 1944, before the winter was over, we were moved to the Cassino front. Two attempts by the American army to capture the formidable heights at Monte Cassino had not been entirely successful. Now the Eighth Army was to undertake the main assault. Our division attacked across the Liri River and went for the lower heights of the monastery, while the Poles were directed along the ridge. After the capture of Cassino and the liberation of Rome, our division was moved in pursuit of the retreating German Army, along the central route to Perugia. Later, the division was moved beyond Arezzo to advance along the west of Route 6 toward Florence.

While I remember little of the operation during that time, my impressions of the year on the divisional staff remain clear. I spent most of my time in the operations caravan. Every time the main divisional headquarters moved, it chose a place as far forward as possible, sometimes just behind the forward brigade. From this position, headquarters could control the next attack and remain until that phase was completed and the troops had gone well forward. As the only armored corps staff officer, I was expected to be on duty at every move. I found our moves exciting, especially when I was free to open the top hatch of the caravan and look out. Such occasions were rare, however, as we moved at night, without lights and often in view of the enemy.

When on the move, the operations caravan remained in constant radio contact with the troops. Every pulse and throb of the battle reached us through the voices reporting on the telephone and the radio. I soon learned to distinguish between words spoken under fatigue and those uttered under stress, between simple fear or a total loss of control, and between someone understating victory because of its cost in casualties among their comrades and someone suffering a mental breakdown. My life ran in a cycle of three days, because there were three third grade operations staff officers who served on regular night duty by turn. During the day I did my regular job of arranging air support for the division, a task not always completed in that time. After night duty, I had time for a quick wash and breakfast before we reported to the first grade staff officer (G1), Colonel Schoolbred, on the night's events. More often than not, we were told to report to General Russell—known affectionately as "the pasha"—who wanted detailed information on one or another aspect of the operations.

The pasha visited forward troops every morning without fail. Sometimes he took the night duty officer with him on these visits, and so I accompanied him on a few occasions. He would first call on the unit that had performed the best and suffered the most casualties. He would ask the commanding officer about the battle, then go forward to an observation point to examine the ground and look at the enemy positions. On the way, he would speak to the officers and the men. He spoke fluent Hindustani and Pashtu and conversed with the men in their native tongue. Such visits were a tonic for the officers and the men. He cared for them and did not just fling them into battle. He lauded success, did not show disappointment at temporary failures, and instead urged his men on to greater effort and inspired them in the cause to win the war.

The pasha had ample proof of his bravery and daring in the decorations he had received. However, as the senior-level commander he was careful in selecting his route in the forward area. As he had said, a senior commander was better alive than dead or incapacitated.

In one operation, his own battalion, 6th/13th Frontier Force Rifles, leading the attack, took very heavy casualties. I was the duty officer and listened to the reports from the brigade duty officer. I had to convey the bad tidings to the pasha, who listened silently. He left quietly at dawn, accompanied only by his aide de camp (ADC), and went straight to his battalion. He spent the whole day with them, watching them bury or cremate their dead in accordance with their customs. But he did not pull the battalion out; instead, he praised the officers and men for their achievements and sacrifices and reinvigorated them for renewed action. In spite of its reduced strength, the battalion made a remarkable recovery and succeeded in achieving its goals. Thereafter, the pasha pulled the whole brigade out, not only his battalion, for rest and reorganization.

I do not recall the pasha ever speaking in anger. But he did expect his staff to work hard and for long hours. Yet he showed a solicitude that won him the affection of his subordinates. After I had been on his staff for about seven months without a day's rest, I had begun to feel tired more readily. But we were preparing for the attack on Cassino and I was busily engaged in planning the air support, while performing my night duty every third night. As we came close to the D-day, hardly anyone slept. Our headquarters was about a mile and a half from the front and the Eighth Army artillery surrounded us. When they started their bombardment, sleep was out of the question. But after three nights the bombardment eased, and I was finally able to get some sleep.

I arranged to be called at 7 a.m. the next morning, which would leave me time to prepare for a meeting with the pasha, at which I would relay the first light-air reconnaissance reports and get his targets for the day's air support. When I finally woke up, with my Pathan batman threatening loudly that if I did not get up he would not continue to offer me tea, it was late in the afternoon. I panicked, as I had missed my meeting with the pasha. I dressed hurriedly and ran to the GI's caravan. On seeing me, Colonel Schoolbred broke out in laughter and said, "You have finally surfaced! No one could wake you up." Eventually the pasha had decided that I should be allowed to sleep. "Go and see the Pasha. He wants to talk to you." Looking at my anxious face, Schoolbred said with another laugh, "Go on! Go to him! It is all right." And then he waved me away. I walked sheepishly to the pasha's caravan. He saw me coming, and with a broad smile he asked me to come in. Before I could say anything he said, "I should have known that you were so tired. I believe you have not slept for a number of days. You had better take a few days off. Why don't you take my staff car and go and see Naples." He had made it so easy for me that I comfortably entered into an enthusiastic conversation about my holiday. I got my rest, and had also learned an abject lesson in leadership.

Although I had spent two years in the Middle East, my experience there was less intense than my exposure on divisional staff to artillery fire and air attack. My visits to the troops after battle, often undertaken at personal risk, revealed the full horror of war. I realized that I had yet to learn two essentials for war. The first was to overcome the fear of being hit. I soon learned that there was fear in all men but one had to learn to overcome it. I had also to learn that most human beings hate to kill or inflict pain. Soldiers have to be motivated to risk their lives and to make war on others. I had two strong motives: to gain battle experience in order to prepare myself for a future military role when India gained independence, and to help the British win the war against their enemies. Like many Indians I was convinced that Nazi Germany, Fascist Italy, and militant Japan were a menace to our world and, in spite of their promises, to the future of India. We gained our independence a little over two years after the defeat of the Axis powers. Thousands of Indians had fought alongside their British comrades. After the war, these same British people elected a Labour government that proved sympathetic to Indian aspirations and led us to our independence. I do not wish to belittle the importance of the role of Indian political leaders and the sacrifices of the people of India that led to independence, but the contribution of the Indian armed forces to victory over the enemies of the British was also an important factor that led us down the road toward independence.

During the rapid advance of our division through the Perugia Valley toward Sienna, 6th Lancers was in the lead. With an open valley, a disorganized German withdrawal provided ideal conditions for light armor to play the traditional role of the cavalry. As the regiment moved on a broad front and mercilessly drove the enemy back, Alan Bond, the signals officer, reported on the radio the excitement of the hot pursuit. In the middle of a report he stopped suddenly, asking me to "wait one", meaning to hold for a moment. When, a few moments later, he resumed his report, he said, "Oh my God! Iqbal's vehicle's been hit! It was a German 88 and it's brewing [burning and exploding]. Will call you later. Out." Lieutenant Iqbal Singh had joined the regiment in Italy and was the youngest of the emergency Indian commissioned officers.

Within a day, another 6th Lancers ICO was killed. Ken Holden had also joined us in Italy. A good athlete and soccer player, he was professionally very capable. He had won the respect of all ranks of the regiment. I was very sorry at his death, especially as I was looking forward to his joining the next sally of us young ICOs into Assisi. This group was already made up of Raghujit Singh, a striking-looking Sikh with a beard and a turban; Lou Fonseca, a handsome, tall, and lean Goan Roman Catholic; and Beli Battliwala, a Parsi who was the spitting image of the American film actor Melvyn Douglas. I was hoping for the addition of Ken, an Anglo-Indian Protestant, to the group, but it was not to be. And so it went every day.

We did have our lighter moments. Our division was on the left flank of the Eighth Army, west of Route 6, on the Arno River opposite Florence. The American Fifth Army was on our left flank. While the Allies and Germans were negotiating to declare Florence an open city and thus avoid damaging its great art treasures, my division and the U.S. 88th Division were coordinating their patrols across the Arno. The pasha decided to send a liaison officer to the Americans on our left flank and chose handsome and suave Battliwala of my regiment for this task.

When Battliwala reached the first American flank patrol, he gave the right password. But when the GI looked at his identity card, he was alarmed that Battliwala claimed to be an Indian, but looked like an Italian and said that he was from a British outfit. When asked to explain, Battliwala told the GI that his regiment was the famous Bengal Lancers. The GI had seen the movie, *The Lives of the Bengal Lancers*. But still bewildered, he yelled for his superior, "Come here, Sarge. I have got a guy here who says that he is a Bengal Lancer." This news traveled fast and Battliwala was received by the American general and returned to his own division having completed his mission.

Some weeks later, General Mark Clark of the U.S. Fifth Army came on a courtesy visit to a flanking outfit. On meeting only the pasha's senior staff, who were all British, Clark teased his ally, "This is an Indian Division, but I don't see any Indian officers." The pasha explained the traditional system whereby Indian officers—designated junior commissioned officers (JCOs) rather than VCOs since the start of the war—had been restricted to commands at troop or platoon levels. The pasha added that there were more than thirty ICOs/EICOs with the units. He also had one on his own staff. So I was called for and presented to Clark. After the first introduction, the pasha, remembering Battliwala's experience, added, "Indar here is my Bengal Lancer."

Clark was effusive in his praise of the Indian troops and said how pleased he was to have the division under his command for the spring offensive. His staff took a lot of pictures. When we received copies of the American forces paper, the *Stars and Stripes*, there was a photograph of Clark with the pasha and his staff. The headline ran, "Bengal Lancers under Command."

As the staff officer responsible for air support in the division, I was always keen to assess the results. Each time we went forward, I was eager to see the results of our air attacks on ground targets. The selection of targets was primarily in the hands of higher echelons of command. The strategic and tactical targets were selected at the theater or army level. At the divisional level, we put in bids for the destruction of targets that were likely to impede our advance. The allies had a large air armada, which supported ground operations. For the assault across the Sangro River some one thousand air sorties were flown by heavy and light bombers and fighter bombers; and for the third battle of Cassino the number of sorties was about three thousand per day. Our targets usually were roads, bridges, and villages. The villages usually sat atop ridges connected by winding roads, and offered passage on narrow streets. Our bombing attacks there invariably blocked our approaches, but offered a convenient way of hitting the well-dug enemy positions. Such attacks also destroyed houses and other buildings, and caused civilian casualties. I was always appalled to see the effect of these attacks and the suffering caused to civilians, especially to women and children, but none of us at that time could think of a better alternative for removing the enemy and minimizing our casualties.

Back with the Lancers

After the Allied troops entered Florence and broke through Hitler's defensive Gothic Line, which ran from Pisa through the Apennines to Rimini, General Russell called me to his caravan for a chat. The pasha said that I had spent more than a year on his staff and it was his practice not to keep young officers longer than a year. He thanked me for my work and said that my excellent handling of air support for the division had kept me there longer than he had intended. But now with winter ahead and war in western Europe in full swing, he expected a quiet period in Italy until spring 1945.

The general asked me what I would like to do next, and without waiting for me to answer said, "I expect you want to attend the Staff College." First, I thanked him for his kind words about my work, and then said that I would prefer to return to my regiment, where I hoped to get command of a squadron. Without further discussion, he picked up his telephone and asked to be connected to the commandant, 6th Lancers, Steffie Robinson. The general spoke briefly: "Steffie, Indar here has done me very well, but has done more than one year here. I want you to take him back." There was a brief silence while Robinson spoke. Then the general said, "Good. We will return him as soon as possible, within the next few days. He is due command of a squadron, isn't he?" There was another answer by Robinson. The general turned toward me and smiled, indicating that I was to get my wish. He said to Robinson, "Good Steffie. I will send Indar back to you soon." That was it. He rose, shook my hand, and wished me good luck.

After attending a sub unit commanders course at Benevento, near Naples, I rejoined the regiment, which was holding the south flank of our division, on the Apennines, southeast of Florence. The 6th British Armored Division was to the south of the regiment. Our Sikh squadron occupied the heights that overlooked Pontasieve and covered the road from Florence to Maradi. Pat Williamson was on leave and I was given command of his squadron during his absence. Lou Fonseca was second in command and Lieutenant Blundell was in command of the rifle troop. The regiment had left its vehicles behind as it moved into the mountains. We operated in a dismounted role. A mule unit was attached to carry our provisions and ammunition. The regiment was responsible for a 6-mile-wide sector, with my squadron, B Squadron, responsible for its northern half.

It was a cold and rainy winter, which was slowing down operational activity. I sent three or four patrols a day and usually one patrol at night to watch the road. Every day, I visited one or two of my forward posts, taking provisions with me. This took up most of the day. At night, we warded off the cold by getting under our blankets fully clothed. Some warmth was provided by foul-smelling kerosene heaters and glasses of sweetened hot rum. Fonseca and I separately or together accompanied the night patrols. He was certain that Maradi was not occupied by the Germans. It turned out that their patrols did visit the town, and one night the inevitable clash occurred, although with little damage to either side. Other than occasional bursts of machine-gun or mortar fire, little happened in the first month, as I spent my time relearning how to command. On Pat Williamson's return from leave, I was given command of headquarters squadron.

Lt. Col. F.H.B. Ingall, my former squadron commander, led the regiment in pursuit of the retreating Germans after the crossing of the Senio by New Zealand troops. Ingall had assembled the regiment south of the river and, as soon as the bridges over the river were completed, he led the regiment across. He left the regiments' 75 mm guns mounted on half-track White armored vehicles to support his advance. The entire operation was supported by Allied air power. In one of the tragic incidents of the war, a group of American light bombers mistakenly unloaded their bomb bays on the Lancers' guns. The bombs not only destroyed valuable lend-lease ordnance but killed most of the crew.

After crossing the Senio, 6th Lancers were driving hard toward the Po, and within days crossed the largest river in Italy. The German resistance had broken, and our troops encountered large numbers of Germans who had given up fighting and were surrendering. After we crossed the Po, I was ordered to move the B echelon, as the administrative tail was called, on to the road to Padua. I would later be told where to harbor for the night. I had already dispatched Burgess, our QM, to resupply the two forward squadrons, advising him to contact regimental headquarters directly for a rendezvous. It was 29 April 1945. Some time during the afternoon, I was ordered to halt and get off the road. The New Zealand Division, which had advanced up the Adriatic Coast, started to go past us in large numbers. Then Ingall told all his units that the war was over and that we were to remain wherever we were until further orders. I tried to raise Burgess on the radio, but got no response. It was almost dark when he came up on the air. He reported that after he had lost radio contact, he had kept going forward. In the absence of any other traffic, he had kept moving until he found himself on the turning point to Venice. He was then overtaken by convoys of New Zealand troops, who told him that he had no business to be where he was—only the Kiwis were to enter Venice. Bravo Burgess. In his usual style, he had put the rear end of 6th Lancers close to Venice first. Later, the regiment was ordered to concentrate at Padua, where we were to harbor.

While I was happy that the war had ended and that we had won, the sudden end at first made it difficult to realize the war was over. But by the following morning, it had sunk in and we were all ready to return home as soon as possible. By now, Ingall and Ian Chauvel had changed jobs, with Chauvel becoming the new commandant and Ingall the pasha's new G1. Pat Williamson and Francis Brock received immediate repatriation, and I replaced Brock in command of A Squadron. I was back with the Jats after three years.

Our squadrons were billeted in different villages. On a walk to see that my men were comfortable in their billets, as I was walking past the carabinieri house, I heard a voice calling me. After some difficulty, my squadron risaldar Hukum Singh and I located the voice coming from the grill of the police dungeon. I walked into the police office and asked after the prisoners. When told that they were Yugoslavs, I ordered their release in my custody. Two men and a woman, disheveled, unwashed, and stinking, emerged. They were flyers for the Chetniks—Serbian nationalists who collaborated with the Germans against the Yugoslav communists under Tito—who had been shot down and captured by Tito's partisans. During a German air raid they had managed to escape to Italy, only to be recaptured by Italian pro-Communist partisans who controlled this particular village and the surrounding area.

I brought the released prisoners to my billet and offered them food, while Hukum Singh sent for clean clothing. While the Yugoslavs washed and dressed, I spoke to my commandant on the radio and asked for his orders. The Italian partisans were friendly but could turn against us. Chauvel told me to take the weapons from the Yugoslavs, if they had any, load them in a vehicle with food and drink, and send them to Brindisi, in south Italy, to the Yugoslav camp. I explained this to Hukum Singh, who went to make the arrangements. The woman pilot spoke English and the other two could conversed in broken Italian, which was also my best. They were grateful for the care and for being sent to the Yugoslav camp. They said that they had to come to terms with Tito's partisans and now was as good a time as any to return to Yugoslavia.

With the war in Europe at an end, I looked forward to soldiering with the regiment in our war against Japan. As expected, our division was ordered to return to India, where after completing our leave we were to reorganize for operations against Japan. With its experience and record of service, the division was expected to be employed for the assault on Singapore and Malaya.

6

Guarding India's North West Frontier

The ten-day voyage home on the P&O's *Empress of Australia*, a large liner, once famous for its comfort, food, and fun, went quickly. On reaching Karachi, we traveled by a special train for Firozpur. The colonel told the officers before we all left for a fifty-six-day furlough that the regiment was to remain with the 8th Indian Division, which was earmarked for assault landings on Malaya. At this time, I was only concerned about the immediate future—a reunion with my family and friends, and a vacation in Dalhousie in the Punjab hills, where my parents had rented a house for the summer.

It turned out to be a wonderful holiday. As a single male, I was in great demand socially. My parents were anxious to see me married and suggested a number of possible brides. I reminded them that we still had to finish the war with Japan. I enjoyed the many socials arranged for my benefit and managed to escape from Dalhousie without getting hitched.

It was during an evening of dancing at the club that the secretary announced that an atom bomb had been dropped on Japan and that the war was expected to end soon. The Japanese surrendered on 14 August 1945. The news of the end of the war came as a tremendous relief, and there was great rejoicing in the town, as elsewhere.

I was sorry when my leave came to an end and I had to return to steamy Firozpur at the height of the monsoons. The war being over, the regiment had received new orders to proceed to Kohat for operational duty on the North West Frontier. By the end of September 1945 the regiment was installed in modern barracks in Kohat. The construction of single officers' quarters and the officers' mess had not been completed before the beginning of the war, so the officers were housed in wartime-built huts, which were reasonably comfortable. We received our compliment of armored cars and other equipment from the Guides Cavalry, who were transferred elsewhere on the frontier. The 6th Lancers, after five years of war, began to settle down to peacetime soldiering, although service on the frontier was operational.

Since the Afghan wars, the British had interests in this rugged, mountainous part of India. The end of the Sikh rule brought the British direct responsibility to administer the area and to protect the Punjab from Pathan raiders. The British built a series of cantonments on the west bank of the Indus River, established military camps forward in the tribal areas, and patrolled the frontier with Afghanistan with paramilitary forces raised entirely from among the frontier men. The tribal people were sturdy, tough, and brave and had their own code of behavior. No power had ever succeeded in bringing them entirely under their control. The British wisely divided the frontier province into administered and tribal territories. The former was further divided into districts, along the same lines as in India, and was governed by the Indian political service; the British Indian Political Department and not the Home Affairs Department managed the tribal territories, in the same manner as they dealt with the Indian princely states. An agent for the North West Frontier, acting on behalf of the viceroy of India, managed subdivisions of the tribal areas that were administered by political agents. These officers, in turn, dealt with the tribal chiefs. Well, at least they tried to.

The British had succeeded in bringing some order to the tribal areas. But every so often a rebel would emerge, causing internecine or inter-tribal warfare. And some tribesmen needed little excuse to fight the British. The job of the army was to safeguard the bases—the main cantonments where families were permitted—maintain forward posts in tribal areas, and keep communications open. The air force, acting from the main bases and a forward base at Miranshah, supported the army. The paramilitary forces manned the border and were on constant patrol.

Kohat was a major army base with a large airfield. It had not witnessed any tribal incident for many years. It was almost a peacetime station, sending only occasional patrols along the roads leading to the frontier. One squadron in the regiment had a more interesting role, on detached duty with the infantry brigade stationed at Bannu. The colonel had sent another squadron there, so I had to wait my turn.

Shortly after the regiment settled down in Kohat, the troops were permitted to bring their families to reside in the quarters in our camp. The British officers had established a system of family care, providing a Regimental Family Center with a nurse assisted by volunteers from among the British officers' wives. But all the married British officers' wives were now in England and had no plans to return because of the uncertain future of India. Except for those promoted from the JCO ranks, the ICOs were all unmarried. Chauvel persuaded a British wife from another unit to help at the family center, but the arrangement did not work well. So the commandant turned his attention to me and suggested that it was time for me to find a wife.

I had considered marriage, but was not sure that I could handle it. Other than casual relationships, I didn't really know the opposite sex. I had been away at school, college, and the academy and then was at war for more than four years. When Chauvel threatened to write to my father to get me married, I quickly wrote to my parents to go ahead and find me a bride.

Meanwhile, Raghujit Singh of my regiment had introduced me to a family at Mussoorie who were on the look out for a suitable match for their daughter, Usha. Her father, Khushi Ram Erry, was an irrigation engineer in the Punjab and her mother, Sheila, was a prominent socialite. In her teens, Usha was already a beauty, a 'belle of the ball' in every respect. With the consent of my parents, I applied to the commandant for permission to marry. When I showed Chauvel a picture of my future bride, he remarked, "She is beautiful! But look at her, Indar, you will never be able to manage her." His words proved prophetic.

I was married at Lyallpur on 5 March 1947, an auspicious day chosen by the priests. An Indian wedding raised considerable interest among all ranks, and this was the first wedding of an officer of my regiment since the war. It was a traditional Hindu wedding. The bridegroom's party included Colonel Chauvel and a number of officers and JCOs of the regiment. I had taken my squadron on detached duty to Bannu, and my bride accompanied me there amid military pomp and ceremony. Soon she was in the center of the cantonment social life in Bannu.

I did two tours of duty on detachment with the Jat squadron in Bannu. One of my troops of three armored cars was further detached with an infantry battalion at Mir Ali, some twenty miles along the road toward the frontier. This troop saw more excitement than the rest of us at Bannu. They were out on daily patrol and encountered tribal opposition. The Faqir of Ipi, a religious tribal leader, had declared jihad against the British and roused some tribes to take up arms. These tribes sniped at camps, attacked patrols, and damaged communications. They also attacked tribes friendly to the administration. Thus, all convoys from Bannu to Miranshah and Razmak, near the frontier, had to be protected. The practice was to have two road-opening days each week, when the infantry, supported by machine guns and artillery, mounted pickets on hilltops that overlooked the roads, while the air force kept vigil from above. Our armored cars provided additional support to the infantry and gave close escort to the road convoys. There were routine incidents but nothing serious occurred during my time there.

During my first tour of duty at Bannu, the first Indian brigadier, K.M. Cariappa, assumed command of the brigade. My officer's mess was near Flag Staff House, the official residence of the general in command. I saw Cariappa there often and we became well acquainted. At the same time, Brigadier Mohammed Ayub Khan was given command of Razmak Brigade. I met him on a couple of occasions when I escorted him between Bannu and his post. Obviously, these men were intended for high positions after independence. Cariappa was destined to be the first commander-in-chief of India and Ayub was his opposite number in Pakistan until he seized power and became the president.

Early in the spring of 1947 my squadron was relieved, and we returned to Kohat. Political developments in the country were in full sail and we on the frontier, although remote from Delhi, were caught up in the wash. Life was mostly quiet, but violence did erupt in

Peshawar and Kohat in response to killings of Muslims in Bihar. Although the Muslim League made a strong plea for the partition of the country and the creation of Pakistan, from Kohat it seemed that the Muslim League was either dreaming or else attempting to leverage the best bargain for the minority Muslim community in a Hindu-dominated India.

In the regiment, the wartime-recruited British officers who had asked for demobilization had already left. The pre-war British regulars had become restless; some applied for the British army while others considered retirement. Chauvel's furlough came through, Sandy Blair became acting commandant, and I was the second in command.

India was hurtling toward independence. Fighting between Muslims and Hindus and Sikhs was reaching an alarming level, and it became evident that India was moving toward a division into two nations. At Delhi, Lord Wavell, the viceroy, had been for some time involved in intensive talks with Indian political leaders. The Indian National Congress was holding out for a united India, with representative power shared by the communities. The Muslim League, under Mohammed Ali Jinnah, stood firm on a divided India and the creation of Pakistan, to include provinces and princely states with a Muslim majority. The strong advocacy of Pakistan by Jinnah had given a militant twist to developments, leading to more communal fighting. To deal with a situation that was approaching anarchy, Clement Atlee, the British prime minister, nominated the popular war hero and cousin of the king, Lord Louis Mountbatten, to replace Wavell as viceroy and governor-general. Atlee set August 1948 as the target date for granting Independence to India.

On reaching India, Mountbatten plunged into talks with the Indian leaders and tried to cope with communal fighting. Kohat, where I was at the time, and Bannu witnessed several political demonstrations, but little fighting.

After their king and country, British officers' loyalties were to their regiment and then to the class of men with whom they had served. Thus, many of the British officers watched the increasingly divisive political scene in India with sadness, for they recognized that the partition of the country would mean the break-up of their regiments, which they had made their home. But there were some among them who viewed the Indian Congress leaders with disdain, felt closer to the Muslim League leaders, and therefore sympathized with the cause of Pakistan. This sympathy was also spurred, understandably enough, by personal considerations. Jinnah could be expected to ask many British officers to stay, whereas it was a foregone conclusion that, with the exception of advisers and trainers, India would not retain foreign officers in its armed forces.

When the cold weather approaches in Kohat, the town looks its best with an abundance of flowers, especially beautiful roses. In 1947, it was at that time of year that the communal fighting was on the rise. In Karachi, the Indian navy and air force had seen near mutinies. Some army units, sent to assist the civil powers, had hesitated to act against rioters from their own community, Hindu or Muslim. With two services already affected and the army showing signs of strain, Britain could no longer effectively continue its rule. Perceiving this vital change in a situation that was already unmanageable, Mountbatten advanced the date of Independence to 1947. Jinnah remained adamant on division, and finally the Indian National Congress conceded: If the creation of Pakistan was the only way to end the fighting, let it be so.

The news of the division of the country was soon followed by orders from army headquarters, Delhi, that 6th Lancers had been allotted to Pakistan. We were to exchange our Sikhs for Muslims from 8th Cavalry and our Jats for Muslims from 7th Light Cavalry, who like us had a distinguished record of service during the last war. One morning in the spring of 1947, Blair told me of his decision to leave immediately. I was to assume acting command until Chauvel returned from his leave in Australia. I did so readily. I had expected something like this to happen, and being committed to remaining in Pakistan, I was prepared to assume this responsibility.

In the dividing of the country, it was agreed that, in the North West Frontier province, where a Congress provincial government held power, a referendum would be held to decide if the region should join Pakistan or remain with India. The Congress, however, decided to avoid contesting the future of a province that was separated from the mainland by such a great distance and withdrew from the contest. In the event, voters approved joining with Pakistan.

I dreaded the day when the transfers of our squadrons would start. I knew these men. I had started my service with Punjabi Muslims, and had acting command of the Sikhs when the squadron had held a part of the Gothic Line. I had commanded the Jats in Syria and again after the war on the North West Frontier. It would be wrenching to see them go, like losing someone from your own family. The transfer of the Sikhs came suddenly. Because of communal fighting in the Punjab involving the Sikh community, Delhi decided to airlift the squadron from Kohat to Delhi. We were told that the Jats would go by train, but there was limited rolling stock, and the railways also had to move thousands of refugees. Therefore, the Jats had to wait, even though they had turned over their duties to the Muslim relief squadron.

Pakistan was to be established officially on 14 August 1947; India was to declare its Independence the following day. In Kohat, we turned our attention to Pakistan's independence day. All officers had been asked to state in writing which country they wished to serve. I kept my promise to the Muslim men and volunteered for Pakistan. Some two weeks later I received a telephone call from the military assistant of the commander-in-chief of British India's Northern Command, General Sir Douglas Gracie. Jinnah had instructed Gracie that no Hindu or Sikh officer was to be permitted in the Pakistan Army. Therefore, Gracie was very sorry to tell me that I would have to go to India. He wanted me to remain in command of the regiment until relieved by Chauvel, who was given a priority passage for his return.

My inability to remain with the regiment and continue my life in the land where I was born and with the people I knew, dampened my enthusiasm for independence. Indian history had proven that people of different faiths and races could live at peace with one another. India's great rulers—for example, Ashoka and Akbar—brought peace and prosperity to the people of this vast land through tolerance and harmony. Rulers like Aurangzeb brought the end of the golden period of Mughal rule by trying to convert Hindus by the sword. Throwing off the yoke of foreign rule by dividing the land with the hope of building separate societies for Muslims and Hindus could weaken the subcontinent. Although I looked forward to Independence, I felt that we were paying too great a price.

I slept fitfully on the eve of Pakistan's independence day. I was unsure of the future and wondered whether our political leaders had the sagacity to lead this vast land between the Indus and the Brahamputra into the future. A poem I read some years later, by the renowned Urdu poet Faiz Ahmad Faiz of Lahore, expresses my thoughts during those times:

These tarnished rays,
this night-smudged light,
This is not that Dawn for which,
ravished with Freedom,
We had set out in sheer longing,
So sure that somewhere
in its desert the sky harbored,
A final haven for the stars,
And we would find it.

7

Partition and Independence of India

I carefully prepared my staff and the troops for celebrations of Pakistan's independence, but having been denied the opportunity to remain in Pakistan myself, I just did not have the heart to participate, regardless of my affection for the troops. An hour before the parade I told my batman to call Major Yusuf Khan, the senior Muslim officer, and tell him I was sick and that he was to command the parade. At 11 a.m., an elated Yusuf and a group of happy officers turned up at my bungalow. In keeping with our usual informality, they were all in my bedroom, hugging me and loudly wishing that I had been there at the head of the regiment. Unable to keep up the pretense, I admitted feigning sickness. They were at first aghast, but then saw my point. This was the day for the future officers of Pakistan.

Chauvel returned as we neared our departure. The Jats were to leave by a special train with other Hindu troops and their families. I was to accompany them, with my family, including my wife's mother and sister, who had come on a visit and had been unable to travel earlier because of the breakdown of railway traffic. Ours would be the first train out of Kohat since then and would have a heavily armed escort. As the time of departure came closer, I hardened myself to the farewells. We pulled out of Kohat on the morning of 27 September, with some 1,500 men and 500 women and children. An elderly British officer who was in charge of the supply depot was the train commander and I was his deputy. The Jats of 6th Lancers were the only combat troops and therefore security became my responsibility. The entire 8th (formerly Indian) Division, under command of recently promoted General Bakhtar Rana, a colleague from the Italian campaign, was to escort us to Rawalpindi. Chauvel, somewhat concerned for our security, decided to send a troop of armored cars all the way to Rawalpindi, and my friend Risaldar Mohammed Yusuf, who was an NCO when I joined the regiment, had volunteered to lead.

At Kohat, so many Hindu and Sikh civilians and their families had begged us to take them along that we had no choice but to do so. I had a compartment for my five family members. Eventually, we were joined by eight of my officers. Each of the three women took a berth, my infant son Ravi stayed in his Grandmother's berth, and the nine men took shifts on duty and in seats in the remaining berth. After we left Rawalpindi we stopped at a wayside station to cook our one hot meal for the day. There being no kitchen car, we had to unload our kitchen utensils and cook on the ground. At the first stop, I learned that the train commander had locked himself in his coupe. When I knocked on his door, he refused to open it and told me that he was quitting India, and since it was my country, I could have it all. I took charge and immediately sent patrols out, one to locate the source of drums beating ominously in the distance.

The monsoons as usual had damaged the rail tracks. Just short of Lahore, a rail bridge was down. While we waited for repairs our train was attacked at dawn by a mob. We were ready for them, and they scattered screaming, dragging their dead and wounded. The Pakistani authorities decided it would be safer for us and their own citizens, who might be tempted to attack us again, if our train was pulled to Sialkot.

When we finally entrained, we went via Montgomery and then across to India for Ambala. On arrival there we were met by officers of 7th Light Cavalry. The Jats had reached their destination and I would soon know where I was to go.

The 7th Light Cavalry was on occupation duty in Japan with Indian troops. They were a pre-war Indianized regiment and had no dearth of senior Indian officers. Lt. Col. Rajinder Singh Sparrow had been appointed the new commandant. The regiment offered little potential for my officers or me, and the cool reception we met with persuaded us to transfer.

On 20 October, in violation of a Stand Still Agreement that set aside six months for deciding the future of the princely state of Jammu and Kashmir (J&K), Pakistan sent into the state waves of raiders recruited from the frontier province. This was bad news and the Jats anxiously waited to hear of further developments while we carried out protection duties at a Muslim refugee camp nearby.

There was a dance at the Sirhind club that Saturday, and a few of us former 6th Lancers decided to entertain my women there. The club was crowded. As Usha and I did our first dance, Arjun Singh, my classmate from college and now in command of the air force station, stopped with his wife to greet us. He said, "I am sorry about Satinder." Alarmed, I asked, "What about Satinder?" Surprised at my question, he told me that my brother had been killed in an air crash on 27 September, the day I left Kohat.

Arjun offered to help me fly to Agra, to see Satinder's wife, Sarla, and their young children. I was at the air station at dawn the next day, while Arjun tried to reach his opposite number at Agra by radio. After an hour's wait Arjun's staff officer told me they were not able to arrange a flight. In truth, Arjun was too shy to tell me what I learned later, that Sarla had already remarried and her two sons had been adopted by their new father to comply with Sarla's precondition for remarriage. In the face of great tragedy, Sarla had made her decision and turned away from Satinder's family, who as refugees had little to offer except their love and emotional support.

The events in J&K soon distracted me from the loss of my brother and friend. Toward the end of October, Sparrow sent for me and told me that 7th Cavalry had received orders to send a squadron to Srinagar. The situation was critical and the armored cars were needed immediately. I was to take my Jats, formerly of 6th Lancers, and a troop of his original Jats. He explained that his regiment was still spread out between Bihar, its concentration area on their return from Japan, and Ambala. He had no choice but to order me and the men I had brought from Pakistan to undertake this mission.

Under attack from Pakistan, India was under a national emergency. Sparrow's reasoning was valid, so I agreed to prepare my squadron. I asked that the men who had no news of their families, and who wished to go home on leave, be left behind. Also, I asked for military transport to take our families immediately to their homes, if they had any, or that married quarters be provided in Ambala. Sparrow agreed. I reminded him that I hoped for an early transfer. He tried to persuade me to change my mind by invoking my loyalty to my men, just when they were to join another battle. Obviously, he was going to be difficult over my departure. But for now we plunged into preparations for the move of my squadron.

I arranged for my wife's mother and sister to leave for Mussoorie. They took Ravi with them, as my wife refused to go. She was independent, and had shown courage on the long, dangerous train journey from Pakistan. Besides, she had acquired a taste for adventure, so she had decided to be a camp follower.

After a meeting with his officers, Sparrow concluded that my squadron should be ready to leave on 1 November, but army headquarters insisted we advance our departure. The squadron and most of the regiment worked round the clock to get us ready. My JCOs assured me that they had talked to the men and those who had cause were to be left behind. I reviewed each case and did what I could to help before we left for J&K. Most men were determined not to miss the first military operation of an independent India. Therefore, only a handful wanted to remain and visit their families before rejoining the squadron in Kashmir.

Having done the trip to J&K via Jammu in a small mountain bus in 1936, I knew the road, which was not the main highway and had not been improved. It was going to be tough going, and our troops already in the valley needed us in a hurry. I did not want to burn out my men before we joined the battle, so I made sure that they had enough rest and good food and that we had all what we needed for the operation.

PART III

Defending India's New Borders

8

Saving Kashmir Valley

My Jat squadron left Ambala on the afternoon of 1 November 1947 and halted for the night at Jullundur. Here we were met by Leslie "Duggie" Sawhney, GSO1, 4th Indian Division. My wife and I were put up at the local hotel where most of the officers of the division and their families were staying. General K.S. "Timmy" Thimayya, his wife Neena, and many IMA classmates and their families gave us a warm reception. My wife received several invitations from my colleagues and their wives to stay at the hotel in Jullundur, but she insisted on continuing the journey with me.

Early the next morning General Thimayya arranged a briefing for me on developments in J&K. The origins of the conflict related to the question of the future of more than five hundred Indian princely states that had the choice to join Pakistan or India. In his advice to the princes, Mountbatten had emphasized that they should bear in mind the religious makeup of their population and contiguity to either country. J&K sat between both India and Pakistan and had a Hindu ruler and a mixed population. The state of Jammu and Kashmir, commonly referred to as Kashmir, has misled the world into thinking of the Kashmir Valley as the former princely state. The Kashmir Valley is indeed a majority Muslim area in J&K, but there are other regions with different demographic make-ups: Jammu, in the south, is a majority Hindu region; Ladakh, in the north-east, and Kishtwar, south-east of the Kashmir Valley, are Buddhist and Hindu, respectively, with Muslim minorities; the northern territories, under Pakistani occupation, and Poonch are largely Muslim.

The tide of communal fighting in neighboring Punjab had spilled across the border into J&K. Both India and Pakistan wanted the state for economic, strategic, and political reasons. Pakistan, which had been gradually losing the territories it had hoped to include, wanted this state badly. With J&K's ruler unable to decide and the two countries unable to reach an agreement, all parties accepted Mountbatten's proposed six-month Stand Still Agreement. But Pakistan's patience had obviously run out, as it allowed the frontier tribesmen to attempt to take J&K by force.

Maharaja Hari Singh, J&K's ruler, turned to India for help. When Sheikh Mohamad Abdullah, the leader of the majority political party, the National Conference, added his voice to the ruler's, India accepted accession of the state and ordered its troops to defend J&K against Pakistani raiders. Hurriedly, India airlifted the 1st Sikh Regiment to Srinagar, and the 50th Parachute Brigade was ordered to Jammu by road.

The situation in the valley was critical as Colonel S. Rai led his Sikhs to Baramulla. As more waves of raiders reached the valley, they spread out in the area, threatening the road to Srinagar and forcing Rai to withdraw to Pattan. Near the airport at Badgaon the situation also had become critical and more troops were flown in, including a battalion of Rajputana Rifles, under the command of Lt. Col. Sarup Singh Kalan, and the 161st Infantry Brigade headquarters, under Brigadier L.P. "Bogey" Sen.

My squadron reached Gurdaspur late in the evening and we harbored for the night in a compound. My wife and I slept on the floor in an unfurnished house. We were exhausted by then and my thoughts were on tomorrow. It would have been easier if my wife had stayed at Jullundur in the first place. Although she did not want an early marriage and children, she had reluctantly followed the custom of our land. We were generally well liked socially and occasionally had some good times together, but our wedded life was far from comfortable. Once married, she wanted independence from her parents and had undertaken this hazardous journey in her desire to be on her own. Now, there was little else for her to do except to return to Jullundur. She left the next morning with Lt. Col. Gurbux Singh, later to become a good friend, who was on his way to Jullundur. My squadron went north on the highway leading to Dalhousie.

At Pathankot, we turned west toward the river, where Lt. Col. Prem Bhagat V.C. and his Bombay Sappers were constructing a Bailey bridge. Already, elements of 50th Parachute Brigade had moved ahead to Jammu, securing the road, the airfield, and the town.

At about 3 p.m. Prem gave me the signal to cross, and in three hours we were in a night harbor south of the River Tawi, in Jammu. We began to work on our vehicles for the mountain driving ahead. I briefed the men on the road and cautioned them to drive carefully. We were the first armor on its way to the valley, where our forces were hard pressed for support. We had to get there as soon as possible.

The next morning, 3 November, we were off at the crack of dawn. On the way, we met the J&K superintendent engineer responsible for the roads, who had been the garrison engineer at Ahmadnagar when I left for the Middle East. He was most anxious about the future of J&K and was determined to get us across the chain bridge over the Chenab River, which took only two-and-half-ton loads. My armored cars carried a bridge classification of seven, and I knew that by stripping them down the load factor could be reduced only to five, which still was too heavy. So we removed all the tow chains from our vehicles and reinforced the bridge with them.

As the last armor went across the bridge, a resounding cheer went up from our throats like thunder echoing far down the river valley. The vehicles of the brigade in the valley waited for us on the other side. They fell in behind us and shortly we were going, our gears screaming, up the ascent to Banihal. We stopped for the night near the foot of the high Banihal pass, which reached some ten thousand feet, tired but content. I felt that we had overcome our worst hurdle. My squadron had handled the frontier tribesman for more than two years, and I felt confident that we would beat the hell out of them.

About halfway to Srinagar, a liaison officer from 161st Brigade caught up with us with a message from Brigadier Sen urging us on. The Sikhs had lost Colonel Rai, suffered quite a few casualties, and were nearly encircled at Pattan. Sen had ordered the Sikhs to withdraw further back. The battle at Bagdaon had not gone well either. The company commander, Major Sharma, whom I knew well, had been killed.

The squadron encamped at the edge of Srinagar airfield, next to brigade headquarters. After settling the men down I went to call on the brigadier. I had not met Bogey Sen before, but he was married to the sister of a friend from the IMA who had been killed in Singapore. When I entered the house they were using as headquarters, I found that Sen was accompanied by Maj. Gen. Kalwant Singh, our newly appointed divisional commander and Singh's GSO1, "Tutu" Bhagat. I was bombarded with questions about the readiness and capability of my squadron. After that, I was briefed on the developments in the valley. The situation had been made more critical because of our slow build up of forces. Demobilization and the dislocations due to the partition of the forces left few organized units available and made airlift insufficient.

Pakistan had the best and most direct road to the valley. The 161st Brigade was preparing for an attack on Shaletung, where the raiders were being held, 6 miles from Srinagar. Some of the raiders had infiltrated to the River Jhelum, which ran through Srinagar, and had even burned a bridge and some houses. We barely held the airfield, but our road to the city was secure, and the raiders were being kept some three miles back along the main highway to Baramula. It did not surprise me when Sen said, "We want you in on this tomorrow. Will you do it?"

Since leaving Ambala we had slept little, driven all day, and taken our vehicles across the most difficult mountain roads. We had done this at the cost of regular maintenance on the vehicles and now some of them required workshop attention. Any breakdown in the battle would result in the loss not only of an armored car, of which there were only eleven, but also of my highly trained, valuable crew. I said I realized the urgency, but explained my situation. Bhagat gave me a look of disdain. Sen watched me thoughtfully, and Kalwant, soon to be popularly known as "K", turned to me and said, "Come on, Rikhye. You have a hell of a squadron and you have made it here against heavy odds. We will take the risk and I want you to go for the raiders tomorrow. Besides, I have an idea that I want to talk about to all of you."

Apparently K and Bogey had already discussed the infantry part of the battle. They intended to use the Sikhs down the main road and the Rajputana Rifles from the airport to attack from the north. They had only two mountain artillery guns, from the army of the princely state of Patiala, and hoped that the air force would spare some eight Spitfires for ground support. My squadron would support the Sikh attack and then break through along the highway. Then K offered the bait, which as a cavalryman I could not refuse. Sheikh Abdullah, the chief minister, was anxious about the security of Bandipur, some 30 miles up the road, near Wular Lake. He had asked K to send some troops there. K knew the area like the palm of his hand, having spent many holidays in Kashmir. I had spent my furlough there after the war. We poured over the map to find a good route to Bandipur. A road from near the airport went around the Wular Lake and then south behind the raiders' positions. K remarked, "That is a typical job for the cavalry, I want you to send part of your squadron to Bandipur and try to outflank the enemy. What do you think?" He had me eating out of his hand.

By the next morning, in spite of all our efforts during the night, we only had nine road-worthy armored cars. I gave my squadron officer, Noel David, three armored cars and the rifle troop to carry out the outflanking maneuver. I formed the remainder into two troops of armored cars to cover the highway and give direct support to the infantry attack.

Noel left when it was still dark and made good progress. An air force reconnaissance flight reported thousands of tribesmen and some 150 vehicles on the west of Shaletung, presumably readying for an attack on the Sikhs. The raiders, in an attempt to preempt our advance, attacked us first. Sen hurried his preparations to advance the time of his attack. Meanwhile, I told Noel to ease forward to Shaletung from the north. The bridge over the spill channel was weak and narrow, but he managed to cross it. His troops were mistakenly accepted by the raiders as Pakistani.

Bereft of armored cars, I had moved my control radio to a Dodge one-ton truck. I had to go forward, but was stopped by heavy machine-gun and mortar fire at the spill-channel crossing. A little after that, Sen and Lt. Col. Sampuran Bachan Singh, of the Sikh battalion, caught up with me. They decided to commence their attack immediately, and Sen gave his staff the orders over his radio.

Noel reported that he had achieved complete surprise and that the raiders had panicked. We pressed our ground attack, with my six armored cars abreast of the leading Sikh bayonet charge. The armored cars attracted heavy fire and all their tires were cut right before our eyes. The crews had closed their turrets but kept up their fire. Although left with only a truck, my instincts told me I should be with my attacking armored cars on the main road. I rushed to the truck, shouting at my driver to start up, but my senior JCO, Than Singh, stopped me: "You are not going forward, Sahib. You are more useful alive than dead." He was right.

It seemed like hours, but the battle was over in twenty minutes. The raiders left behind about 475 dead and some 140 vehicles. We suffered only light casualties, including two of my men. Later in the afternoon, the Sikhs and Noel's troops occupied Pattan, which had been abandoned by the raiders. They retreated to Baramula, which they abandoned during the night. Before they left, they had pillaged the local convent, raped and murdered four nuns, and abducted hundreds of women and children.

After the victory at Shaletung, my squadron assisted in the taking of Uri on 14 November. Later, we helped relieve a state forces garrison in Poonch, before returning to Uri, which was then under attack from the raiders.

On a visit to the troops, Prime Minister Nehru informed us that any advance toward Muzzafarabad was likely to invite the Pakistani army to join the war, a development he wished to avoid. He said that the Indian Government was considering bringing the issue of J&K before the United Nations.

I received a letter from Colonel Walter Schoolbred, commandant of Hodson's Horse at Meerut, whom I had served with for a year on General Russell's staff in Italy. I had written Schoolbred to ask if he had a vacancy for me in his regiment, and now he was offering me a job. I spoke to Sen and told him of my intention to leave. He was very disappointed. He felt that I deserved to be decorated for bravery and leadership, but suspected that if I left, the regiment would not put up my name. I explained my difficult relationship with the regimental officers, and he consented to my transfer, but most unhappily. When I met Sparrow, he had received my posting orders to Hodson's Horse, and he too tried to change my mind. But when he realized my decision was irrevocable, he allowed me to leave 7th Cavalry.

I collected my wife from Jullundur and joined Hodson's Horse at Meerut. All commands were now being Indianized and Schoolbred had already been replaced by Hari Badhwar, formerly of 3rd Cavalry and a former Japanese prisoner of war. I was to be his second in command, a position I expected to enjoy. But within three months I was ordered to take over the Royal Deccan Horse (RDH) from Duggie Sawhney, who left on promotion.

The Pakistan Army was by now involved in the fighting in J&K. I took over RDH at Ambala early in May. Its Jat squadron was on detached duty at Jammu, and the rest of the regiment soon joined it there. Pakistani tanks from Sialkot and Gujarat had sallied into J&K territory, threatening the delicate line of communication with Naushera and beyond to Poonch. I was soon engaged with Pakistani armor west of the Chenab River.

One afternoon, Pakistani tanks moved to attack Chamb. We had anticipated such a move, and the resulting battle turned out to be the only tank-versus-tank engagement of the operation. While we were in the midst of the battle, the army commander, stationed in Jammu to deal with the fighting, received orders from Delhi for a cease-fire. As I had given away my rear link tank to one of the squadrons, there was no way to relay the news to me directly as I was on the radio frequency of my assaulting tanks, and so I continued to harass the Pakistani armor. The commander sent an air observation plane to find me, inform me to cease-fire, and then bring me back to the commander's headquarters. Within an hour, I was standing before the army commander, with no remorse. I relaxed when I noticed an approving twinkle in his eye.

Little did I know, this day's action would turn out to be my last battle.

9

With the Black Elephant

In early 1948 my personal finances began to worry me for the first time in my life. When I joined the army, because of the lower pay scales for ICOs, my parents had borne all my expenses except for my daily living. My clothes, uniforms, holidays, and all other expenses had been taken care of. During the Second World War, the British had increased salaries of ICOs to a level equal to their British counterparts, and there was little to spend my money on while I was away overseas. When I returned to India I was a well-paid major and by all reckoning I could more than afford to get married. And when I did marry, my wife came loaded with clothes, jewelry, and cash. The loss of our family estate after Partition required us to tighten belts, but what had a much graver impact on our lives was that after Independence the Indian Government withdrew wartime benefits and reverted ICO emoluments to pre-war scales. This cut my salary by half.

Many ICOs in my circumstances appealed to the authorities to reconsider the pay scales, but without effect. Quite a few quit and sought jobs in civilian life. I could not. I was married with a son and had another child on the way. My parents and their families were all refugees and had little money. My father was considering going into private practice. It was then that he received the invitation from Lord and Lady Mountbatten to assist in organizing medical facilities for a new industrial township at Faridabad, near Delhi. With the ready consent of my mother, Father accepted, for the job would provide them with additional income and an opportunity to serve fellow refugees from the Punjab. On one of my trips to Delhi, I saw my parents roughing it out in the hot weather in a large tent, in the middle of a sea of tents that housed some hundreds of thousands of refugees. My parents' tent had a grass-mat shade over it, electricity, fans, and a refrigerator. They were comfortable and happy.

Early in 1951, I was posted to the Infantry School, Mhow, as an instructor on a new mandatory course for senior officers. I had completed about three years in command and had planned to apply for admittance to the staff college, but this posting would delay such an attempt by at least a year.

A year earlier I had attended a Unit Commanders Course in Mhow. I was back with my family, including a second son, Bhalinder, born on 19 September 1950. Once into the routine of life as an instructor, I would have time to prepare for the entrance examination to the staff college.

I was well into my studies when I received a telegram from my sister Indra. Father had been taken seriously ill and I must come immediately to Rajpura refugee camp, near Patiala, where he had been sent by Lady Mountbatten to open a new hospital and ancillary medical support services.

I reached Rajpura at about 7 a.m. after a sleepless eighteen-hour journey. Some fifty close relatives were already there. I was told by Indra that Father had in fact died before she sent me the telegram. She and Mother had decided that the news of Father's death might be too much of a shock if I received it when alone at Mhow. Instead, I was to be told of his death when my family surrounded me. Mother was distraught but in control. She was greatly relieved to see me.

We said our final prayers at *kirya*, the tenth day of Father's death, and gave alms to and fed the poor. All our guests left that day. The next day we took Mother to Mhow, where, with the help of Indra and her family, we gradually brought her out of her grief. Meanwhile, her mother had received a grant of land at Semla, near Ambala, 100 mile north-west of Delhi, as compensation for her losses in Pakistan, and she gifted a quarter of the allotment and part of a house there to my mother. Anxious to occupy herself at her new home, Mother decided after about a month in Mhow to leave with Indra and her family.

I took the staff college entrance examination and managed to win a place. The college, located at Wellington, Nilgiri Hills, in south India, had mostly rental housing for students with families. The house allotted to me in nearby Conoor was a small English-style cottage with a neat garden. The near-year-long course constituted a major advance in the career of most military officers. But as the most senior student, it did not take me long to realize that I had come too late in my service for the college to be of help to me. The course was designed primarily for mid-level staff officers; I, like a number of other students, had already commanded a unit. In my last appointment, I had been an instructor for the training of a higher level of officers. And what made it even more difficult to adjust was the atmosphere, which was more like a middle school than a college.

Complicating the situation further were my family circumstances. Barely able to cope with my own family, I inherited the mantle of my deceased father. About a year before he died, he had helped my two younger brothers lease a farm near Bareilly, Uttar Pradesh. In addition to the investment required for farming, the costs of board and lodging for my brothers had to be covered. Just like any small business that moves in cycles, farming required a constant flow of capital. The choice before me was to either support this venture or pay for the boys' return to college, an option they had already rejected. So choosing the first course, I borrowed money; but even before I left the staff college, the venture collapsed because of the failure of the monsoons.

At the end of my course, I was posted as the GSO1 at the 1st Armored Division at Jullundur Cantonments, Punjab. I had first been associated with the division when I commanded the Royal Deccan Horse. The "Black Elephant", a charging bull elephant on a gold background, was the sign of the 1st Armored. The division proudly wore the sign on its uniforms and vehicles while on service up-country. With unending tensions between India and Pakistan, the division, India's primary ground strike force, was strategically located less than two hours' drive from the Pakistani border. The divisional commander, Maj. Gen. Mohinder Singh Wadalia, was tall and athletic, and one of the nicest senior officers that I had had the good fortune to be associated with. He and his charming Belgian wife, Martha, kept a lovely home and neatly pulled the many threads of the division together, largely focusing on the senior officers and their families. General "Wad" (as he was known) spent most of his time helping to ready the troops for combat. It became clear to me at the outset that he expected me primarily to support his efforts to boost the combat efficiency of the division.

As the political climate between India and Pakistan calmed somewhat, and after the raising of new armored units, the division was transferred to Jhansi, Uttar Pradesh, where the accommodation was better, the training areas were relatively free of crops, and the field firing ranges were the best in the country. Among the joys of a posting at Jhansi was that the forests nearby had some game.

The division also received a new commander, as General Wad was appointed chief of the general staff, under the newly appointed chief of staff Thimayya. Although General Wad would be missed, his good posting meant that he would watch over our interests. His loyalty to his comrades, especially his friends, never ebbed. Our new commander was General Daulet Singh, who had commanded the independent armored brigade.

Daulet worked long hours and was attentive to the details of running the division. He continued with Wad's high level of training and made a special contribution by further improving administration at all levels. Daulet enjoyed a daily, hour-long walk, on which I happily joined him whenever I could. This afforded a wonderful opportunity to talk and exchange ideas. We ended our walks at his house, where I would have a seasonal beverage and sometimes stay for a drink with his wife and children.

It was during this time that I attended an Indian cavalry reunion in Delhi. Among the few former British officers, I was glad to find Pat Willamson of my old regiment, 6th Lancers. He was the managing director of Williamson & Magor, the largest manager of tea estates in the free world and a major owner of tea gardens in India. I had known that he was an important businessman, but was not aware that he was the chief executive of one of the major British ventures in India. We had booked rooms at the same hotel and spent an evening reminiscing about our time together during the war. It was when he asked me about the break-up of the regiment and my last days with 6th Lancers that conversation turned to my family. I gave him a brief account of the changed circumstances. Without hesitation, Pat offered to take both the younger boys as tea garden management apprentices. He said my brothers would solve a problem for him because foreign-owned businesses were under government pressure to Indianize. He had taken in some Bengalis and Assamese to oblige local officials and politicians. But none of them had the qualities to rise in their professions. While I demurred at my sudden good fortune because I wanted to be sure that my brothers were up to Pat's expectations, he persisted: "Come on, Indar. You will be doing me a great favor. I want good Punjabi *goondas* [rascals] just like you in my firm."

Comforted by his insistence I offered to send Jeshi first, and if it worked out well I would send Hemi after a year. Pat ordered brandy to celebrate, and we stayed at the bar until closing time. In a display of one-upmanship over the old Indian army, Pat said that he intended to offer my brothers the same emoluments as his British employees. I could not thank him enough. I would now be left to pay off my outstanding debts, which would still take some time.

After General Daulet had commanded the division for a year, he was appointed quartermaster general at Delhi and was replaced by Maj. Gen. K.P. Darghalkar, a former prisoner of war under the Japanese. The ill treatment of prisoners of war by the Japanese was a tragedy too well known to repeat here. Even those among such prisoners who were able to continue service in the armed forces lived with their scars. General "Drag" (his nickname) could eat only boiled, unspiced food and could drink no more than one diluted whiskey. A man of discipline and integrity, he lived alone with his spaniel dog and household staff. His sparing habits had a profound effect on official and social life in the division.

General Drag enjoyed his lunches in the divisional officers' mess, often alone. I joined him occasionally. At the start of the hot weather, when my wife and our younger son Bhalinder left for Shimla (where Ravi already was attending school), I joined the general for lunch regularly. Like his predecessor, Drag daily took an hour-long evening constitutional, and I regularly accompanied him. Usually, we spent another hour at the end of the walk for a cup of tea and a chat. On one such sultry evening in June 1957, as Drag and I sat on the lawn in the gentle breeze, he told me that the military secretary at Delhi had telephoned him to say that my promotion to the rank of colonel had been approved and that I should expect a posting to the Directorate of Military Operations, Army Headquarters. I was pleased at the news but not happy about going to Delhi. I said so to Drag adding, "You know I can't afford to live in Delhi." He replied, "Your posting is due by September. Thimmy hasn't given his final decision yet. You just have to wait. I will see to it that they do well by you."

When the time came for my posting, Drag received a call that the chief of staff wanted to see me at Agra. I took the train and stayed overnight with the Parachute Brigade. It was this brigade that had provided its 3rd (Kumaon) Parachute Regiment for duty with the UN Emergency Force (UNEF) in Gaza and the Sinai after the Suez War of 1956. The battalion had completed a year's service in the Middle East and was being replaced by 1st (Punjab) Parachute Regiment. Chief Thimayya was coming to see them before their departure.

Early next morning, the chief arrived by a special flight. After his official reception, he took me aside and said, "I am here for a very short visit and I must return to Delhi for urgent business. I did want to see you personally. First, I want to tell you that you did a fine job for the armored division. You took good care of three commanders and two of them are my PSOs [personal staff officers]. I was pleased to promote you. I was going to bring you to my MO [military operations] branch. But I required a colonel I can really trust for a special assignment. As you see, I am here to see the 1st Para and attached services off to Gaza. You will go with them as their contingent commander."

The chief could see the turmoil in my face at the suddenness of the news and he explained, "I had chosen you earlier for this appointment, but you know the PM [prime minister] takes personal interest in international affairs and he is particular about the UN, and especially Egypt. I had to press the defense minister for a decision on your posting and it was only after I told him that the next contingent was due to depart for Egypt in about a fortnight that he spoke to the PM."

The chief now explained to me the circumstances that led to my selection: "At the end of the last conference of the Commonwealth chiefs of staff in England, I stopped in Gaza to see our troops. We had received complaints from Sarup Singh Kalaan, the contingent commander, and Onkar Deva, the battalion commander, about each other, and from Kalaan against the commander of UNEF. I found our troops in good shape, well cared for, and heard nothing but praise from other contingents and Egyptians. My talks with our officers convinced me that we have to be more selective in senior appointments."

Referring to General E.L.M. ("Tommy") Burns, head of UNEF, the chief continued, "I said to him that since we had provided the largest contingent, he should have an Indian COS. He was receptive. With his dry humor, he said that if I sent him a good contingent commander and he thought him suitable, he may choose him for the post. On my return to Delhi I went through the list of present colonels and I put them aside, because they were either due for promotion or to be retired. Then I looked at the list of those recommended for promotion and I found your name. I decided that you will do. Now you'd better do well and get the COS position. Good luck and keep me informed."

I returned to Jhansi to complete arrangements for the move of my wife and son Bhalinder for the year that I was to be away. I was hoping to take advantage of my posting abroad to reduce my financial obligations. The house in Shimla was still occupied by tenants and the rooms available were not up to the standard for my family. My wife chose to stay with her parents to start with. She later rented a portion of a bungalow in Patiala. My sister Indra, at Dalhousie, offered to take Bhalinder so that he could continue his kindergarten class at the local convent.

The entire contingent was housed in the Transit Camp, Colaba, not far from the center of Bombay. We were there for nearly a week before we boarded the ship. My younger brother Sodarshan, now turned a professional gambler, managed a cards club and was a racehorse bookie—but he did not have any license for either. His second wife, Vera, a former WREN (a member of the Women's Royal Navy Service), was a fashion model, and an editor of the popular society magazine *Eve's Weekly*, and her younger sister, Joan, also a fashion model, took charge of my entertainment. Joan, whose Indian name was Madhu, eventually succeeded her sister in my brother's affections and became his third wife. My mother's two younger brothers, Major Krishan Kumar Sudan and Raj Kumar Sudan, were also in the city with their families. Many army friends were there as well. It was a social whirlwind and I was glad to board the ship and recover from the high life that I had led in Bombay.

PART IV

Peacekeeping with the United Nations

10

Commander, Indian Contingent, UNEF

The Middle East was always of special interest to India. Our country, with its close ties with the Arab peoples, depended heavily upon the Suez Canal as the main surface link with the western markets so vital to our nation's development plans. And besides our historic and national interests, the Indian Army had inherited a tradition of meritorious service in the Middle East under the British. Many of our famous regiments proudly carried names of familiar places in that region, such as Gaza, and others less well known, as battle honors on our standards. Previous generations had served in the different lands of the Middle East, and some had remained behind in the Commonwealth cemeteries. Some of us had served in Persia and Iraq; or in the Ninth Army in Syria, Lebanon, and Palestine; or in Eighth Army in the Middle East Command. And now India had provided the strongest contingents of troops to UNEF in the effort to bring peace to the area.

The first UNEF Indian contingent included an infantry battalion, 3rd Parachute Battalion (Kumaon), supply and postal units, transport, ordnance, and signal platoons, a military police detachment, and a number of staff personnel. Colonel Sarup Singh Kalaan, a friend and colleague of many years, had been placed in charge of the contingent and appointed liaison officer to UNEF. After the first contingent had spent nearly a year in UNEF, a rotation program for troops was decided upon, and I was sent in command of the second Indian contingent, composed as the previous one had been.

The first Indian contingent, which was sent in a hurry, was airlifted, whereas my contingent traveled to UNEF in the SS *Muzzafri*, a British Indian Line Haj ship. The new battalion was the 1st (Punjab) Parachute, under the command of Lt. Col. Inder Singh Gill. Inder, while studying for a higher degree in his mother's native Scotland during the Second World War, had joined the Royal Engineers. He later transferred to the British Commandos and was captured by the Germans during an operation in Greece. He transferred to the Indian Army after Independence. I had first met him when he led a local militia unit during operations in J&K.

Our voyage was uneventful, except for a brief stop for refueling and a short visit to the British troops at Aden. On reaching Suez, we were met by a UNEF staff officer and an Egyptian pilot who guided our ship up the canal. On reaching Port Said on the other side, we were entertained to a large lunch. Here I was introduced to an Egyptian brigadier general, Amin Hilmy El Tani, chief of the liaison staff to UNEF. With his confident air and sparkling eyes, he easily stood out from among the others present. We were to work closely together over the years and become lifelong friends.

An Egyptian Army band provided music, playing many Arabic tunes, novel but pleasing to our ears, including "Moustafa", composed by an Egyptian expatriate to the United States. This song had achieved almost the same popularity with the UN soldiers as the wartime hit tune "Lilly Marlene" (first introduced in North Africa by Rommel's troops) enjoyed among troops of the Eighth Army, who had adopted the tune on their march from El Alamein to Berlin.

The advance party of my contingent had been sent by air to Gaza about a month before. They had taken charge, and it was to their credit that the rotation began speedily and was completed smoothly. Kalaan and I left Port Said by car late in the afternoon and made very good time along the newly paved road built by the Egyptians through the Sinai to El Arish and Rafah. We drove quickly through El Arish, with its belt of date palms around a mass of mud huts, new villas by the sea, and military barracks. Here the road followed close to the sea, which washed over some of the loveliest sandy beaches along the eastern Mediterranean. UNEF had a Canadian air transport unit and some Indian troops stationed here.

Beyond El Arish, we drove past the Yugoslav camp and entered the Gaza Strip at Rafah. Driving through small towns and refugee camps, we encountered heavy pedestrian and vehicular traffic. Ruddy-faced school children sat by the road doing homework, using edges of the tarmac for slates. Clusters of people sat near the refugee camps transacting business, which I later learned consisted mainly of trading in rations that had been provided by the United Nations. Before crossing into the Gaza Strip, we drove along the boundary of a huge UNEF camp that Kalaan explained was UNEF's maintenance area, with Canadian and Indian support services. We continued to Khan Yunis and beyond, where human endeavor had slowly but surely overcome nature. Many acres were under cultivation, and one could see date palms, almond and fig orchards, fields of vegetables, and citrus gardens.

I was returning to this town after fourteen years, having last traveled through it in a cattle rail truck with the 8th Indian Division from Damascus to Alexandria, en route to Italy in September 1943. Gaza had changed from the mud huts that I then knew into a bustling township. It had grown enormously and now had a modern shopping center, villas, paved roads, piped water, and electricity. Kalaan drove me through the town to his villa, which faced a small park opposite the offices of the Egyptian governor-general. It was cold inside Kalaan's room, which I was to share, sleeping on a narrow and uncomfortable "hospital" cot. We washed quickly and went to call on UNEF's chief of staff, Swedish colonel Erik Rosengren, who lived in an adjoining villa. The force commander, General E.L.M. Burns of Canada, was away from headquarters.

Before coming to Gaza, I had heard about the difficulties that Kalaan had encountered in his role as the senior Indian officer and liaison officer to UNEF, and now I heard from Kalaan himself. What had especially incensed Kalaan was that the force commander did not invite Kalaan and other national contingent liaison officers, all of them lieutenant colonels or colonels, to join his mess and had left them in a common mess for the remainder of the staff. Kalaan and the other national liaison officers had protested against this "discrimination". On Kalaan's suggestion, to lend more dignity to the post and perhaps secure me an invitation to the commander's mess, my official designation had been changed from contingent

liaison officer to commander Indian contingent, although my role
had altered but little.

It was time Kalaan and I repaired to "our" mess to quench our
thirsts and satisfy our appetites. The headquarters mess, or "B mess",
as it was usually called, was on the edge of sand dunes overlooking
the Mediterranean. A wide door led to a sparsely furnished anteroom.
Beyond the anteroom lay a long bar lined with liquor bottles and a
dining room with small tables. The place looked more like a cafeteria
than a mess. The view through the windows, overlooking the short
beach and the Mediterranean, was out of a picture book.

In the crowded bar, I was introduced to a number of people,
including the national contingent liaison officers. With the exception
of a Yugoslav colonel, they were all of my father's generation. But
they were a jovial group and I felt sure that life in Gaza would not be
dull. Over liquor and cheap food, I became acquainted with the
problems of my ilk.

The main problem, apparently, was that the home countries
considered their national liaison officers to be their senior officers
for all purposes. The force commander, however, dealt with unit
commanders directly and preferred to restrict his contacts with national
liaison officers to national matters, such as the dietary habits of troops.
Furthermore, the national liaison officers were directly responsible
to their governments and not to the force commander. Since the
position of liaison officer was akin to that of an attaché, the force
commander did not feel obliged to look after the liaison officers
except for providing some material assistance unavailable from local
resources. This problem was not resolved until eight years later, after
I had assumed command of UNEF.

I had spent my service life as a regimental officer, on the staff
close to the general officers during the war, in military cantonments
and in schools of instruction, and I had always enjoyed a privileged
position. After my recent appointment, I had left India amid
ceremonial fanfare and after meetings with several high-ranking
government and military officials. Indeed, my appointment had
propelled me swiftly, if briefly, to national attention (only once before,
during the early part of Kashmir operations, had I appeared on the
front pages of our national daily newspapers and All India Radio

news bulletins). I had been spoiled for days on the voyage to Egypt as the most important guest aboard. But this evening I sat in a bar full of people of many nationalities, mostly clerks, drivers, mechanics, radio operators, and junior civil and military officers. With time, I learned to like the place. Although the mess lacked a sense of cohesion, because its members belonged to disparate groups, it possessed spirit. In the years to come, many people (myself included) attempted to improve the mess, but none of us was entirely successful. Depending upon the personality of the mess committee, the place would be presented as an army mess, a cafeteria, a restaurant, or just a club. But it always had life for its members, and it provided the heartbeat for the body of UNEF.

I was introduced to the senior civilian and military staff by the commander's aide de camp, Captain Vipin Khanna of the Guards. He emphasized cooperation between the civilian and the military staff and the contingents. He was most encouraging and I learned later that he had done a lot to smooth my future at UNEF.

Shortly after his return to Gaza, General Burns invited all national liaison officers to join his mess. Although I was happy at this "promotion", I was sorry to leave B mess and often returned there to meet many of the staff members whom I had come to know.

It was not until Kalaan and his troops departed from Port Said that I was able to get down to establishing my routine. There was a lot to learn about UNEF.

The events that had led the year before to armed action against Egypt by Israel, and subsequently by Britain and France, can be traced to the Palestine problem, Egypt's nationalization of the Suez Canal Company, and Egyptian support for Algerian independence. The birth of the state of Israel had led to the first Arab-Israeli war in 1948. After negotiations lasting more than a year, Ralph Bunche, the UN mediator, forged a series of General Armistice Agreements (GAA) between Israel and each of its Arab neighbors in 1949. A UN Truce Supervisory Organization (UNTSO) subsequently monitored the armistices and attempted to deal with complaints. Lack of compliance with the agreements, along with the other factors cited above, prompted a renewal of fighting in 1956. After Britain and France, who were parties to the conflict, vetoed the course of action proposed by the Security Council, the General Assembly, acting under the Uniting for Peace resolution of 1950, called for a cease-fire and authorized an emergency force to implement the resolution.

Burns, then chief of staff of UNTSO at Jerusalem, was called upon by the UN Secretary-General to take command of this force and to submit recommendations for its composition and organization. The eventual shape of the force turned out to be somewhat different from what Burns originally proposed, because only a limited number of nations, none of them major military powers, were eligible as contributors to this force. It was agreed that the permanent members of the Security Council should not contribute to the force. The outline organization of this force would be a headquarters (Headquarters UNEF) that would directly administer eight units, each of a battalion size. Only Canada and India offered administrative and technical troops, and it was decided that Canada would contribute the bulk of them. India also agreed to supply elements of the service corps and ordnance, military police, and signals personnel, while Norway offered to supply a medical company.

General Burns, on reaching Cairo, proceeded to establish a cease-fire. The next step was to separate the combatants, for which purpose UNEF troops were interposed between rival forces. Once UNEF moved into the Gaza Strip and along the international frontier, both the Israelis and the Arabs in the area came to know peaceful conditions again. The Israelis, on the one hand, and the Egyptians and Palestinians in the Gaza Strip, on the other hand, went about their routine business without disturbance. Similarly, shipping into the Gulf of Aqaba, to the Israeli port of Elath, and to the Jordanian port of Aqaba was restored. A few incidents of theft, sabotage, and cross-border infiltration did disturb the peace, but they were minor.

The presence of the force provided protection to both Egypt and Israel. Before UNEF's arrival, all Israel's kibbutzim opposite the line of camps held by UNEF lived in a constant state of emergency. While the presence of UNEF did not use physical force to maintain peace, there was no doubt about its moral force since, being an instrument of the United Nations, it had the support of member-states. Besides, the members of UNEF enjoyed excellent relations with the local inhabitants and contributed to the local economy in many ways.

The creation of UNEF was novel in the history of mankind. For the first time, different countries had voluntarily surrendered elements of their armed forces to a paramilitary organ under UN command and far from their homes to interpose themselves between two antagonists. This force was symbolic of the hopes and the desires of the peoples of the world to attain peace, a condition essential for the development and improvement of mankind. And while the final settlement of the wider political issues involved did not rest with soldiers of UNEF, the presence of the force in the Middle East provided a measure of political stability. However, as long as political agreement between Egypt and Israel was not forthcoming, it was difficult to forecast the future of UNEF.

For my part, I soon realized that my position was somewhat anomalous in the chain of command, so I decided to stand aside. I did, however, advise all my unit commanders and officers on staff to keep me informed of developments. This arrangement proved most satisfactory except for minor, albeit irritating, problems of adjustment between the Canadian and Indian administrative units, which were required to operate closely and sometimes as a single administrative service. These problems were invariably resolved jointly with the Canadian contingent commander, Colonel W. Chapelle, a fine officer.

The approach of Christmas generated a great deal of excitement among the Canadians, Scandinavians, Brazilians, and our Christian staff. There were probably forty officers and men of the Christian faith in my contingent. After consulting my senior officers and receiving the consent of my men, I had a word with Burns. I conveyed the Indian contingent's offer to take over observer and force administrative duties along the Armistice Demarcation Lines to relieve the units in the Gaza Strip and Rafah Maintenance Area for twenty-four hours to enable them to enjoy a complete Christmas holiday. This offer was gladly accepted. When Christmas Day came along, Indian sentinels manned the entire Armistice Demarcation Lines. This step, though it required considerable extra effort, created great goodwill between my troops and other contingents, who reciprocated in many ways, including helping the Indian contingent during one of our festivals. It was to become a regular practice in UNEF.

Dag Hammarskjöld arrived amid the gaiety of these celebrations.

He visited every contingent, and electrified the entire force. He expressed his appreciation to the Indian contingent for standing duty and was greatly impressed with the efficiency of our troops.

The rotation of contingents generated considerable military and social activity, keeping most of us fully occupied for several days at a time. And sometimes the force commander, on his official flying visits to neighboring capitals, would offer us space on his aircraft so that we might take leave. Many of us took advantage of his generosity.

Appointed Chief of Staff

UNEF had decided to open a summer leave camp in the hills at Broumana, Lebanon. Toward the end of March 1958, the Lebanese Tourist Department had invited the commander, his staff, and contingent commanders to see the location. Burns invited me to travel to Beirut in his plane and to dine with him that evening at the hotel. After dinner, the general asked me of news from India and I said there was little to add to the newspapers. After a few moments of silence, he said that I should have received a communication from Delhi by now. Before I could ask why, he said, "Before leaving Gaza I had word from the Secretary-General approving my recommendation that you be my next chief of staff. This has your government's approval. You will take over from Rosengren as of 1 April." Excited as I was to hear this news, I gave a skeptical laugh because Burns had earlier mentioned April Fool's Day. The general showed a flicker of a smile that conveyed that he was not joking. I had fulfilled General Thimayya's wish.

I prepared myself as well as I could for my new job. I had a very useful discussion with Burns as to how exactly I should operate as his chief of staff. He wanted me to conduct myself as the senior staff officer in the usual military manner. I would be responsible to him for the implementation of all operational plans. The coordination of the logistics and supply services was complicated and delicate and I was to assist in every possible way, but in the main the force commander himself would handle these matters. Similarly, the force commander would deal with the important task of relations with the Egyptian authorities, but it was up to me to strengthen the good relations he fostered. Because UNEF had not received Israel's permission to deploy on its side, contacts with Israel were a sensitive issue, especially for the Egyptians. Therefore, the force commander decided that he alone would continue to deal with the Israelis.

I gave special attention to patrolling and to maintaining equipment and vehicles. In isolated camps and under hard living condition, morale was a problem, which we sought to address by offering sports, recreational activities, leave camps, PX facilities, regular mail, and a good diet. Contributing nations sent entertainers, who made a round of all contingents. When a Swedish soprano came to sing for the troops, Inder Gill's battalion was included on her itinerary. Just before the soprano was to appear on stage, Gill stood up to explain the show to his Sikhs. His introduction was brief. He said, "Look fellows. You won't understand a word of what she sings. But she is very pretty. Have a good look and enjoy it. Since you won't know when she concludes her songs, when I clap, you clap." She received a thunderous applause at the end of each aria. When she concluded her performance, Gill rose to cheer her and so did his several hundred men. The soprano was overwhelmed with the ovation, and she turned to Gill and said, "Thank you, colonel. You have made my day. I had no idea that opera was so popular in India."

Before my appointment as chief of staff some dramatic developments had caused the Middle East once again to hurtle toward crisis. The growing influence of Egyptian president Gamal Abdel Nasser had led to a union between Egypt and Syria—the United Arab Republic (UAR). This caused the kingdoms of Iraq and Jordan to join in an Arab Federation. Yemen decided to join the UAR, and King Saud of Saudi Arabia gave the ministry of foreign affairs to his brother Prince Feisal, who was known to sympathize with Nasser. The changes in the region reignited an age-old conflict between the Muslim Druz and Christian Maronites in Lebanon, upsetting the delicate communal balance and leading to a civil war. In this environment, Camille Chamoun, whose term as president of Lebanon was about to expire, sought to amend the constitution and run for another term.

American and British concerns in the Middle East led the United Nations to act, and in 1958 the Security Council authorized an observer mission, the United Nations Observer Group in Lebanon

(UNOGIL). The UN headquarters in New York instructed UNEF to assist UNOGIL with UN Field Service personnel, communications equipment, and other material. John Birckhead, our dynamic chief administrative officer, was responsible for carrying out these orders.

I was instructed to go to Beirut and meet the triumvirate in charge of UN operations in Lebanon: Galo Plaza, former president of Ecuador; Rajeshwar Dayal, formerly India's permanent representative to the United Nations; and General Odd Bull, former chief of staff of the Royal Norwegian Air Force. The three worked remarkably well together and were assisted by David Blickenstaff, an experienced UN official, who was the principal secretary for the mission. The group was most interested to learn of developments in the area, particularly in Egypt, and was anxious to be kept informed on a regular basis. Like UNEF, UNTSO had been asked to establish close working relations with the Lebanese operation, and the Israeli–Lebanese Mixed Armistice Commission, located in Beirut and with observers responsible for the Israel–Lebanon border, served this purpose.

During his visit to the Middle East in June 1958, Secretary-General Dag Hammarskjöld met with Chamoun and other leaders in Lebanon. He went on to Amman, Jerusalem, and Cairo and in between paid UNEF a brief visit. Concerned that the civil war in Lebanon could threaten peace and security in the region, he sought and obtained assurances of cooperation from all the parties concerned.

UNOGIL persuaded Rashid Karami, the Muslim leader in northern Lebanon, to assist in facilitating its operations in the rebel-held border areas, and gradually the level and capability of UN patrolling had increased. Also, Plaza and Dayal had obtained from the Lebanese an agreement for elections and for General Fuad Chehab, popular among all factions, to be presidential candidate.

Lebanon was not to remain the only country in the region in political turmoil. On 14 July 1958 army officers seized control of Iraq in a bloody coup. Fearing his own ouster, Chamoun called for military support from France, Britain, and the United States. The next day, U.S. Marines landed at Beirut beaches. Fearing the same fate as his Hashemite relative in Baghdad, King Hussein also sought help from

5. With the 6th Lancers, 1942.

6. Sodarshan (*left*) and Satinder, brothers of the author, 1942.

7. The formidable foursome. *From left to right:* Lt. B.S. Battliwala, Lt. Raghujit Singh, Lt. L.C. Fonseca and Capt. B.C. Marsh, who replaced the author on his posting to divisional headquarters.

8. A visit to UNEF by Ralph Bunche, Gaza, April 1959. *From left to right*: the author, then UNEF Chief of Staff; Ralph Bunche, UN Under-Secretary for Special Political Affairs; Lt. Gen. E.L.M. Burns, UNEF Commander; and Brig. Gen. Amin Hilmy, Chief of Egyptian Liaison Staff in Gaza.

Britain and the United States, and the British landed two thousand troops in Amman, backed by U.S. fighter aircraft.

Chamoun's main problem was the political support that the rebels received from Nasser, on top of the ceaseless radio war conducted by Cairo against him. In seeking the help of the United States, he complained that the "communists" (by whom he meant supporters of Nasser) were gaining more power and threatened to take over Lebanon. At a time when the U.S. Secretary of state, John Foster Dulles, was building a "southern tier" to stop the spread of communism, the United States responded by dispatching its Sixth Fleet and landing its marines on the beaches of Beirut. Such an action by a superpower caused reverberations throughout the region and beyond. UNOGIL had to coexist with the marines, and we in Gaza placed our troops on maximum alert. But it was obvious that political problems needed political solutions. Chamoun was persuaded to hold elections and General Chehab, the chief of staff, was elected president. This government was immediately recognized by the United Kingdom and the United States.

When peace was restored in the aftermath of Chehab's election, Hammarskjöld visited the Middle East again to begin dismantling the UN operation in Lebanon and to set up a UN presence in Jordan headed by the experienced and able Ambassador Pier P. Spinelli, head of the UN office in Geneva. UNOGIL added another feather to the United Nations'—and Hammarskjöld's—cap. The Lebanese operation, however, had been different from other observer operations and from UNEF. The crisis in Lebanon was primarily political and internal, and the UN mission there was limited to Lebanese borders. In Gaza we were greatly relieved to see the end of the Lebanese crisis and the return to peace in the region. It also pleased us to note that in spite of turmoil in the region, UNEF had emerged as a highly successful peacekeeping tool.

Close liaison with Egypt and Israel was essential for UNEF's operations. Since Egypt had agreed to the deployment of the force on its territory, liaison arrangements with that nation took on an even greater importance. Accordingly, liaison offices were established at Cairo, Port Said, and UNEF headquarters in Gaza. A liaison team was established with the Israeli Defense Force (IDF) at Tel Aviv to overcome political problems related to the non-recognition by most UN member-states of Jerusalem as the capital of the Jewish state.

After I took over as the chief of staff, the IDF repeated an invitation for me to meet my opposite numbers in Israel. Burns and the Secretary-General decided not to allow me to go to Israel, for fear of prejudicing the Egyptians against me. I was comfortable with my superiors' decision on this matter.

But several months later, at the insistence of the Israelis, the Secretary-General authorized me to visit the IDF. As the United Nations had feared, Israeli radio announced my visit and I was met by the Israeli press at the UNEF's Ashqlon checkpoint on the border. I had nothing to say of any value and continued my journey to the Dan Hotel in Tel Aviv.

Colonel Chaim Herzog, director of military intelligence, and a delegation of Indian Jews met me at the hotel. While Herzog was warm in his reception, my former countrymen complained of ill treatment by the European Jews and offered me a petition to convey to the Indian Government. Herzog turned to me and said, "This is a free society, you know." Since I too came from such a society, I turned to the Indian Jews and told them, "You made your choice and came here. You know that your homes and property in India are kept in the custody of the Indian Government [and could thus be reclaimed if the Indians returned to India]." Then turning to the question of their petition I said, "I am here to represent the UN. Therefore I cannot help you with your petition. You can easily mail it to Delhi, if you so wish."

Herzog took me to a private dining room where chief of staff General Chaim Laskov waited to welcome me and to host lunch. It was a good session and it proved very helpful for us all to get acquainted. After that, all our communications were infused with that degree of personal warmth so important to establishing smooth working relations. The day after my return to Gaza, Hilmy came to my office on another matter. He was bound to have heard about my visit to Israel. As he rose to leave he asked about my trip. I replied that it had gone well.

The Israelis were most concerned with the ever-increasing influence of Nasser. Syria and Yemen had joined Egypt, and Iraq's new military leaders were pro-Nasser. Chamoun's failure had provided a fillip to the Muslims in Lebanon, and it seemed that the country might swing into active opposition of Israel. Only Jordan remained outside the Nasser camp, presently propped up by the British with American help. But the young king was growing ever more attentive to the voices of Palestinians within his country—and the Palestinians kept their radios tuned to Cairo.

Storms Brew in the Sinai

UNEF had a quiet year in 1958, and a visible peace prevailed in the region. Despite our success, the financing of UNEF became a major cause of concern. In Gaza, we spent our time streamlining the force, which was reduced to the minimal level needed for it to continue to carry out its mandate.

Taking advantage of the relative calm in UNEF's area of operations, Burns went on home leave. A few weeks later, the Egyptians brought in MIG fighters at El Arish, a move that led to an increase in overflights by both sides. The rise in Egyptian air activity greatly concerned the Israelis, who had hoped we could persuade the Egyptians to withdraw their fighter aircraft unit west of the canal. In October, the Israeli troops held a field firing exercise as part of their training maneuvers in the Negev and, as a matter of routine, brought troops to the area for exercise. Suspicious of the large number of IDF troops concentrated in the Negev, the Egyptians responded by moving additional troops into the Rafah–El Arish–El Auja triangle. The GAA had limited the number of Egyptian troops in this area to about a brigade of three battalions and border police. The Egyptians informed UNEF of their movements and started to patrol the area. Not surprisingly, an Egyptian patrol clashed with a UN patrol of Canadian troops; both sides suffered one casualty.

As we anticipated, the Israelis protested, and I sought instructions from New York. I was advised to argue for withdrawal of Egyptian forces on three grounds: (1) the increase in the number of Egyptian troops in the area constituted a violation of the GAA; (2) Egypt had agreed to UNEF's assuming responsibility along the international frontier and the Gaza Strip and therefore the presence of Egyptian troops violated this arrangement; and (3) UNEF could not share patrol responsibilities along the frontier.

Remy Gorgé, UNEF political and legal adviser, and I realized that the negotiations that I was to enter into with the Egyptian High Command at El Arish would be my first high-level talks. We thoroughly prepared ourselves for the meeting. Remy had gone over all the political and legal issues and briefed me on the process and style of negotiations. His approach was essentially based on agreements and international law. However, when I met the commander of the Egyptian Eastern Army, representing Commander-in-Chief Field Marshal Hakim Amer, the scenario was not what I had prepared for. The general received me with great courtesy and warmth. I was only a colonel, but he greeted me as an equal and an honored guest from India. After the usual cup of coffee and a glass of coke, he reminded me of the good relations between our two countries. When the general turned his remarks to UNEF and our being guests of Egypt, I immediately understood the thrust of his conversation.

I had made sure that I had read everything related to UNEF. I was clear on the question of the sovereign rights of states. Furthermore, Hammarskjöld's statement to the UNEF Advisory Committee during the preparations leading to the establishment of UNEF was engraved in my mind: "For my whole operation, the very basis and starting point has been the recognition of the General Assembly of the full and unlimited rights of Egypt." Therefore, I was able to put the general at ease. Apparently, recognition of Egypt's sovereignty was the key to our negotiation.

When I presented the United Nations' arguments to the Egyptian commander, he accepted the second and third points, but not the first. He said that Israel had violated the GAA by occupying the El Auja demilitarized zone, and therefore, he argued, Egypt had no obligation to comply with limiting its force in the El Arish area to a brigade. He saw good reason, however, to avoid shared patrol responsibilities with UNEF along the frontier. He also emphasized that by permitting UNEF on its soil, Egypt had not abrogated its sovereign right to move its troops freely in order to defend its territory.

After an exchange of messages between New York, Cairo, and UNEF, an agreement was reached reaffirming UNEF's patrol zone of five kilometers by day and two kilometers by night along the international frontier. No Egyptian troops were to be stationed in or were to patrol these zones. The Egyptian sovereign right to deploy its forces in the Sinai was at least tacitly reaffirmed, and it was made clear that UNEF was there with Egyptian consent.

After a few weeks, Egyptian troops appeared to have returned to the Sinai in strength. I reported to New York on 10 November on a conversation I had just had with Hilmy. When I had asked Hilmy why Egyptian troops in El Arish had exceeded the limit, he had explained that they were there on training. However, it was clear the troops had taken up defensive positions in the area of El Sir airfield, Abu Aweigla, and Jebel Libni. Hilmy had assured me that the Egyptian troops would keep away from UNEF's 5 kilometer zone of operations along the frontier. Hilmy had been warned by Cairo of Israeli military preparations and he asked me if I had any information on this matter. I had said I had no knowledge of any military alert in Israel at that time.

Hammarskjöld responded to my cable on the same day. He felt that the Egyptians were alarmed because they had received a warning by a third party (presumably the Soviets) about supposed Israeli intentions. He did not believe that there was any basis for the warning. Meanwhile, General Carl Von Horn, chief of staff UNTSO in Jerusalem and the UNEF liaison officer with IDF, confirmed to me that there was no basis for anxiety on the part of Egypt.

On 16 November, Hilmy wrote to me to say that, as part of their desert training, young officers would become acquainted with the terrain in the Sinai. Their activities, he noted, would come as close to UNEF's troops as Kuntilla. Clearly, young Egyptian officers did not have to come all the way to the Sinai to familiarize themselves with the desert. After all, the Great Eastern Desert lay just outside their barracks at Cairo. 'Desert training' had to be subterfuge for attempts by Egyptian officers to reconnoiter the Sinai, where their troops were to be deployed. This was getting to be a serious matter.

I ordered a special air reconnaissance flight over the Sinai that day. Major Jafferson, a Canadian armored corps officer and my information officer, returned from the flight to report no increase in the number of Egyptian troops, but they did note that there were additional antitank guns, T-34 tanks, and anti-aircraft artillery. El Arish airfield had fifteen MIGs, some SU-100s, and some medium anti-aircraft artillery. In any case, Egyptian deployment appeared to be defensive in nature. By now, my concern at the possibility of a clash between the Egyptian troops and UNEF had grown considerably. I phoned Hilmy to express my concerns and he agreed to speak with the chief of staff, Eastern Army, Ismalia. After that, I was assured that Egyptian troops would remain outside the UNEF area of operations.

On 16 November, Hilmy informed me that some two hundred Israeli trucks had been seen traveling a road along the frontier south of Nizzana, opposite El Sabah. I immediately sent two air sorties, at an one-hour interval, but they saw nothing to report.

All this time, I had received no reports on Egyptian movements from the Yugoslav contingent of UNEF, who were responsible for the frontier south of El Sabah. They informed me that they had nothing to report, and when questioned on movements farther west, they said that they were authorized only to keep vigil along 5 kilometers of the frontier and that therefore they did not observe or report on movement outside the area. Strictly speaking, they were correct. However, my responsibilities were wider and so I had to rely on other eyes.

On 18 November, a diplomat travelling by road to visit his national contingent arrived at Gaza to report heavy movement of Egyptian troops across the Suez canal. He estimated that an armored and an infantry division had crossed the canal. Since I was not authorized to order an aircraft to this area, I called Jafferson to my office and asked him when he had last been to Cairo on leave. He had not been there for some time, and therefore it would make sense for him to go there. Since we reported all our troop movements to the Egyptian liaison staff in Cairo, Jafferson had good reason to visit. Off he went, knowing exactly what I expected of him. He cabled me from Cairo to confirm the information that we had received from our visiting diplomat. I passed this news on immediately to New York, getting more anxious about the increasing gravity of the situation.

At the same time, our liaison officer in Tel Aviv reported that he had been informed by the U.S. military attaché that the U.S. Government had advised Israel that "any breach of peace" by Israel would result in "cessation of economic aid by the United States".

The Americans had informed Egypt of their views and urged them to call off their military alert in the Sinai. I was relieved to learn this, but kept up our patrols and air sorties. Over the next few days, activity appeared to lessen, but we had no evidence that Egypt had reduced its troops in the area.

In fact, the number of Egyptian troops was not reduced for many months. Although tensions in the area lessened, Egypt was later to maintain that the events of these months had established a precedent for its sovereign right to defend its territory and deploy its troops for such a task regardless of the limits imposed by the GAA. Egypt further maintained that the United Nations had accepted this interpretation of arrangements between Egypt and UNEF. Seven years later, in May 1967, Egypt was to argue for the return of its troops to the Sinai on this basis, leading to the withdrawal of UNEF and the June 1967 war.

On 3 December 1959, the Secretary-General, at the request of the Canadian government, released General Burns to join the Canadian delegation to the disarmament talks in Geneva. The Secretary-General requested the Government of India to submit the name of an experienced officer of the rank of a general to serve as commander, and consequently Maj. Gen. Prem Singh Gyani was submitted for the approval of the General Assembly. This was heartening news, as it permitted my return to national service, and I was already due for promotion and command of combat troops. The departure of Burns put an end to a chapter in the life of UNEF. I assumed acting command until February 1960, when Gyani arrived and I was able to return to India.

11

An Interlude from Peacekeeping: Guarding Ladakh

It was a five-hour flight from Beirut to Delhi, where I arrived in the afternoon. I was invited by General Thimayya to stay at the Army House, his residence as chief of staff. Next morning I was asked to join him at breakfast and there I found General Wad as well. After a warm reception, Thimmy told me that he had again specially selected me for a new posting, command of the new 114th Infantry Brigade Group, to be deployed in Ladakh.

During the conversation, he asked after my wife, which suggested to me that he knew of my delicate marital situation. Clearly, I was being posted to a non-family station. With Wad's consent, and in the knowledge of my situation, Thimmy had chosen me for the most challenging Brigadier's operational command then available in the Indian Army.

Thimmy added enthusiastically, "Look, Indar, it is not just another infantry command in the most impossible terrain. There are sensitive political aspects to this job. Ladakh is mostly Buddhist among a majority of Muslims who run J&K. The second-most important lama in J&K, Kushak Bakula from Leh, is a minister of state and has direct access to Nehru. The cease-fire line ends at a point near Kargil and thereafter there is no line of demarcation in the territory in which you will deploy your troops. And then there is a new conflict with China. We intend to push our troops to the line of control without provoking China. Also there is the Buddhist question. The Dalai Lama is in India and the Chinese are massacring his people. You will be involved in assisting Tibetan refugees. A political officer will administer the frontier region and you will have to handle him with care. This is a challenging job, Indar. You have a good record as a soldier. You love the mountains. You have gained political experience with the UN. You are the right man for this job, and I want you to take it."

I had begun to recognize that my marriage had failed. Given the constraints of a Hindu marriage and Indian social custom I had to make arrangements for not only my wife but also my two boys. Meanwhile, I had no other choice than to accept my posting to Ladakh.

I traveled to Shimla with some trepidation. My wife was living with my mother there, and the boys were at Bishop Cotton School. My visit with my wife proved difficult. I gave her the news of my posting. She knew Thimmy and Wad well and wanted to know exactly what they had said about our situation. When I told her, she responded by offering me a divorce. But the conditions under which Hindu law permitted a divorce were far too humiliating for us to accept. I needed time to figure it all out. After visiting my boys at school and spending a couple of days with my family, I left for Chandigarh to fly to Jammu and then go by road to Udhampur.

The Chinese troops had entered Tibet on 7 October 1950. India initially protested, but finally recognized China's sovereignty over Tibet in an agreement with China in 1954. Both countries consolidated their positions until 1959 when differences over the boundaries became public. India refused China's proposal that India withdraw its troops to 20 kilometers from the border, thus creating a demilitarized zone pending settlement of the boundary question. Talks between Chou En Lai and Nehru in New Delhi in 1960 also failed to resolve the issue. At this stage, India decided to embark on a "forward decisive policy" that meant building new outposts on the frontier. The operations for which I was responsible were part of the overall implementation of this policy.

My staff had already established the brigade headquarters at Udhampur. Major Bansi Lal Kapur was my brigade major and Major Gurcharan Singh was the deputy assistant adjutant and quartermaster-general. The brigade was under the direct command of XV Corps, commanded by Lt. Gen. Shiv Varma, who had been my armor superior when I commanded the Deccan Horse. He assured me that I now had a more challenging job than command of an armored formation or a school and that I would gain an experience that I would not regret. The eyes of the government were on the deployment of troops in Ladakh. He would do all that he could to save me from visiting dignitaries, but I should be prepared for such visits and organize myself so that there were minimum interruptions of the buildup of troops.

Within a week, I flew to Leh, where I decided my first priority was to improve the airstrip with the help of my engineers. All material and supplies for the troops and pack animals would have to come from the Kashmir Valley, an hour's flight or two days by a road that was open from the end of April until the snowfall, around October.

14th J&K Militia was already deployed on the eastern border, near Tibet. As the other battalions arrived they were pushed to their forward posts, supported by animal transport and aircraft. Meanwhile, I called on Kushak Bakula at his monastery, some five miles above Leh. He was a young man, educated at Varanasi, articulate and intelligent. I knew immediately that he and I would get along well. Afterwards, I drove to the Hemis monastery, a larger monastery twenty miles east along the Indus. Its head lama was away in Tibet, a prisoner of the Chinese. Hemis was well known for its religious dance festival, and I gladly accepted the invitation of the monks to return for the event.

The brigade officers' mess was located in the old British residency building. The British had built an attractive house for political officers to spend the summer here when the silk trade with China opened toward the end of the nineteenth century. Caravans made a stop here, where the political officer collected customs duties and valuable intelligence.

Thanks to General Shiv's warning, I was prepared for VIPs. I received the top brass, including the chief of staff, the Defense Minister, and the Prime Minister. They were satisfied with the progress of deployment and I never hesitated to request what was needed. The purchase of one hundred C-111 aircraft from the United States made stocking speedier.

I received information that the Chinese were in strength along the China–Ladakh–Tibet road and were conducting large-scale operations to subdue Tibet. The Tibetan fighters, called Khampas, were putting up a strong resistance with some help from us and the U.S. Central Intelligence Agency. Our plans required that there should be no further Chinese encroachment on our territory, and where possible, we should try to go forward without a fight. But our army resources were scarce. India's emphasis on national development under Defense Minister V.K. Krishna Menon had reduced the armed forces and their budget. The increase in air transport was the first effort to enhance the potential of our forces to cope with the border problems. However, many in the government were opposed to any action that might suggest to the Chinese that India was changing from a close friend to a competitor.

I was allotted two militia battalions, good troops but poorly equipped, and 1st/8th Gurkhas, a first-rate battalion. Another regular infantry unit possibly would join me later. I had all the services and ancillaries but no machine guns, mortars, or artillery. I could call for air support, but considering the distances involved and the range of fighter aircraft, the support would be limited. My troops could provide only a screen, but by keeping the Gurkhas in reserve, I could cope with an emergency. We needed some helicopters and forward landing strips for emergencies and for me to visit troops.

By early July the airfield had improved sufficiently to enable us to increase our troop lift. Shiv had planned a conference for mid-month with the chief of staff, Western Army, and a representative from air headquarters. Besides receiving a regular news summary from the corps headquarters, we listened to All India Radio (AIR) news and the BBC. The Belgian Congo had gained its independence, and its army, called Force Publique, had mutinied. We were so busy with our work that this news made little impression. On 13 July the evening AIR news informed us that the UN Security Council had authorized a peacekeeping operation in the Congo. Kapur, who prided himself on his prophetic powers, burst out, "We are going to lose our brigadier! He will be off to the Congo!"

I scolded him for starting rumors and said, "It's out of the question. How could I go back into UN service when I have just returned to national service after more than two years in Gaza? As far as I am concerned, I am not going to move." No more was said on this subject, and the next morning I left for Udhampur, not knowing I was never to return.

After the meeting at Udhampur, my sympathetic corps commander gave me a week's leave to attend to my many personal chores in Shimla. On the second afternoon there, I received a call that the military secretary had asked for my immediate return to Delhi. I was told it might have something to do with a foreign posting for me. I had barely started to deal with my family problems and I had to leave again. There was nothing more I could tell my family as I packed.

The next morning I left by car for the railway terminal at the foothills of Kalka and took an overnight, air-conditioned coach to New Delhi, arriving in the morning. I was taken straight to Army House, where General Thimayya informed me that I was to leave immediately for New York to join Hammarskjöld's staff. He said that I was to see the prime minister later that morning, and that I would get my final orders from him. He advised me meanwhile to get all my shots and have my passport in order.

Prime Minister Nehru received me at noon the same day and confirmed what Thimayya had already told me, adding that I was to be Hammarskjöld's chief military adviser on the Congo. Nehru didn't know what the job entailed, but he advised me to serve the Secretary-General loyally. As an international staff member I was to accept instructions from the organization alone. This advice stood me in good stead when conflicts arose later with representatives of my own country and those of other countries.

The Staff Duties Branch, Army Headquarters, responsible for the army's involvement in UN peacekeeping missions, was processing my travel documents and had arranged for my immunization shots. With my departure set for midnight of the following day, I phoned Usha, suggesting that she take a train down from Shimla for us to discuss our future arrangements. While I was in Ladakh she had joined St. Bede's College and was enjoying her studies. When she arrived in Delhi I informed her of my new appointment and its temporary nature. I thought I might well be with the United Nations when the boys were on their winter vacations and I would try to arrange for her to bring them to New York. I suggested that if I stayed longer in New York, she might take some courses in the United States. Uncertain of my own future, I could discuss only possibilities.

I left for New York on 21 July 1960, by an Air India Super Constellation. During the twenty-one-hour flight I had ample time to wonder what the future held for me. What on earth was a military adviser supposed to do at an organization like the United Nations? I was soon to find out.

12

Military Adviser to Hammarskjöld for the Congo

On my arrival at Idlewild airport, New York, I was told by the UN staff member sent to receive me that the Secretary-General (SG) wished to see me immediately. On reaching the UN Secretariat on the East River in Manhattan, I was warmly received by Hammarskjöld's personal staff and asked to wait until the SG was free. While I waited, Andrew (Andy) Cordier, the Secretary-General's executive assistant and the highest ranking international staff aide, stopped in and extended his welcome. Short and round, with a background in academia and the U.S. State Department, Andy was endowed with tremendous patience and tolerance.

Hammarskjöld emerged from his office. He wore a white silk suit, providing a contrast to his blue eyes and the flush of tan on his face. He held a sheaf of papers and a small cigar in his left hand. In the courteous manner of the Swedes, he almost came to attention, and with a slight bow said, "Hullo Indar", shaking my hand warmly. Then he gave me the papers and said, "These are some cables from the Congo. Will you please work on their replies? We will discuss them at our evening round up." Then he left through the same door as he had come from. I just stood there, not knowing what had hit me.

I sat down and read through the cables. They made no sense to me at all. The SG's staff told me that I had been given an office in Ralph Bunche's suite, and one of the receptionists took me there. During my first visit to the United Nations, I had had a room in this wing and had become acquainted with Bunche's staff, who had handled my work while I was with UNEF. Some of them were present in the office and greeted me as if I had only been gone a short time. Bunche was away "as our man in the Congo", and his political aides were with him in Leopoldville. There was a pile of Congo reports and documents on my table. As I perused them, a picture of the crisis in the Congo began to emerge, yet I was only beginning to understand the complexity of the crisis.

The transfer of power in the Congo from the departing colonial power, Belgium, to the government of the newly independent state did not turn out as the Belgians had envisaged. They had hoped that they would be asked to play an important role in the newly independent state. They had not fostered any indigenous leadership, as the British had done in their colonies, nor had they established a cadre of *évolués* (highly educated nationals), as the French had done.

As the nation moved toward its independence date of 30 June 1960, law and order were already breaking down. Within a week of independence, the Congolese security force, previously known as the Force Publique but renamed the Armée Nationale Congolaise (ANC) at independence, mutinied against its Belgian superiors. Civil war erupted throughout the land and the entire administrative infrastructure collapsed amid chaos and bloodshed. To appease the ANC, Prime Minister Patrice Lumumba arranged the departure of Belgian officers and non-commissioned officers. Lumumba then appointed Victor Lundula, a former medical warrant officer, as the new force commander and Joseph Mobutu, a journalist who had served as a quartermaster's clerk, as chief of staff. He then allowed the soldiers to elect their own officers. Having appointed their officers, the Congolese soldiers promoted themselves to a minimum rank of lance corporal, becoming the first army in world history with no privates.

In the mineral-rich province of Katanga, President Moise Tshombe opposed the center–provincial relationship as established in the Loi fondamentale (the Congolese constitution). With the backing of the departing colonial power and economic interests, Tshombe proclaimed Katanga's own independence on 11 July. Meanwhile, Belgian troops, which had remained at the bases permitted them under the Treaty of Friendship signed on the eve of independence, were joined by metropolitan forces from Belgium, and together they intervened to protect European life and property. Fearing that the Belgians intended to reoccupy the country, the Congolese Government sought help from the United States, which advised them to turn to the United Nations. On 13 July, Lumumba requested military assistance from the UN Secretary-General, and in the meantime he asked Ghana for help as well.

The crisis in the Congo presented a novel challenge in that the legitimate government of the newly independent African nation had applied to the Security Council for assistance. This request was strongly endorsed by the United States, and other permanent members of the council did not actively oppose it. Interestingly, the two superpowers had initially agreed to the dispatch of a UN peacekeeping force. Although differences between the two arose later over the role of the UN mission, there was never a call by a permanent member for the removal of the force from the Congo.

The United States' support for the UN Congo Operation (known as ONUC, the acronym for its French name, Operations des Nation Unis au Congo) was clear and strong, in spite of differences over the conduct of the operation with the United Nations. Adlai Stevenson, the U.S. permanent representative to the United Nations, expressed the American view plainly during a Congo debate in the Security Council: "the only way to keep the Cold War out of the Congo is to keep the UN in the Congo".

While the United States saw a threat from the Soviet Union, acting through states such as Egypt, Ghana, and Guinea, the Soviets emphasized the continuous presence of the Belgians in the Congo as a threat to decolonization. Thus in agreeing to UN intervention, the superpowers were avoiding a military confrontation, but their ideological rivalry permeated every aspect of ONUC, making the work of the world organization and its Secretary-General most difficult.

I was called to Hammarskjöld's meeting at 7.30 p.m. in the conference room adjoining his office. The SG was already engaged in dealing with the cables and interrupted the discussion to introduce me to the others in the "Congo Club". Besides Cordier, there were Constantin Stavropoulos (Greek), the legal counsel; Heinz Wiechoff (U.S.), political adviser; Sir Alexander MacFarquhar (formerly Indian

Civil Service), adviser civilian affairs; and Count Wilhelm Wachmeister (Swedish), special assistant to Hammarskjöld.

That evening, we learned from the SG that President Kwame Nkrumah of Ghana was sending his British-seconded chief of staff, Maj. Gen. Henry Alexander, with recommendations for improving ONUC command. Bunche's cables had already given me a good idea of the problems of command in the Congo. General Carl Von Horn of Sweden was on his way from his post as chief of staff UNTSO, Jerusalem, to head ONUC, and in the absence of a force commander and a headquarters, Bunche, as the special representative of the Secretary-General (SRSG), dealt directly with contingent commanders as they arrived. When Alexander arrived with Ghanaian troops, Bunche asked him to deal with some difficult matters, including plans for the withdrawal of the Belgians. It was on the question of handling the ANC that Bunche disagreed with Alexander.

It became apparent that the ANC was regularly provoking confrontation with UN troops. Alexander concluded that since the ANC itself was a major law and order problem, it should be confined to barracks and its weapons should be stored. Bunche disagreed. Alexander also offered a command and control plan that Bunche deemed unacceptable. This plan divided the overall command between a supreme commander, who would deal with political, international, and strategic matters, and a field commander, who would be in charge of operations.

It soon became evident to me that Alexander had a good understanding of the situation in the Congo. His military expertise gave him insight that others lacked. On my request, he spent some time briefing me in military-related developments in the Congo. In discussing the command and control of ONUC, he admitted that he had little confidence in Von Horn's ability to manage the mission. Since Von Horn already had been appointed commander, he could perhaps be left to deal with political and international relations, but it was important that a capable and qualified commander be appointed to conduct operations.

I was impressed with Alexander's military knowledge, but it was apparent that he had scarce understanding of the politics of peacekeeping. The Congo was his first exposure to peacekeeping and he looked at the crisis through the prism of imperial policing.

His perspective was: The Congo is falling apart—let us fix it. But the United Nations was not an imperial power nor did ONUC have the authority that Chapter VII of the UN Charter had given the operation in Korea, in which the British had participated, and that would allow the United Nations to enforce its will on the Congolese.

I explained to Alexander the role of the United Nations. The task of disarming the ANC was very difficult, given that some forty thousand Congolese troops were deployed across the vast land. Katanga had seceded, with the support of Congolese troops in the province, and there were other regions where revolts were bolstered by elements of the ANC. Disarming the ANC would help the United Nations in Leopoldville, but there were many more thousands to disarm, requiring a UN force many times the size of that envisaged. In any case, countries that had recently gained independence would oppose such disarming and the Soviets would surely veto any attempt to disarm because the United Nations had been invited to help the ANC and not to disgrace it by taking its weapons.

Alexander's proposal to appoint a supreme commander, I felt, would cause an overlap with the duties of the SRSG. However, I did agree that Von Horn's lack of experience in operational command was a serious handicap, but there were few alternatives. The permanent members of the Security Council had a tacit agreement not to participate, so there were only a few countries that might provide a suitable commander, and for one reason or another none of these countries was acceptable. As an alternative to replacing Von Horn, I already had in mind to select a suitable chief of staff and other key staff officers to ensure that the operation was well managed.

I briefed Hammarskjöld before he saw Alexander and the Ghana permanent representative to the United Nations, Ambassador Alex Quaison-Sackey. The Ghanaian delegates heard the same arguments in fewer words from the SG than I had offered to Alexander. Hammarskjöld sent his visitors along with his appreciation for the Ghanaian contingent. Otherwise, Alexander left disappointed.

On a visit to the United States, Lumumba came to the United Nations. Among the many meetings arranged for him was one I attended that dealt with the role of ONUC and UN assistance to the ANC. The meeting was tense and it was evident that Lumumba had little understanding of the United Nations. At the evening round-up with the Congo Club, the SG gave vent to his frustrations. Disciplined man that he was, he seldom allowed his own feelings to influence his judgment and actions. He expressed the hope that when he went to the Congo he would have a better opportunity to explain to Lumumba the ways of the United Nations. This proved difficult, if not impossible.

Hammarskjöld decided to visit the Congo and sent me there ahead to get acquainted with the land, our troops, and the people we were dealing with. On my arrival at Leopoldville, John Olver, the chief administrative officer (CAO), met me. John was CAO, UNEF, when I first joined it and we had become friends. Tall, handsome, and taciturn with a dead-pan humor, he was experienced and ideally suited to administer a large peacekeeping force across a huge country. John briefed me on the main administrative issues. Unlike UNEF, the ONUC administrative staff was having a difficult time with the military.

I was immediately taken to see Bunche in his office. Though he showed the strain of long working hours and exhausting dealings with the Congolese, this had not blunted his charm and courteous manners. Like Hammarskjöld, Bunche was among the great men in world affairs of our times and it was a pleasure and an honor to be associated with him. I looked forward to my visit and hoped to address some of the perplexing issues we faced.

Brian Urquhart and F.T. Liu, Bunche's political aides, were seated with him around the dining table, which appeared to be groaning under the weight of cables, papers, reports, and a telephone. In my associations with senior commanders, I had never seen such a disorganized office in emergency operations. Pauline Lascerte had her own table with a typewriter, on which she was busily engaged in finishing a document. I soon learned that Ralph liked to have things he required around him, including his staff. This room acquired the label "snake pit", yet it was the nerve center of ONUC. In spite of the disorder in the room, it managed ONUC in an efficient and methodical manner.

There was little time for pleasantries and Ralph went straight to his concerns. His problems with Von Horn had already begun. Ralph had no desire to continue to manage the peacekeeping force once the commander arrived. But the commander was more concerned with personal comforts and matters of prestige than with the conduct of operations. Ralph was anxious to consult and coordinate with the military, not only in the conduct of operations but also in establishing linkages with the ANC.

Ralph asked me to work on the two military matters while he completed preparations for the SG's visit the following day. He explained his efforts to persuade Patrice Lumumba and his ministers to help keep the ANC from hindering the work of UN peacekeepers. He was also engaged in negotiating his own visit to Katanga with Moise Tshombe and the Belgians in control there.

I arranged to see Von Horn after my visit with Bunche. I had met him frequently during my posting at UNEF. Von Horn had already made himself unpopular with two important pillars of ONUC. Bunche had problems dealing with him and his political staff was getting nowhere with him. The administrative staff was mutinous. Von Horn had brought a handful of observer officers with him and appointed them to key positions for which, with few exceptions, they demonstrated little ability. His French Canadian military assistant, Lt. Col. Fred Berthiume, acted like a chief of staff, although an able Ethiopian, Brig. Gen Iyassou Megansha, held that position. Olver and his assistant, Virgil De Anglis, explained that the general and his staff from Jerusalem were more interested in their comforts and daily allowance than the care of the troops. Besides, the general was rude and had even insulted a couple of the senior UN staff.

Von Horn greeted me warmly and then launched into his complaints against the UN staff. I asked after the operations of the force, but he returned to administrative matters. After his long complaint, I was able to identify two issues he was concerned with. The first was the daily allowance. He and his UNTSO officers had failed to understand that, unlike observer operations, in which individuals were given a per diem and had to fend for themselves, in a UN peacekeeping force all facilities were provided, and an out-of-pocket standard allowance was given to all ranks. His second complaint concerned his relations with Bunche. Obviously, Von Horn had no previous experience of working with a civilian chief of a mission. I said that I hoped to get acquainted with the ways of ONUC and would attempt to complete my recommendations in about a week. I intended to fly to key towns to obtain first-hand knowledge and check out available facilities for UN troops. I assured Von Horn that I would discuss my suggestions with him before I referred them to Bunche and then forwarded them to the SG.

My next call was on Sture Linner, a Swede who coordinated UN agencies and worked to establish working relations with NGOs and bilateral governmental aid programs. A Greek scholar, he had served with American mining interests in Liberia and turned out to be different from the typical Swedish diplomats and military officers that I had met. Charming, cultured, and courteous, he briefed me on civilian operations. From our conversation, it was obvious there had to be close cooperation between the UN force and civilian operations, and that I had to make necessary arrangements to achieve this.

At dinner, Von Horn returned to his complaints against the UN civilian staff. I made a few attempts to talk strategy and organization of the force, but in vain. My host returned to his earlier refrain. When I told him some of Hammarskjöld's ideas for the operation in the Congo, he said, "You are Dag's military adviser. You know what to do. Just go ahead and do it." Somewhat mellowed by now, he added that I should have been his chief of staff. I was not flattered.

The next day, when I asked him if he had spoken to his staff on some of the matters that we had discussed, he simply repeated what he had told me the evening before. I was to go ahead and tell the staff what I had to say. I was amazed. He was asking me to do his job. From then, I dealt directly with ONUC staff and gradually took command of ONUC in all but name.

I had by now arrived at my immediate concerns: the first was the organization of ONUC; the second the establishment of an effective political-military linkage to provide military advice to Bunche and interpret his political and strategic directives into military terms to be conveyed to the force staff, and through them to the troops; and the last was the organization of support services. Taking advantage of the free rein given to me by the commander, I walked through the force headquarters asking questions of all the chiefs of sections. By the end of the day, I was meeting with Olver and his field services staff to discuss a variety of administrative and financial issues. A picture of a staff organization for ONUC began to emerge. But more time was required to think it through.

A day after Hammarskjöld arrived, he announced plans to send Bunche to Katanga to open negotiations with Tshombe for the entry of UN troops in Katanga. I had a good session with the SG and his comments helped me develop a plan to improve linkages between political, administrative, and civilian operations. He authorized me to implement the plan immediately. So I drafted several cables and sent them to New York for dispatch to contributing states.

The outline of the organization was to place the force commander parallel and equal to the chief of civilian operations, under the SRSG. The military staff was to be as large as the staff for a division-size force, with brigades responsible for one or more Congolese province. A political/civilian officer would hold positions that paralleled the military organization, so that the two could better coordinate their activities. Military and civilian charter aircraft would be placed under a commander, ONUC Air Force, directly under the force commander. The deputy force commander would be responsible for training the ANC. The responsibility for liaising with and advising the SRSG would belong to the deputy chief of staff, who would be assisted in this duty by the chief of military operations. The latter two were also to work closely with the chiefs of political, legal, and other civilian divisions. Finally, the chief of logistics was to be the link to administration and finance.

I had informed the SG of the problems of command. He approved my recommendation that the UNTSO officers return to Jerusalem, although Von Horn would be allowed to keep his military assistant and ADC. I had already asked for some key staff for early dispatch to ONUC, to be contributed by member states, and six selected staff officers from UNEF to fill key positions until they could be replaced. Taking Von Horn at his word that I could go ahead and implement high-level decisions, I made these arrangements with members and UNEF.

When I told Von Horn of the arrangements, he objected to returning the officers he had brought with him and insisted that he have the final choice in selecting his staff. I replied that I had only acted on his word giving me freedom to implement decisions of the SG, and that he would have to ask the SG to change these arrangements. But apparently he would not ask Hammarskjöld for redress.

While Hammarskjöld, assisted by Bunche, continued his negotiations with Lumumba and Tshombe to arrange an ONUC presence in Katanga, I started my tour of the Congo in a twin-engine Beechcraft flown by a former Belgian air force pilot. Everyday, on my return, I would join the SG and others to learn of the progress of the negotiations.

On 4 August 1960, Bunche flew to Elisabethville, Katanga. After an unceremonious reception and negotiations that went nowhere he decided to return. Hammarskjöld cabled Cordier to request a Security Council meeting to deal with the Katanga issue and left for New York without waiting for Bunche to return. Before leaving, he instructed me to remain in Leopoldville on completion of my visits around the country. He said Bunche wanted my help and that I should work with Von Horn.

Back in New York, the Security Council confirmed the authority conferred upon the Secretary-General by previous resolutions, called on the Belgians to withdraw their troops from Katanga, and stated that entry of ONUC troops was necessary provided they not interfere in the internal affairs of the Congo. Three days later Hammarskjöld returned to the Congo and personally led ONUC troops into Elisabethville to take over security duties from the Belgians there. I accompanied Hammarskjöld on this venturesome trip. We flew in a group of three chartered DC-4s with the SG's aircraft in the lead. As we descended to land at Elisabethville, air control told us that we did not have permission to land. The SG and I had a quick conference and he decided that we should try again. At some two thousand feet we could see a cluster of troops on the tarmac and barrels across the runway blocking our path.

We made another circle around the airport. The SG asked me for my views. Tshombe had not refused the SG's visit, I pointed out. The cluster on the tarmac could be a reception party including men in uniform. Would Tshombe and his Belgian advisers dare to shoot at the SG? I did not think so, because the consequences for Katanga and the Belgians would be grave. And if the SG did not insist on landing it would make it harder to enter Katanga in the future.

In a precise tone, Hammarskjöld asked, "Do you advise that we attempt to land?" I said that was the only choice if we wanted to succeed. In a calm and deliberate voice, the SG said, "You will tell the captain to inform air control that I intend to land."

I went forward to the crew cabin and spoke to the captain, who in turn spoke to air control. After listening to control, he turned around to me and said, "I have Major Weber on the phone and he has ordered me not to land." I took the microphone from the captain and said, "This is the military adviser to the UN Secretary-General. He has ordered the UN aircraft to land together with three hundred Swedish troops. Please clear the runway." After some moments, he returned to the phone and gave us permission to land.

The SG's reception resembled an act out of a comic opera. White officers with drawn swords stood in front of Katangese troops. A rag-tag military band, hurriedly assembled for this ceremony, with a white conductor played what was presumably the national anthem of Katanga. Dark-suited Katangese leaders, with sun glasses hiding their eyes, escorted by their Belgian advisers, stood in a row behind the guard of honor. A Katangese official accompanied by a burly Belgian military officer stood on the tarmac waiting to greet the SG. The scene seemed to be out of a Hollywood movie. Bill Ranallo and I edged closer to the SG. He seemed to have no worries as he stood at attention, with a faint smile, seeming to wonder if all this was real.

The following morning, the SG received urgent appeals for help from Katangese workers at Jadotville, a mining town thirty miles west of the state capital, who were opposed to Tshombe and were under threat from their Lumumba opponents. The SG immediately responded by asking me to lead a Swedish platoon there to protect them. Over the objections of the local Katangan official and his Belgian adviser, I left them there. I learned to understand Hammarskjöld's great diplomatic skills and his keen sense of when to place his personal prestige on the line. However, despite his efforts, the Belgians remained in Katanga, the secession had by no means ended, and Hammarskjöld's relations with the Congolese Government, tenuous from the start, worsened because he had refused Lumumba's demand that Congolese representatives and military be included in the UN advance elements in Katanga.

One day, when I was alone with Cordier, he raised the issue of Von Horn. I had been anticipating this moment. I gave Cordier my frank appraisal of Von Horn, that he was beyond help and therefore must be replaced. While Cordier did not say so in plain words, his response led me to understand that Hammarskjöld was going through a difficult time. The Soviets had challenged him openly on his handling of events in the Congo, and many Africans and Asians were critical. He was also under pressure from Western friends of Belgium. At this time Hammarskjöld needed the goodwill and support of the Nordic countries, especially of his own, Sweden. Therefore, we had to keep Von Horn for a while.

As Bunche's relations with Lumumba and his government reached a low ebb, Bunche informed the SG that he—Bunche—could no longer be effective and should be replaced. After a few days searching, Hammarskjöld, with the consent of Prime Minister Nehru, chose Rajeshwar Dayal, then Indian Ambassador to Pakistan, to replace Bunche. Dayal had served as India's permanent representative at the United Nations and as a member of the triumvirate appointed by the Security Council to deal with the crisis in Lebanon in 1958.

Bunche was keen to return by the end of August and Dayal was not available until early September. I was back in New York by this time, and Hammarskjöld told me to be ready to return to the Congo and fill in before the arrival of the new SRSG. When Bunche's return was arranged for the end of August, Hammarskjöld told us at a Congo Club meeting that now Cordier would go to Leopoldville as acting SRSG, allowing him an opportunity to learn the organizational problems of ONUC. I was glad to hear this, as Cordier would also have an opportunity to get personally acquainted with the problems of military command. I was still to proceed to Leopoldville to help Carl deal with some critical operational problems. I left immediately, soon followed by Cordier.

On returning to Leopoldville I was delighted to find several of the staff I had requested from member states. They included some of my associates from UNEF and UNOGIL and friends from India. This team saved ONUC from the follies of its commander and helped the force to achieve the measure of success that it did. It was a great relief for me to have them to organize ONUC operations and to have an occasional opportunity to join them for an evening of relaxation whenever I was in Leopoldville.

By early September, a constitutional crisis had developed, with catastrophic consequences for the Congo. Lumumba, frustrated by the United Nations' refusal to quell the Katanga secession by force, decided to do so himself and mobilized the Congolese army, aided by Soviet aircraft and ground transport that had been made available for the civilian administration. Lumumba's ill-prepared force, lacking access to airfields in Katanga, landed in the neighboring Kasai province and immediately became embroiled in internecine fighting with Baluba tribes. Many Balubas were killed; others were made homeless and became refugees, further adding to the critical problems facing the UN aid agencies. The Congolese president, Joseph Kasavubu, opposed Lumumba's action. As the difference between their views widened, Kasavubu dismissed Lumumba under the authority given him by the Loi fondamentale. Unperturbed, Lumumba 'dismissed' the president. Declaring Lumumba's action against him invalid, Kasavubu replaced Lumumba as Prime Minister with Joseph Ileo, the senate president, who proved ineffective in the face of political squabbling and the collapse of Congolese authority. Alarmed at the threat of civil war, Cordier closed the airports to prevent movement of Congolese troops and shut down Radio Leopoldville to prevent political leaders inciting the public.

Dayal arrived amid this crisis. Somewhat stunned at first by these developments, he seriously thought of returning to New York to withdraw from his assignment. I urged him to remain and weather the storm, and I was glad when he finally decided to take over from Cordier.

On 16 September, Colonel Mobutu, the army chief of staff, staged a coup, neutralizing Kasavubu and Lumumba and dismissing Ileo's government. Lumumba was arrested and removed to the ANC camp at Thysville. The coup announcement was made from Radio Brazzaville, obviously with the help of Belgian and other foreign advisers. Somewhat scared of the consequences of the announcement, he came to visit Dayal at the Royal (an apartment complex used for UN offices and residences) at the crucial hour. There had been talk in the air of a coup, but I had hoped that Mobutu would resist the pressures and the temptations offered. Now after his brief announcement, which took all of us by surprise, Mobutu had another trick up his sleeve. He asked Dayal for the United Nations' help to institute military rule. Dayal, always quick to respond, replied, "This is a military matter. At moments of crisis a general should be at his command post." A disappointed Mobutu left the Royal never to turn to the United Nations for help again. However, he managed to find other friends.

Two days earlier the Soviets, bitterly critical of Hammarskjöld for closing the airports, had introduced a resolution in the Security Council requiring the Secretary-General to remove the ONUC force commander. At a special session of the General Assembly to discuss the Congo crisis, many heads of state were present. The ensuing debate was tumultuous. Hammarskjöld was severely attacked by the Soviets in a campaign personally led by Chairman Khrushchev; they called for his removal as Secretary-General and his replacement by a troika of representatives of the major three blocs. Hammarskjöld, however, not only survived this attack with the help of the Western nations and Third World countries but was requested by the special session to continue his efforts to implement previous resolutions and to appoint a conciliation commission (composed of represen-tatives to the African and Asian countries that had contributed troops to the peacekeeping force). Meanwhile, the General Assembly recognized Kasavubu as the constitutionally elected president of the Congo by accepting the credentials of his delegation. Having failed in the attempt to oust Hammarskjöld, the Soviets thereafter opposed Kasavubu's every move, making Hammarskjöld's task ever more difficult.

On 8 October, Hammarskjöld requested that the Belgians withdraw their personnel from the central government. The same day, he re-quested of Dayal that either he or I should visit Tshombe to personally deliver a letter asking him to reduce his number of Belgian advisers and to negotiate a cease-fire in north Katanga, where fighting had broken out between the Balubakat and Luandas. Since I had already met Tshombe, Dayal asked me to go. On reaching Elisabethville, I discussed the situation with Ian Berendsen, ONUC representative; Colonel Henry Byrne, the Irish ONUC commander; and Swedish colonel Mauritz Möllerswäld, chief military observer of the group I had deployed in north Katanga to monitor a cease-fire between warring groups there. They confirmed what I had suspected all along, that the gendarmerie, determined to reimpose its control, had fueled the fighting in north Katanga. Led by Belgian officers, these troops behaved in the notorious fashion of cruel colonial regimes. The key to resolving this human disaster was to resolve the issue of Belgian personnel first.

I called on the Belgian resident representative, Robert de Rothschild, and found him willing to negotiate. Apparently, Hammarskjöld's efforts to persuade the Belgian Government to remove Belgian nationals and cease interference in the internal affairs of the Congo were bearing fruit. Allowing for enough time for Rothschild to contact Tshombe, I called on the president of Katanga, accompanied by Berendsen. Tshombe was all smiles and sociable. We agreed to continue our dialogue at the working level with the gendarmerie officers and UN troops. We soon reached an agreement.

The arrangement required the deployment of more troops in a delineated neutral zone in North Katanga, hereafter known as the "Rikhye Zone". Byrne had to move his area HQ to Albertville to be near the neutral zone and I appointed the commander of the Swedish battalion in the Elisabethville area to be Byrne's deputy and take charge of all the rear elements.

Hammarskjöld asked Dayal for a report on ONUC for submission to the Security Council. Dayal knew that the members, divided as they were, would attack the report if it did not favor their side. He decided to prepare a report based on facts in as diplomatic a language as he could manage. But when we read the final draft, it was evident that the hyenas from the right and the wolves from the left would eat the UN leadership alive. The unabashed way that member-states were blaming the United Nations for their own actions and failings had to be reported, regardless of the consequences to individuals responsible for the operations.

The report created a great furor in the international community. Hammarskjöld called Dayal to New York as reinforcements and instructed that either Linner or I should take charge of ONUC in the interim. Linner told Dayal and me that he was so overwhelmed with his own work that he had little time to learn the intricacies of political and military affairs. I stated my reservations to my assuming control— namely, that UN civilians at ONUC Headquarters were generally antimilitary, often for good reason. Besides, Von Horn, because of his claim to seniority, would be most unhappy to have to answer to me. Eventually, however, Dayal appointed me because I knew his and the Secretary-General's minds, and because he knew I would perform with a modicum of modesty.

On assuming the office of acting head of the mission, I called on Linner for help and guidance, which he gave me generously. Similarly, respecting Von Horn's seniority of age and service, I had always gone to his office to obtain his approval on proposed actions. But now, he was no longer affable.

We had all hoped that it would remain relatively quiet during Dayal's brief visit to New York. But, each day brought a new crisis, which, however, we were able to cope with. On 17 November the Congolese *Sureté* (the criminal investigation department) insisted that Ghana's chargé d'affaires, Andrew Welbeck, leave the country. He, like several other diplomats sympathetic to Lumumba, was actively engaged in politicking, and a member of his embassy was caught carrying large amounts of cash, presumably meant for buying support for Lumumba. Hammarskjöld advised me to give the same protection to the embassies as we were giving the Congolese leaders. Accordingly, we placed the Ghanaian compound under the protection of a Tunisian battalion. The following day the Congolese threatened to expel Welbeck by force. I cautioned them against this, as ONUC was obligated to offer the Ghanaian diplomat our protection. In the meantime, Nkrumah had decided to recall Welbeck and an aircraft was being arranged to collect him.

But on 21 November the chief of Congolese security went to the Ghanaian embassy and served Welbeck notice to leave. Not having been informed of Nkrumah's decision, Welbeck told his visitors that he had no instructions to leave. Shortly thereafter an ANC unit arrived and surrounded the house. The Tunisian platoon requested re-inforcements and I agreed. A stream of visitors prevented my going to Von Horn's office, so I requested he come to see me. But he was not in his office. As the crisis escalated, I needed the force commander to take charge of his troops, but he was unavailable.

In a telex conference I kept the SG informed. Later in the afternoon, while I was engaged in an exchange of views with the SG, firing broke out. I ended our conversation and turned to find that General Alexander, accompanied by Ghana's permanent foreign secretary, had arrived with instructions from Nkrumah to bring Welbeck back. Alexander offered to join me and we rushed to the embassy. The ANC was all over the place, shooting in every direction, including that of their own troops. Alexander and I abandoned our car and crawled to the embassy to find the Tunisian platoon commander dead, shot by Colonel Nokokolo, the ANC commander in Leopoldville. Tunisians coming to the aid of their officer shot Nokokolo dead. Otherwise, casualties were few. Welbeck was safe but shaking and ready to go home. I was glad to see Alexander take him away.

Attur-ur-Rahman, the chargé d'affaires from India and a respected friend, came to see me one morning. He was well versed in military affairs. He said, 'Indar, why don't you fix this situation. You have the military capability to do it. If you put an end to this nonsense you will be remembered as a great hero in India.' I told him that I was following my instructions. The Indian authorities would have to approach the SG to change his instructions to me. I always recognized that such conduct on my part would never get me any medals. My rewards were a job well done in accordance with what I was told to do and within the framework of international law. Besides, I was doing what Prime Minister Nehru had told me to do—loyally serve the UN Secretary-General.

Dayal returned in a few days and I had instructions to remain to help him. He shared my primary concern of finding a suitable replacement for Von Horn. I suggested Maj. Gen. Sean McKeown, chief of staff of the Irish Army, then visiting his troops in ONUC. A short, plain-speaking professional soldier, he was popular with his troops. Dayal agreed that McKeown was a deserving candidate. When asked, McKeown expressed his willingness to accept the appointment provided his government approved. Dayal wrote to Hammarskjöld, who accepted our proposal, and after some weeks had the approval of the Irish. The SG had decided to return Von Horn to UNTSO, where his old post had remained vacant. My next assignment was to settle in the new commander and then to return to New York.

Lumumba had not been inactive meanwhile. He enjoyed considerable political influence and was able to rally the soldiers at the prison to his side. Mobutu transferred him again, this time to

Tshombe's custody in Katanga. Deeply concerned for Lumumba's safety, Hammarskjöld sent instructions to ONUC to do everything possible to protect his personal rights. Lumumba was last seen by UN troops on his arrival at Elisabethville airport being mistreated by the Katangese as they took him away. On 13 February 1961, Lumumba was killed by his captors.

I returned to New York amid the turmoil at the United Nations caused by Lumumba's murder. At the United Nations, the pro-Lumumba states in Africa (such as Ghana and Egypt), many non-aligned states, and the socialist bloc had earlier called for Mobutu's ouster by ONUC and the restoration of Lumumba to his elected office. On the other hand, the West and many African states were sympathetic toward Mobutu. Hammarskjöld had strong faith in law and, at his suggestion, the Security Council on 21 February 1961 took several important steps to ensure the rule of law. The council specifically authorized ONUC "to prevent the occurrence of civil war" and for this purpose to use force as a last resort, but not limited to self-defense; called for the withdrawal of Belgian and any other foreign military and paramilitary personnel, political advisers, and mercenaries; and urged the convening of the Congolese parliament and the reorganization of the ANC to put an end to its interference in the country's political life.

Lumumba's death led to further splintering of the fledgling nation and the intensification of civil war. The United Nations was blamed for this result, and Hammarskjöld advocated new measures to confront the problem. Hammarskjöld felt that the 21 February resolution gave ONUC sufficient authority to launch a major initiative to deal with the civil war, restore the economy, and help the Congo Conciliation Commission to start the negotiating process leading to the convening of parliament. The African nations, however, became impatient with the pace of developments and divided in two main groups. The first, known as the Casablanca group, called for a deadline to be set for the convening of parliament, after which enforcement action should follow; and the second, named Tenerife, supported the more cautious approach of the Congo Conciliation Commission. A similar rift developed among non-African, troop-contributing countries.

A UN General Assembly resolution of 15 April also urged that the Congo National Assembly be convened and that necessary measures be taken to protect it—a measure with particular relevance because of the threat from Katanga, where large numbers of mercenaries, not only from Belgium, were being inducted into the Katanga gendarmerie. This mercenary menace was to become a major factor in determining the subsequent actions in and against Katanga, which now became the focal point of ONUC's attention.

The goal of reconvening the Congo National Assembly—essential to the reestablishment of normal political life in the Congo—was achieved, largely because of the good offices of the United Nations and because of the security guarantees for the delegates provided by ONUC. Thanks to these measures, the assembly was able to meet and conduct its business. Cyrille Adoula was elected prime minister on 2 August and continued in that office throughout the remainder of ONUC's stay in the Congo. Antoine Gizenga, the leader of the Lumumbist faction in Stanleyville, recognized the Adoula government shortly after normal political control of the country's affairs had been resumed, and Gizenga subsequently became vice prime minister.

In another resolution, the General Assembly called on the Congolese to desist from seeking a military solution to their problems and to prevent the introduction of military hardware into the country. The Congolese were to release members of parliament and the provincial assemblies who had been detained and convene parliament. Last, the General Assembly decided to appoint a Second Conciliation Commission to end the political crisis.

With a new political incentive in Leopoldville, it was possible for ONUC to concentrate on implementing the provisions of the Security Council resolution of 21 February to end the secession of Katanga and remove foreign mercenaries. On 28 August, in a surprise move called Operation Rum Punch, ONUC rounded up 338 of the 442 European officers who were known to be serving with the Katangese forces and who occupied key positions in Elisabethville. The next day Tshombe capitulated to the expulsion demand, broadcasting an endorsement of the United Nations' move. But Tshombe's action was wholly deceptive, for within a very short while the European officers were once again leading his gendarmerie.

Two weeks later a second intervention by ONUC, named Operation Morthor, sought the arrest of Tshombe and others and resulted in eight days of severe fighting in Katanga. The senior

commanders involved in the operation informed me that both
Mohamoud Khiary of Tunisia, the chief of the UN civilian operations
who played a lead role in the political management of the operation,
and the UN representative in Katanga, Connor O'Brien, told them
that the Secretary-General had approved the action in Katanga. The
commanders further understood that the objective, as far as Khiary
and O'Brien were concerned, was to end the secession. The entire
issue of the authorization of the UN action in Katanga remains
controversial. Hammarskjöld had approved the general plan
submitted by Khiary and O'Brien and had permitted limited action
"to take over the Katanga radio, if necessary, and at the same time
ensure that gendarmerie, Sureté, police, and mercenary-led groups
could not oppose the UN's action or disrupt public order".

Hammarskjöld decided to fly to Elisabethville to deal personally
with the crisis. In his book *Hammarskjöld* (New York: Alfred A, Knopf,
1972), Brian Urquhart confirms my memory of events leading to
Hammarskjöld's journey to the Congo, tragically his last. Urquhart
wrote: "Hammarskjöld certainly had no idea that any major and
drastic action might be taken before he himself arrived in the Congo.
His authorization to Linner to go ahead with the plan they had
discussed omitted any precise guidance on timing, but it specifically
referred to Khiary's message, saying that no action would be taken
before consulting with the Secretary-General in Leopoldville."

This collaboration between UN representatives Khiary and O'Brien
and the Adoula government was a direct departure from the
prescribed limits of ONUC's mandate. The Security Council had
given ONUC a mandate to "assist" in the ending of secession, "by
the use of force, if necessary, in the last resort," but Khiary and
O'Brien had exceeded Hammarskjöld's instructions that "no action
will be taken before consulting with the Secretary-General in
Leopoldville. Therefore, it was not surprising that the UN action
provoked strong reaction from supporters of Katanga. The operation
failed because it had lost the element of surprise and was mounted
hastily. Tshombe and three of the ministers avoided arrest; the UN
troops were subsequently forced to hand back the installations they
had secured; and ONUC's military posture was badly shaken, not
least by the fate of a two-hundred-strong company of the Irish

contingent, which was encircled at Jadotville, forced to surrender, and held captive for five weeks before being released on 25 October.

The controversy over Operation Morthor continued over the years and led to reaffirmation of the notion of UN peacekeepers as best suited to a role that does not involve the use of force. This role has come to be known as "traditional peacekeeping". Operation Morthor solved nothing; the situation became worse, if anything. Tshombe resumed where he had left off, and mercenaries continued to operate in large numbers in Katanga.

The tragic death of Hammarskjöld, who was killed in an air crash at Ndola, Northern Rhodesia, on 18 September while flying to meet Tshombe, cast a dark shadow over the Congo scene and dimmed hopes of an early settlement of the Katanga problem. Nevertheless, in his planned meeting with Tshombe, Hammarskjöld had intended to renew the process of negotiation, at which he was especially adept, to encourage reconciliation between Tshombe and the Congolese government. Now, more time would be needed to create conditions for negotiations to resume.

Dag Hammarskjöld had two goals for ONUC: first, to restore law and order; and second, to enable the Congolese people to determine their own destiny under their own government. In structuring the peacekeeping force, the Security Council had provided a military force for the first goal and a civilian technical assistance program for the second. Hammarskjöld intended that the two elements would become fully integrated and complementary to each other. This was achieved to a great measure.

When ONUC arrived in the Congo, it was faced with a rapidly deteriorating security situation, a major economic crisis, a serious health problem caused by the departure of Belgian and other foreign medical personnel, and a complete breakdown in the civilian machinery of government—public services, communications, labor administration, social security, judiciary, and supply. As the military operation got under way, the civilian operation was able to start picking up the pieces.

There is enough evidence to show that, if the United Nations had not intervened, the Congo would have become a cauldron into which other African states, the United States, the Soviet Union, and other major powers would have been drawn on one side or the other, and that the Congolese themselves would not have acquired the stability on which they could build their independent nation-state. Mongi Slim, former foreign minister of Tunisia, touched on this point in delivering the Hammarskjöld Memorial Lecture at Columbia University in 1963:

> Much controversy arose on the merits of such operations, with many pros and cons. But what can be asserted beyond any doubt is that the UN presence prevented the Cold War from settling in the Congo, that the unity of the Congo was reestablished thanks in large measure to the UN's effort, and that the UN helped to avoid an impending chaos that threatened peace and security, not only in the Congo but in the whole of the African continent.

Hammarskjöld's name has become synonymous with peacekeeping. His commitment to this process stemmed from his realization that these operations could be developed into an effective tool for furthering the process of the peaceful settlement of disputes. Hammarskjöld often spoke of his understanding that the resolution of conflicts through mediation and conciliation was based not only on the prevailing mood of the UN members but also on a conviction of the uselessness of war.

Hammarskjöld had many other gifts besides his gift for diplomacy. He needed only a few hours of sleep per day and for relaxation on long flights he would work on his translation of Martin Buber from German to Swedish or read other literature. His quiet humor, his sympathetic word here and there on his visits to missions, and his willingness to join the working men and women of the United Nations at their meals or on a joyful occasion endeared him to all. He took care of the peacekeepers and established an easy rapport with civilians—great and rare qualities in higher leadership. What I admired most in him was that he was a courageous man. He wrote in his notebook, *Markings*, "Do not seek death. Death will find you. But seek the road which makes fulfillment."

Hammarskjöld's last flight in the Congo was the only one during this time for which I was not in his party. He died, but I live with the joy of having been so fortunate to have been closely associated with such a great man.

13

Military Adviser to U Thant:

Congo Operation concluded, Ruanda-Urundi, West Irian, and Cuba

U Thant Assumes Office

I first became acquainted with U Thant after he was elected chairman of the Congo Conciliation Commission. A good Buddhist, he was kind and tolerant. However, he made certain that his politeness was never mistaken for weakness. In his gentle and quiet manner, he gained the respect of his colleagues and others associated with him.

Familiar as he was with the developments in the Congo, U Thant wasted no time in setting his own style in the conduct of the operations. He was primarily interested in the politics of peacekeeping and avoided involvement in its management. Since Hammarskjöld's death, Bunche had assumed the pivotal role for managing peacekeeping in general and in the Congo in particular. As U Thant gained knowledge of the working of the UN secretariat system, he became engaged in giving political direction to the operations, allowing Bunche to continue day-to-day management of the operations.

It was important for me to know exactly how I fitted into the channels of command as the military adviser in the new set up, and so I arranged to see U Thant. His role, he said, would be similar to the one he had played in the Congo Conciliation Commission, namely, providing political direction. However, I would continue to be his military adviser and I would enjoy direct access to him. Unlike his predecessor, for whom he had great admiration and respect, he was determined not to let the Congo preoccupy his attention and lead him to give scant attention to other crises, both old and new. Bunche, he added, would continue to deal with the Middle East and the Congo and might have to assume other duties.

There was a second under Secretary-General for special political affairs and U Thant intended for him to take on some new duties. Only weeks before Hammarskjöld's death, realizing that the Soviet attacks on him could prove yet more damaging, Hammarskjöld had sought to widen his circle of advisers (his two top aides were both Americans) by bringing in C.V. Narasimhan, a brilliant former Indian Civil Service officer, as his chef de cabinet. Popularly known as "CV", he was retained in this position by U Thant. While I was U Thant's military adviser, when it came to implementing policy I had to work with Bunche for peacekeeping operations and CV for overall coordination.

When I asked U Thant how any disagreement between my military and Bunche's political views was to be resolved, he said with a laugh, "But you must settle your differences." Since I had great respect for Bunche and no desire to find myself locking horns with him, I looked at U Thant to say that I needed a fuller answer. With great amusement he added, "You can always come to me for advice for a change, instead of my wanting yours all the time."

Congo

The UN role in the Congo had become highly controversial, and although U Thant was careful not to identify himself with the mission to the same extent that Hammarskjöld had done, he was not always able to avoid political controversy. In particular, he became embroiled in controversy over the withdrawal of UNEF.

On 24 November 1961, the Security Council approved a resolution on the Congo that was probably the strongest and most direct authorization for the use of force ever issued by that body. The resolution gave the Secretary-General authority to take vigorous action, including the use of requisite means of force, to apprehend for deportation all foreign military and paramilitary personnel and political advisers not under the UN command, as already authorized in the 21 February 1961 resolution. Despite this forceful resolution, the situation continued to deteriorate. In December 1961, following a skirmish between the gendarmerie and UN troops on the outskirts of Elisabethville, ONUC launched another operation. Both sides suffered casualties.

Some critics claimed that the UN force had gone beyond the Security Council mandate. U Thant strongly denied the charge, pointing to the harassment that the UN troops had suffered at the hands of the mercenaries and gendarmerie over a long period. The UN operation in Katanga was concluded with the signing of the Kitona Accord on 21 December 1961, by which Tshombe recognized President Kasavubu as head of state, the indissoluble unity of the republic, and the central government's authority over all parts of it, and agreed to place the Katangan gendarmerie under the authority of the president. The secession appeared to be over, but within twenty-four hours the Katanga cabinet declared that it could not authorize President Tshombe to make such an agreement. A few days later, fighting between ONUC and the Katanganese flared up again in the north of the province. The deadlock over Katanga continued throughout 1962.

U Thant proposed a program of national reconciliation. First Adoula and then Tshombe accepted the idea, but the latter again defaulted. The final chapter of the secession story began on 27 December 1962 and ended after only thirty-six hours of fighting. In the tradition of renowned Asian rulers, demonstrating his determination to enforce the law, U Thant authorized another military operation to create an environment for implementing national reconciliation. The operation was carried out successfully and all mining installations were safely secured. On 21 January 1963, the United Nations announced the end of military operations and of Katanga's secession and declared that all important centers in Katanga were under UN control. In a prior statement issued the same day in New York, U Thant had stated that the military phase of ONUC operations had been completed and that UN troops would gradually be withdrawn from the Congo.

U Thant sent me to Leopoldville to assist General Ironsi, the Nigerian commander of ONUC, with instructions to end the operations in the Congo by 30 June 1964. The officer-in-charge, Bibiano Osario-Taffal, a highly experienced Mexican and a veteran of the Spanish civil war, was to continue with his peacebuilding tasks as the resident representative of the United Nations Development Programme (UNDP). ONUC withdrew after a most complex and difficult four-year operation. Had its length, manpower commitment, and financial cost been foreseen, there is little doubt that it would never have taken place—the cost alone would have deterred the member states.

The balance sheet of achievement is difficult to draw up. Those who were lukewarm at the start were the first to raise their voices at any sign of ONUC exceeding what they considered to be the limits of its mandate. As the operation proceeded, the limitations of the UN machinery for managing such an enterprise became increasingly evident. The large number of different nationalities on the UN force and their wide differences in military experience and other characteristics posed political, command, and administrative problems and markedly affected the conduct of operations. The haste with which the force was collected and deployed posed an unprecedented command-and-control problem for the ONUC force commander and his staff—a problem exacerbated by the fact that the ONUC headquarters staff itself was assembled piecemeal as the operation proceeded and was not fully staffed until six months into the operation. Add to this the size of the territory covered, which made overall coordination virtually impossible, and the differing loyalties governing the actions of certain of the contingents, and it is a wonder that anything at all was achieved.

Of the many lessons of the Congo operation, perhaps the most important is the need for the United Nations to organize peacekeeping operations suited to the specific needs of each situation. Each conflict is different; each requires its own diagnosis and treatment. UN peacekeeping forces can prove effective only if the Security Council tailors the forces' mandates and resources to the needs of their missions.

Ruanda–Urundi (Rwanda-Burundi)

Ruanda and Urundi were German colonies taken over by the League of Nations, and subsequently the United Nations, under Belgian trusteeship. The Belgians established administrative and economic linkages between the two mountainous territories and their own colony—the Congo. The population of the territories was made up of Bahutus (85 per cent) and a very small group of Batwa pygmies (1 per cent), both of whom had for generations been controlled by a feudal elite, the Watusi (14 per cent). Both countries were populous, together supporting five million people, but poor. There were one million cattle, which bestowed high status on their owners but yielded little meat or milk. The main crop was coffee.

In November 1959 a virtual civil war erupted between the two main ethnic groups in Ruanda. The 1959 elections organized by the UN Trusteeship Council led to a republic and a constitutional monarchy under the traditional ruler, Mwami (King) Mwambutsa IV. While Urundi had remained quiet, Ruanda had to guard its borders from Watusi raids and threats to public law and order from within.

The UN Trusteeship Council selected 1 July 1962 as the provisional date for independence for the two nations. A UN Ruanda-Urundi Commission concluded that the main concerns on independence would be maintenance of law and order, technical assistance for development, and financial and economic aid. ONUC was to organize a military advisory group for the commission, and General McKeown established its headquarters at Usumbura, Urundi, and a sub-office in Kigali, Ruanda.

The Belgian-organized, one-thousand-strong armed force in the two countries was inadequately trained and had fewer than ten indigenous officers. ONUC, preoccupied with its responsibilities in the Congo, could not spare troops. Retaining Belgians was a poor decision, since they were no longer wanted. However, the United Nations was agreeable to helping to train the security forces if necessary.

The government of Urundi declared that Belgian troops must depart by 1 July, whereas Ruanda expressed its desire to retain Belgian troops for the interim, fearing across-the-border attacks from refugees. Meanwhile, the Soviet Union was insisting that all Belgian troops leave the territories. In the last week of June the General Assembly, after intensive negotiations, decided to free Ruanda-Urundi as of 1 July. It requested the Secretary-General to set up a minimum UN presence and stabilize the area politically and economically. It also gave Belgium one month, not three months as requested, to withdraw its troops. At the end of this assembly session, no one was in doubt that the United Nations had by this resolution risked another Congo.

Taghi Nasser, an Iranian with UNDP experience, served as SRSG and reported the smooth transfer of power. The last action, but not least, of the UN Commission for Ruanda-Urundi was to ensure the departure of Belgian troops from the two states. The chair, Angie Brooks of Liberia, decided to visit the two states and U Thant asked me to accompany her. I met Brooks at Leopoldville and together with a small staff we flew to Usumbura. The Belgian troops had mostly gone, as had most of the Belgian civilians and other foreign nationals, except for a small number of Greek and Indian traders. The next day, we flew to Kigali and while Brooks and Nasser met the government, I spent the day with the military team. After listening to numerous reports, I was saddened to learn that the Belgians had made very little effort—less even than in the Congo—to prepare these colonies for independence. A dreadful fate awaited these people.

We returned to Usumbura that afternoon. While our work was mostly done we had yet to pay our courtesy call on the Mwami. We finally caught up with him, playing the drums in the band at a restaurant-night club on Lake Tanganyika. As he played, Angie Brooks and I enjoyed a couple of twirls on the dance floor.

West Irian

U Thant had been at the helm of the United Nations for barely a month when he had to divert some of his attention from the Congo to the fighting that had broken out in Dutch West New Guinea, or West Irian, governed as part of the Dutch East Indies, which included Indonesia. On Indonesia's independence in 1949, President Sukarno claimed West Irian as part of Indonesia, but the Dutch argued that the territory should be allowed to determine its own future. A crisis was in the making. Although the dispute was brought to the General Assembly, no agreement was reached.

Some twelve years later, Indonesian fighters landed on the Dutch East Indies islands and sporadic fighting between the Dutch and Indonesian infiltrators was reported. A series of appeals by U Thant and President Kennedy led to talks that concluded on 1 August 1962 in an agreement at the American University, Washington, D.C. U Thant had kept me informed of the progress of the talks and in the summer of 1962 he told me to join Ambassador Ellsworth Bunker, the UN mediator, and assist him in the final military phase of the talks.

Bunker, former American envoy to India, brought me into his small entourage and by the following day we had worked out a plan, and had secured the approval of the parties involved, for the military part of the protocol. The Dutch military would withdraw and Indonesian fighters would be collected at the five major ports in the territory before being returned by the United Nations to Indonesia. An Indonesian brigade would be allowed to enter and reside in a camp monitored by the United Nations. Security for the island would be provided by a one-thousand-strong Pakistani contingent, including an infantry battalion and supporting arms. Pakistani naval personnel would replace the Dutch crews and man vital coastal shipping. The plan also included detailed arrangements for the turnover of civilian administration and security to the United Nations.

After receiving the approval of the General Assembly on 15 August, the agreement was signed in the Security Council. U Thant sent me to the Dutch East Indies via Tokyo to take charge of the UN observer mission. On reaching Biak on 20 August, I was informed by the Dutch that their naval aircraft were pursuing two Indonesian submarines. The Dutch military were certain that the Indonesians were not yet fully trained to man the underwater craft and therefore they were certain that Russians were aboard. Regardless, the Dutch viewed the presence of the submarines as a threat to their fleet and were determined to destroy them. The Dutch understood that the cease-fire had come into effect and therefore they had anxiously awaited my arrival to obtain my consent to attack the submarines.

I didn't think for a moment: "No, you can't do this. You suspect that there are Russians aboard. If Russians are present do you want to involve them now in your colonial war?" The chief of staff of Admiral Leender Reeser, the commander of the Dutch East Indies

Forces, thought for a minute or so and said, "No. I don't want to start a war with the Russians or anyone else. But, General, you must get these submarines out. We cannot accept the risk of their presence in these waters."

I asked if he could connect me to the Secretary-General and I gave him the number at his residence in Riverdale, New York, where he would be in the early hours of the day. Half an hour later I was speaking to U Thant. The Secretary-General said that I must not allow fighting to resume and that he would immediately call Sukarno to have the submarines removed. I flew to Hollandia the next morning to establish my headquarters. At the Sentani airport, I was greeted by thirty-four hundred Papuan demonstrators. Contrary to the press reports, the crowd was friendly and more inquisitive than angry. Later in the day Admiral Reeser and the Dutch army chief of staff, Brig. Gen. W.D.H. Eckhart, came to call. They informed me that the submarines had left the area and were heading toward Indonesian waters. For my part I called on the Dutch governor of West New Guinea, P.J. Plattel. He was most helpful and assured me of his support in the implementation of the agreement.

I now proceeded to arrange the collection of the Indonesian fighters and to work out the future of the Papuan Volunteer Corps, who had been recruited by the Dutch from among Papuan aborigines. Information from the Dutch on the zones in which the Indonesian fighters had been dropped was vague and covered vast areas. The Indonesians, I hoped, would have more precise information. I had to locate the Indonesian fighters, inform them that the war was over, persuade them to report to collection points for assistance, and arrange for their removal from West Irian. It would be best if I could obtain a recorded statement by Sukarno so I would be believed by his fighters. This required my going to Jakarta and seeing Sukarno. As to the Papuan battalion, the Dutch officers, ably led by Colonel William van Heuven of the Dutch Royal Marines, showed great concern for their future welfare.

The Indonesian foreign minister, Subandrio, had already suggested in New York that I visit Sukarno in Jakarta soon after my arrival in West Irian. My observer group now had access to the international telephone and telegraph system at Hollandia via Amsterdam, so I cabled Narasimhan that I had successfully concluded my negotiations with the Dutch officials and that I was leaving for Indonesia to call on President Sukarno. The CAO arranged for me to take a KLM flight from Biak to Sydney, and then for me to go by Qantas to Jakarta.

I arrived at Jakarta on 24 August to a ceremonial airport reception and Indonesian hospitality. The next morning I was driven to Sukarno's palace at Bogor, thirty miles out of the city. Sukarno received me in an audience hall, attended by his cabinet and the chiefs of the armed forces. After breakfast, he led me to an anteroom. I reported on the progress of the operation and then brought up my two problems. I said that I proposed to airdrop leaflets outlining the main points of the Dutch–Indonesian agreement. Sukarno offered to have them ready in bulk for airdrop before my return to West Irian. He also agreed to broadcast a statement from an Indonesian island nearby to instruct his fighters in West Irian to report to the UN centers. As for the Papuan battalion, he said that they would be absorbed by the new West Irian police. Sukarno readily agreed to my suggestions that an Indonesian liaison team should be posted at Hollandia and communications established between Jakarta and Hollandia.

On my return to Hollandia, I caught up with cables from New York and was pleased at the smooth progress of the operation. A few days before the United Nations took over temporary administration, I received a cable from Narasimhan asking me to close the observer operation and inquiring when I proposed to return. José Rolz-Bennett, an able former Guatemalan diplomat on U Thant's staff, would take over from me as the acting head of the mission. What intrigued me was that the cable expressed interest in my travel plans. It was only after I returned to New York that I learned that the Indonesians had put forward my name as a candidate for the post of administrator of West Irian and the Dutch had agreed. But at this juncture Pakistan's permanent representative, Sir Zafrullah Khan, told U Thant that, although there was no objection to me personally, it was not politically acceptable for Pakistan to have their troops placed under command of an Indian general.

A couple of days before closing my observer operation, the Pakistani commander arrived. He turned out to be Brigadier Saeed-ud-din Khan, my course mate from the IMA. Saeed's staff could not-restrain him from spending his free time with me, not only to talk about old times but also to get the "gen" on West Irian. I recognized a significant difference in attitude among the Pakistani fighting arms units in Saeed's contingent compared to that of the Pakistani services units in ONUC. The bitterness over the recent Jammu and Kashmir war was more than apparent in the behavior of the fighting troops. But I was not going to allow this to spoil my last hours in Hollandia and the fun I was having in Saeed's company.

In a cable, Narasimhan instructed me to meet Sukarno, stop at Karachi to visit army headquarters there, and then go on to the Netherlands to see the Dutch government and finalize arrangements for the implementation of the agreement.

In West Irian, as it was called now, Rolz-Bennett replaced the Dutch governor Piet Platteel and a few weeks later turned over the administration to Ambassador Djalal Abdoh of Iran. I returned to New York. There, I was pleased to have a fine soldier, Lt. Col. Shirin D.K. Niazi of Pakistan, on my staff to deal with the UN Temporary Administration in West Irian (UNTEA). Testifying to the peculiarities produced by the Partition of India, Niazi discovered that Piki Dastur, the wife of Lt. Col. K.K. Dastur, military adviser to the Indian mission to the United Nations, was from Dera Ismail Khan in West Pakistan, Niazi's home town, and was fluent in his dialect. Mrs. Niazi did not know English. Here we were citizens of divided countries. I was one of the few who could speak Punjabi with Sir Zafrullah and Piki Dastur was the only one in our circles who could converse in the dialect of the Niazis.

I caught up with events in the Congo, especially with U Thant's determined efforts to push forward his plan for reconciliation and ONUC's emergency plans for an operation in Katanga, in case Tshombe became obdurate. The month of October 1962 was a month of crisis. The Berlin blockade threatened military confrontation and nuclear exchange between the superpowers. War between India and China led me to speak to U Thant, asking permission to return to India—India had not asked for me, so U Thant did not think that there was need for me to return; and, in any case, the war ended quickly. There was also fighting in Laos. The United Nations, however, was not invited to engage itself in any of these crises.

Cuban Missile Crisis

On 18 October, Andrei Gromyko, the Soviet foreign minister, met President Kennedy. They mostly discussed the Berlin crisis. Two days later, Admiral John McCain, commander-in-chief of the U.S. Eastern Fleet and chief military adviser to Ambassador Adlai Stevenson, U.S. permanent representative to the United Nations, came to see me. McCain said that he had been authorized by the Pentagon to inform me in strictest secrecy that the United States had definite proof that the Russians had moved nuclear missiles to Cuba. For security reasons, Washington had decided to use me as the channel to convey this information to U Thant and to no one else. I was able to see U Thant almost immediately. He realized that the transfer of Soviet missiles to Cuba was potentially a dangerous move. He thought aloud what the United Nations could do to cope with this catastrophic threat to world peace.

Relations between Cuba and the United States had continued to worsen since the Castro-led revolution in the island state. Earlier in the year, a CIA-supported invasion of Cuba, by U.S.-based Cuban dissidents, had failed, resulting in recriminations and heightened tensions. But the introduction of nuclear missiles was an extremely dangerous move.

On 20 October, Admiral McCain requested through me that U Thant arrange a meeting with Stevenson. In the meeting, U Thant learned that Kennedy was going to make a statement and that it would be very tough.

That evening, I joined U Thant in his suite to listen to Kennedy. The president told the American people that the Soviet Union, contrary to promises, was building missile and bomber bases in Cuba. His tone was indeed tough and he declared a commitment to act alone against the threat posed to his country by the missiles, which had a range of two thousand miles.. He declared a unilateral quarantine on the shipment of weapons to Cuba. The world was at the brink of a catastrophic war. The President called on Chairman Khrushchev to withdraw his missiles and weapons and said that he was asking for an emergency meeting of the Security Council. The same day, Cuba also requested a Security Council meeting to consider the grave threat to its security as a result of American actions.

After the speech, U Thant said, "It was the grimmest and gravest speech I have ever heard a head of state make." In his memoirs (*View from the UN* [1978]), he wrote that he was reminded at the time of a speech he himself had delivered in San Francisco a few years earlier: "The vitality of the American people [the speech declared] is reflected in the extraordinary pace of your everyday life, the vehemence of your reactions and your feeling and the fantastic growth of your economic enterprises. This vitality, this vigor, and this exuberance of your national character have been in the past both an asset and a liability." U Thant now wondered whether President Kennedy's vigor and vitality—and the vehemence of his reaction—were reassuring or frightening.

Greatly concerned with the fate of mankind, U Thant decided to issue an appeal to Kennedy and Khrushchev for a moratorium of two to three weeks on military activity and for a voluntary suspension of arms shipments to Cuba. He also made himself available for whatever services that he could perform.

The debate in the council was highly emotional and confrontational. After allowing the opposing parties and the Latin American member on the council to speak, U Thant informed the council of his appeal and urgently called on the parties to hold negotiations.

Later in the day, U Thant received responses from both parties agreeing to his proposals. U Thant had discussed with me and his other staff the danger of a confrontation between rival ships. I had by now been fully apprised in secrecy by a high-powered American military operations team of their estimates of the deployment of Soviet troops, aircraft, and missiles in Cuba. The American briefing was supported by air photographs, which I was trained to read. By now I was certain that if these weapons were not withdrawn war was inevitable. I was not certain at this stage that the war would turn nuclear, because the air photographs showed that the Russian missile systems were still incomplete.

Although an American nuclear strike was a possibility, the Americans had the capability to fight a conventional war in the Caribbean, which they would surely win. As far as I was concerned, the immediate priority was to prevent a direct confrontation between the two parties on the high seas off Florida.

These considerations led U Thant to send another appeal. He asked Khrushchev to order Soviet ships steaming to Cuba to stay away from the interception area temporarily and asked Kennedy to avoid direct confrontation with Soviet ships. Both agreed.

By this time, I had received information regarding the construction of major military installations in Cuba, notably those designed to launch medium and intermediate-range ballistic missiles. I briefed U Thant and persuaded him to send a message to Castro informing him of the encouraging replies from Khrushchev and Kennedy and asking for the suspension of the deployment and construction of launch pads during the period of negotiations. Castro offered a courteous reply, but asserted Cuba's right of self-defense. He also invited U Thant to visit Cuba for direct talks.

It was true that other nations—for example, Turkey, Pakistan, Thailand, and Japan—had received missiles from the United States, but they had all received them openly, as opposed to the secrecy and denials that accompanied the deployment of Soviet missiles in Cuba. Cuba would soon find itself a pawn between two superpowers, helpless to influence the final outcome of the crisis.

The United States, anxious to have a legal basis for possible future action in Cuba, obtained a resolution by the Organization of American States (OAS) calling for the immediate withdrawal and dismantling of missiles and other weapons in Cuba. The resolution further recommended that the member-states take all measures, including the use of armed force, to ensure the dismantling of all weapons and to prevent Cuba obtaining additional weapons from the Sino-Soviet bloc. This resolution was transmitted to the Secretary-General, consistent with Article 54 of the UN Charter. It should be noted that Article 52 of the charter, in referring to regional organizations, states that such action may be taken "provided that such arrangements or agencies and their activities are consistent with the Purposes and Principles of the United Nations". I found the discussion of this action at U Thant's lunch meeting that day interesting. Members of his staff pointed out that the Soviets had resorted to this approach in their invocation of the Warsaw Pact to justify Soviet actions in Hungary in 1956. Later, the United States used the same approach in its intervention in the Dominican Republic in 1965 and the Soviets used it for their intervention in Czechoslovakia in 1968.

The United States sent John McCloy, a skillful diplomat known to be tough on communists, to assist Stevenson at the United Nations. Apparently, Washington thought Stevenson was not tough enough to deal with the Soviets. But I had heard Stevenson deliver his speech on the introduction of missiles in Cuba, which was recorded as one of the sternest speeches ever given by a delegate in the council, and it seemed obvious that there were other reasons for McCloy's appointment. U Thant had met McCloy before and, although the American was known as a hard-liner, U Thant thought highly of him. Indeed, Stevenson had many admirers in the United Nations, including most of the Secretary-General's staff.

The Russians sent V.V. Kuznetsov, the first deputy foreign minister, to cooperate with the Secretary-General in his efforts to resolve the conflict. This was a welcome change from Valerian Zorin, the permanent representative of the Soviet Union to the United Nations, who had severely criticized U Thant for his first appeal to deal with the crisis. Zorin was not much liked on the thirty-eighth floor of the United Nations.

U Thant began his consultations with McCloy and Kuznetsov without delay and created an ideal environment for the two sides to supplement and discuss details of continuing negotiations between the heads of governments. Kuznetsov was a highly experienced diplomat with old European courtesies of diplomacy, whereas McCloy, an intelligent man with a successful business and a diplomatic background, was more combative. While I sympathized with McCloy's concerns, for it was the United States that was under nuclear threat, I found it hard to see any advantage in his excessively hard-line approach and displays of ill temper. U Thant had said to us at a meeting that Stevenson had described McCloy as a "hard old frontiersman". This seemed to fit the man. There was more than one occasion on which U Thant had to intervene to cool down the discussions, using the excuse that it was time to quench our thirst with a daiquiri, his own favorite.

As secret negotiations between the United States and the Soviets proceeded, U Thant's meetings were smoothing out the details of implementation. But just as secret diplomacy was helping narrow the gap between the United States and the Soviets, the media announced that Russian withdrawal of missiles was to be linked to American withdrawal of U.S. missiles in Turkey, creating a public furor. The American temper began to rise and I received information that the U.S. military were just short of launching an air assault on Russian targets in Cuba. I alerted U Thant in the middle of the night after McCain confirmed this news.

The Soviets had told U Thant that although they would not object to UN observers monitoring the removal of missiles, they preferred that the International Committee of the Red Cross (ICRC) undertake this duty. I presumed that the Russians believed some Western or pro-Western observers would take advantage of the opportunity to increase Western knowledge of their weapons systems, whereas the ICRC had been used before as a civilian observer system and was viewed with less distrust by the Soviets. U Thant agreed to let the ICRC monitor the transport of missiles on the high seas (the United Nations would monitor the removal of missiles from Cuba itself), and found that the ICRC was willing to accept this responsibility.

On 27 October, Kennedy wrote to Khrushchev that the United States would generally accept U Thant's proposals, and the Soviets should remove their missiles and weapons under appropriate UN observation, with suitable safeguards established to halt further introduction of such weapons in Cuba. The United States, for its part, would end its quarantine of Cuba and give assurances against an invasion of the island. There was a positive response from the Soviets.

Thus the crisis had been resolved and now arrangements had to begin for the two superpowers' implementation of their agreement. The question of inspection by the United Nations, agreed to by both, had to have the consent of Cuba, which was excluded from negotiations between the two superpowers.

U Thant, having already received an invitation from Castro to visit Cuba for direct talks, informed Castro of his intention to visit Havana. Castro responded positively and the travel arrangements were set in motion. With Omar Loutfi, U Thant's highly respected Egyptian senior political adviser, we determined an agenda. After hearing Cuba's responses to moves at the United Nations and between the superpowers, U Thant would discuss the monitoring arrangements for the withdrawal of the weapons. If these were accepted, I was to remain with three officers (two from my staff and another borrowed from the Swedish mission to the United Nations).

On 30 October our party of some twenty left by air for Havana, where the Secretary-General was received by Foreign Minister Raul Roa and several diplomats, notably General Albino Silva, special envoy of the president of Brazil to Cuba. At the first meeting that afternoon with President Osvaldo Dorticos and Premier Fidel Castro, U Thant was accompanied by Loutfi, Brazilian chief of UN information Travers de Sa, and me. Attending the Cuban leaders were Roa and Ambassador Mario Garcia Inchaustegui. As expected, the Cubans had a lot to say. U Thant, in explaining his mission, emphasized the basic requirement of the consent of the host country. First Castro and then Dorticos raised issues beyond the immediate crisis, but U Thant again stressed his mission's purpose.

Castro summed up Cuban views. Cuba was opposed to the proposed UN presence in Cuba. The Soviet pledge to withdraw its strategic arms should be accepted as binding and as such Cuba was opposed to any inspection of its ports. As for inspection of missiles on the high seas by the ICRC, that was a matter for the Soviet Union to decide. As for the American pledge not to invade Cuba, Castro questioned the right of the United States to do so in the first place and wondered why the United Nations even considered this a concession. Convinced that the negotiations were going nowhere, U Thant interrupted the meeting and proposed another the following morning.

On our return to the guest-house the Soviet ambassador was waiting for U Thant. The ambassador informed the SG that he had received instructions to dismantle the missiles and launching pads. The ambassador then went to fetch the general in command of the missile forces, while the SG sent for me to join the meeting.

The Soviet ambassador was youngish, to be expected of the representative to a small though strategically important country. The Soviet general was in his forties, a relatively young man to hold so high a post in the Soviet military. I had not met a Russian commander of nuclear forces before. This man was articulate, spoke well-accented English, and was precise. Apparently his instructions were to cooperate with the

Secretary-General. Unlike in the James Bond movies, where the man with his finger on the nuclear button is always sly and devilish, this Russian had an open and honest face and proved to be so in his conversation.

The Russian general told us that all weapons except those that were excluded from the U.S.–Soviet agreement were being withdrawn. In fact, the last missile was being loaded at that time and he invited me to witness the event. "What about the American air reconnaissance?" I asked. He said that the Americans were conducting low-level flights and on the high seas their helicopters hovered over Russian vessels, with missiles tied to their open decks. I added, "What about supersonic aircraft? I am told that you are leaving some behind concealed in caves." He said that no supersonic aircraft were being left behind.

In an attempt to check on information that I had received before my departure from New York, I asked how the Russians were maintaining the secrecy of their weapons systems and what role the Cubans were playing in Soviet activities there. The information I had from American sources was gleaned from counterespionage, double agents, and radio intercepts—the usual bag of tricks of intelligence services and not the most reliable of sources. Accordingly, I was keen to find out what suspicions I could discount. The Russian general's replies were most intriguing.

At the outset, the general said, the Russians had decided that the missiles and other sophisticated weapons were going to remain strictly under their own control. The area of deployment was under Russian security, for which they brought their own troops. The port, the access to the deployment area, was also kept under their own control. Therefore, Russian labor and technical services were brought in. This ensured that only Russians saw any part of their weapon systems. No Cuban, even military chief Raul Castro, was permitted in the area of control. If the general was telling the truth, then the Americans could rely only on two sources of information: radio intercepts and double or turned agents.

By the time U Thant and I had finished speaking with the Soviet ambassador and the general, we had all the information that we wanted. This alone made U Thant's journey to Havana most valuable. U Thant attended the next morning's meeting by himself, but it made little progress and he decided to return to New York. The United Nations's inability to deploy observers in Cuba concerned the Americans. Having little confidence in the veracity of the Russian General's reports and understandably concerned with leaving the fate of their nation in the hands of three diplomats and a Brigadier—all from the Third World—they continued to seek information vital for their national security from other sources.

For our part, would we have learned more by leaving behind an observer group? I was convinced that there was little left to add to our knowledge, although a presence typically provides "negative information" (by confirming, for example, the absence of potentially hostile deployments) and builds confidence, which is so vital in ending a conflict. U Thant immediately received praise from President Kennedy and Chairman Khrushchev for his efforts. But this praise did not last long. The many books published on the Cuban crisis barely mention U Thant and the key role played by the United Nations. All too often UN contributions to diplomatic successes are denied their proper recognition.

14

More with U Thant

Yemen, Cyprus, Spinelli-Rikhye Mission to Israel and Jordan, and the Dominican Republic

Yemen

Just as U Thant was engaged in ending the secession of Katanga, he had to attend to a crisis in Yemen. In September 1963, Imam Ahmed Bin-Yahya died and was succeeded by his son, Imam Mohammed Al-Badr. A few weeks later a military-led coup ousted the new imam and was accorded recognition by the UAR (Egypt) and the Soviet Union. No other nation recognized the rebel regime. The imam escaped to Saudi Arabia and, after obtaining help from friends, launched a fierce guerrilla war against the rebels. The military regime in Saana alleged that the imam had Saudi Arabia's aid, while the imam accused the Egyptians of helping the military. The UN General Assembly decided in favor of the president of Saana, and recognized his regime by the end of the year.

U Thant sent Ralph Bunche on a peace mission to Yemen, and the United States dispatched Ellsworth Bunker in search of a solution. The combined efforts of these two skilled negotiators led to an agreement calling for a cease-fire and deployment of an observer group. Since General Von Horn was in Jerusalem, he was nominated to go to Yemen, Egypt, and Saudi Arabia to consult on the implementation of the accord. He recommended that the observer group be over one thousand strong and include light armored reconnaissance and aircraft. I thought the numbers were excessive. As it turned out, the costs of the operation, which Saudi Arabia and the UAR agreed to share, and the nature of the mission led to the assignment of a smaller group of about two hundred personnel and a small air unit. Von Horn was appointed commander. At first, I could not believe it. But I later learned that he was being eased out of his post at UNTSO at the behest of Israel. I felt certain that this time Von Horn's shortcomings would be exposed.

Shortly after the start of the mission, Von Horn began a dispute with the UN administration, much as he had in the Congo. He sent cables to New York threatening to resign if his demands were not met. U Thant accepted his resignation, ordering Von Horn to hand over charge to his deputy. Von Horn was to proceed to Cairo, where I was to meet with him and make arrangements for his departure home. In replying to the Secretary-General's cable, Von Horn stated that he wanted to be released sooner than the 20 September date proposed. He added that his deputy, Colonel Pavlovic of Yugoslavia, had declined to take over from him and that his operations officer, American major L.P. David, had asked to be returned to UNTSO.

Von Horn arrived in Cairo a couple days after I did. He was accompanied by the observer group's finance officer, his Swedish secretary, and Yugoslav captain D. Krajger. The Yugoslav sought a separate meeting with me to inform me that Von Horn had brought him to see the Yugoslav Ambassador to support Von Horn's position. Krajger emphasized that, although Yugoslav troops would like some additional support, they were quite happy. As for Pavlovic, he had at no time refused to take command of the group. This made me wonder whether David, too, had really asked to leave the mission. The fundamental problem, it seems, was that both the general and his operations officer were out of their depth and failed to grasp the nuances of this sophisticated political operation, of which the military observers were only a part.

For the next ten days or so Von Horn argued the merits of his complaints against the UN secretariat, which I was obliged to report to New York. He visited various embassies, making his case, but U Thant did not change his mind. It was a bitter Von Horn who left for Beirut on his way home. On his arrival at the Hotel Phoenicia in Beirut, he went public with his criticism of the UN command. Also, a lengthy interview appeared in the *New York Times* with a person who, though unidentified, apparently had access to Von Horn's cables to the Secretary-General and was critical of the United Nations. Although I learned later who the anonymous interviewee was, since the affair was relatively inconsequential, I preferred to let sleeping dogs lie.

My stay in Cairo was hardly enjoyable, and for having put up with all the unpleasantness I was told to go to Saana and assume acting charge of the mission. Saana, a typical Middle Eastern town and at high elevation, required some physical adjustment. The UN office and commander's residence were in a "palace"—a palace with small rooms and a narrow staircase. The bakery on the ground floor served as the mess. The walls were covered with writings from the Holy Koran and I felt it would be a sacrilege to consume alcohol in these surroundings.

The Royal Canadian Air Force flew me around to visit the observer posts, see the Yugoslav unit, and view the terrain. I also paid a call on the Saudi foreign ministry in Jedda. The area of operations was too large to be covered by the limited number of aircraft available for aerial reconnaissance by day, and only a limited number of approaches could be kept under observation at night. In fact, the UN presence was more or less token. Once I had seen all that was important, I was ready to return to New York, and was glad to learn that the Secretary-General had arranged for General Prem Singh Gyani from UNEF to take over responsibility.

Eventually, lack of financing and the failure of the parties to come to an agreement persuaded U Thant and Bunche decided that the observer group should be replaced by a negotiator. Accordingly, Pier Spinelli, head of the UN office in Geneva, was appointed SRSG. After about a year, the results of these efforts did not warrant continuation of the mission and, in September 1964, the UN Yemen Observation Mission was disbanded. In a frank report, U Thant informed the United Nations that the mission had failed to achieve its goals.

Cyprus

Cyprus gained its independence from Britain in 1960 based on the Zurich agreement of 11 February 1959 between the heads of the Greek and Turkish Governments, and the Treaty of Guarantee, signed by Cyprus, Greece, Turkey, and the United Kingdom on 16 August 1960. These agreements recognized the special rights of the Turkish minority, which made up 18 per cent of the population of the island. The application of several of the provisions of the constitution encountered difficulties from the start. The earlier attempts by Greek Cypriots for *Enosis*, a reunion with Greece, as Cyprus progressed toward its independence had left arms scattered around the island. Within three years of independence, efforts at reconciliation between the Greek and Turkish Cypriots had failed and violence had broken out. The day before Christmas 1963 the Turkish garrison of 650, stationed in Nicosia under the Treaty of Guarantee, moved out of its barracks and redeployed in north Nicosia, a predominantly Turkish area. The following day, Cyprus reported low-level Turkish overflights, and for the next several days there were reports of troop movements on the south coast of Turkey and of naval shipping offshore.

Responding to the crisis in Cyprus, the guarantor powers offered their good offices to the parties of the conflict, and they both accepted the offer. A cease-fire was called on 26 December and a neutral zone, called the Green Line, was established between areas occupied by the two communities in Nicosia. The Security Council asked the Secretary-General to appoint a special representative to observe the peacemaking arrangements previously decided. Accordingly, U Thant dispatched General Prem Singh Gyani, commander UNEF, to Cyprus. After the negotiations failed, a UN peacekeeping force was arranged by the Security Council with the consent of Cyprus. Gyani was appointed commander. The council also appointed a mediator to promote a peaceful solution to the Cyprus problem.

The peacekeeping operation in Cyprus—the United Nations Force in Cyprus (UNFICYP)—had several novel aspects. The UN force was to replace an existing peacekeeping force and retain a number of British troops already deployed on the ground. The British military bases were to provide logistics support, offering the best of such services ever experienced by the United Nations. An RAF component was readily available in case of an emergency. Also, the British were a permanent member of the Security Council and as a major power had ready resources to support the operation. And all of these arrangements existed within the overall framework of a conflict between two communities whose mother countries were members of NATO. These factors made the management of UNFICYP challenging and different from other UN peacekeeping operations.

Another important aspect of the mission regarded the preparation of guidelines for the UN force's presence. I was determined to avoid relying on Security Council resolutions alone to guide the force commander and labored hard to define the mission and provide rules of engagement. The insistence of Canada on establishing such guidelines helped to ensure that, for the first time, they were laid down in writing. This proved to be an important step in the development of techniques for managing peacekeeping.

Within weeks of the deployment of the force, Gyani asked to retire from the United Nations for personal reasons. General K.S. Thimayya, former Indian Army chief of staff, replaced him. U Thant instructed Thimayya to make it a priority to address the issue of the National Guard. Allowed by the agreements to establish a National Guard consisting of both communities, President Makarios was recruiting only Cypriot Greeks to the force. He was also importing weapons for it, in violation of international accords. This had caused the Turkish Cypriot community to bolster its forces, thereby further destabilizing the island. U Thant told Thimayya, "You must try to stop the development of the National Guard and the Turkish community's response."

President Makarios received Thimayya warmly when he made his first call. While discussing the security situation, Makarios referred to his efforts to strengthen the National Guard. "General Thimayya," he said, "you are very experienced in military matters. I would like you to visit the National Guard and I will be grateful for your advice how to improve it."

Momentarily surprised at the request to see the National Guard, which had hitherto been kept hidden from the United Nations and foreign observers, and in light of Makarios's welcoming remarks, Thimayya decided to be blunt. He said, "Sir, I don't have to visit your troops because I can give you my advice now."

"Pray what is your advice?" asked the president.

Thimayya answered, "My advice, Mr. President, is that you should disband them."

Stunned by Thimayya's frank and simple reply, the President only took a moment to recover. He said, "I have heard that you are a naughty man."

Amid laughter and mutual assurances of cooperation the meeting was concluded.

Before leaving for Cyprus, Thimayya had asked U Thant to spare me for a few days to help Thimayya settle in. I spent two weeks in Cyprus during the summer of 1964. On arrival, Natalie Thomas, Thimayya's personal assistant and a friend of mine from New York, warned me that Nicosia was a hotbed for eavesdropping. The only safe places for conversation were in the UN office, a car, or a crowded restaurant. Natalie, knowing my fondness for swimming for exercise and recreation, added that the pool at our hotel was equally safe for conversation. The hotel being on the Green Line, the two communities had posts on either side of the pool and watched the hotel guests through binoculars. Since Natalie was going to check my cables from New York, she suggested that we meet at the pool in the afternoon to swim and work.

Thimayya asked for my help on several matters. For instance, he asked me to review procedures for reporting to New York and within the force; recommend improvements in information collection and procurement; and evaluate his performance and suggest how he might improve upon it. I had to travel all over the area where the force was deployed, meet the political leaders on both sides, see the troops, and visit the British bases. In the evenings, I accompanied Thimayya for cocktails and dinners, where he did most of his work. When we met at restaurants, Thimmy was first to join the dancing and the singing of Greek songs that he had already learned.

My afternoons at the pool soon drew the attention of the Greek and Turkish sentries and other observers. Since Natalie had her own friends and social contacts in the communities, she was asked by both sides what I was doing in Nicosia. I was seen to spend a good part of my time daily at the pool, as if I was on vacation.

I was coming to the end of my work helping Thimayya and improving support of the operation from New York. Besides, cable traffic from New York about the Congo was on the increase and I thought it was best that, with Thimayya's consent, I inform New York that my work here was done and that I was returning.

The UN force in Cyprus was able to prevent a renewal of fighting but was unable to halt all incidents between the communities. Both sides violated agreements on freedom of movement, especially at critical times. The Turkish Cypriots did not participate in the police and other civil duties and little progress was made in finding a solution for durable peace. Both communities, the guarantor powers, and the major powers wished to avoid a major crisis that could threaten peace and security in the region, and were anxious to retain UNFICYP.

I was very saddened to learn of Thimayya's sudden death toward the end of 1965. With the approval of U Thant and Bunche I arranged with the Field Service to have a party of Indian troops from UNEF fly to Larnaca and accompany Thimayya's remains to India. En route to his home in Coorg, his remains were received in Mumbai (Bombay) with the full military pomp and honors that a great hero of India deserved. A grateful Cyprus, where he was much admired and loved, issued a memorial stamp to honor a great peacekeeper.

Spinelli-Rikhye Mission

Concerned with heightening tensions in 1965 along the Armistice Demarcation Line (ADL) between Israel and Jordan, U Thant began intensive consultations with the permanent representatives of the parties. He decided to send a special mission consisting of a diplomat—Pier Spinelli—and me as the military adviser. While the mission was independent of UNTSO, for practical reasons it looked to UNTSO to provide communications and general support. Our mission was to consult with the appropriate authorities in Amman and Jerusalem about the causes and nature of recent incidents and about means for avoiding a recurrence of them, and to study the situation from both sides of the ADL. The mission was to remain in the area for a week or ten days and was to report to the Secretary-General on its consultations, observations, and conclusions.

Spinelli and I flew over the border between the two states from Lake Tiberias to Eilat, on the Gulf of Aqaba. We walked the entire dividing line through the city of Jerusalem. In Israel we talked to leaders— Levi Eshkol, Golda Meir, Yitzhak Rabin, and others. In Jordan, we met King Hussein twice, and met with his ministers and military commanders. Located as we were at UNTSO, in the old Government House, we had easy access to the staff of General Odd Bull, who was home on urgent personal business.

As we immersed ourselves in the issues, we realized that we needed more time than had been anticipated. In the end, it took us three months to complete our mission. Happily, Odd Bull returned in time for us to exchange views with him, which was helpful in finalizing our report.

In our report to the Secretary-General we stated that the two parties appreciated our efforts to foster better mutual understanding and had expressed strong interest in avoiding serious incidents. There was room for further negotiations. Israeli assurances of a reduction in aggressive patrolling and a reaffirmation of the no-firing agreement between the parties were clearly important.

Mount Scopus, on the edge of Jerusalem and occupied by Israel, was a sensitive issue with the Israelis. We recommended a return to the General Armistice Agreements there, a reduction in IDF patrols, and an easing of restrictions on Arab villagers in the area. Lastly, we recommended that the Secretary-General take up the recommendations of the report with the permanent representatives of the parties and personally communicate with the governments.

U Thant immediately acted on the report, and in the following months the tide of violence seemed to recede along the ADL. However, if there was a respite, it was only brief. Incidents across the ADL never ceased completely, and IDF retaliatory action against Jordanian troops at Es Samu in November 1966 became the trigger for the June 1967 war between the Arabs and Israelis.

Dominican Republic

The Dominican Republic had a history of invasions and revolutions. Eight years of military administration by U.S. Marines, ending in 1924, were followed in 1930 by the presidency of General Rafael Leonides Trujillo Molina. His authoritarian regime achieved economic stability and administrative reform at the cost of human rights and individual freedoms. His assassination in 1961 by Dominicans led to the appoint-

ment of Joaquín Balaguer as president, although the real government
power was in the hands of General Rafael Trujillo, Jr.

In 1962, the reformist Dominican Revolutionary Party (DRP) of
Juan Bosch, a historian, novelist, and poet, won the national election.
Now, denied the privileges of the past, the business community and
the military raised a storm. Meanwhile, the Left protested at the slow
pace of promised reforms. The United States threw its weight against
agrarian and other social reforms, and viewed with displeasure Bosch's
support for the principle of non-intervention by one state in the
affairs of another and his reluctance to take any measures against
Cuba and its policies in Latin America.

Within seven months of his inauguration, Bosch was overthrown
by a military coup led by an air force colonel, Elías Wessín y Wessín,
based at San Isidro airbase. A number of attempts to form a
government by the military and political leaders failed and the military
split in two: one group, under Wessín, wanted to install a military
junta; the other, under Colonel Francisco Caamano, wanted the return
of Bosch. The leftists seized two military camps, took over the armory
at Ozama fort in Santo Domingo, and distributed weapons to the
public. Wessín sent his troops down the road to Santo Domingo,
where they joined battle with the rebels and strafed rebel strongholds,
reportedly killing thousands.

Threatened by a possible takeover by leftists, President Lyndon
Johnson ordered the U.S. Navy to evacuate American citizens through
the port of Haina. On receiving further reports of the worsening
situation and on the recommendation of his ambassador, Tappey
Bennette, President Johnson ordered the marines ashore on 28 April
1965 and on 30 April flew in the 82nd Airborne Division, who
reinforced Wessín's troops who were fighting Caamano's forces.

At the request of the United States, the Organization of American
States (OAS) met and heard from Ambassador Ellsworth Bunker
of the dangerous developments in Santo Domingo, including the
fictitious 'sacking and burning' of the American embassy. The OAS
called for an immediate cease-fire and the establishment of an
international security zone for the protection of embassies and foreign
personnel. The American troops immediately advanced to expand
the areas under their control and established an international security
zone in the eastern part of the city down to the ocean.

The OAS resolution gave an impetus to negotiations led by a papal nuncio. Joined by Ambassador John Bartlow Martin, the nuncio and Bennette pressed for a cease-fire and were able to obtain the consent of air force colonel Pedro Bartolome Benoit, the nominal head of the San Isidro junta; Wessín, the real chief of the junta; and Caamano, the chief of the rebel Constitutionalist High Command.

To have an international flag flying over the unilateral U.S. military intervention, the United States pushed through a resolution for an Inter-American Peace Force (IAPF) by the OAS. A precedent for such a force had been established by the Russians when they reached a similar agreement with most communist-dominated East European states to invade Hungary in 1956. At its peak, the IAPF consisted of twenty-two thousand U.S. troops, sixteen hundred Latin Americans from Brazil, Honduras, and Nicaragua, and twenty-one civil police from Costa Rica. General Hugo Panasco Alvim of Brazil was appointed force commander and General Bruce Palmer, the U.S. commander, was deputy force commander. Alvim, contradicting the stated goal of the OAS and the U.S. government, declared on his arrival that the IAPF would eradicate communism from the country; Palmer was restrained in his statements.

After a prolonged and a bitter debate between the U.S. and Soviet delegates, the Security Council on 14 May called for a cease-fire and, for the purpose of reporting to the council, requested that the Secretary-General send a representative to the Dominican Republic. While U Thant was deciding on his representative, he asked me to take an advance party immediately to Santo Domingo.

I left the same day with a small staff, stayed overnight at Puerto Rico, and reached Santo Domingo the next day. We landed to a chaotic scene at the airport, which was crowded with people fleeing the conflict-ridden city. Luckily, I was received by the UNDP resident representative, who arranged to get us out of the airport quickly. The U.S. chargé d'affaires, William Connette, who happened to be at the airport, offered a seat in his helicopter, which I gratefully declined, as I wanted to remain independent. As we drove into the city, groups of people, on seeing the UN flag, cheered us along. Wessín's troops were few and scattered except for an infantry company and a few tanks at the eastern end of the Duarte Bridge over the Ozama River.

Beyond there, the junta troops were north of the main highway to the embassy area, while rebel troops were in the old city. The International Zone under control of the IAPF included the embassies, the hotel area, the polo ground (for helicopters), and the area down to the beach to Haines. Our mission was billeted at the Hotel Embajador, which also was in use by the IAPF. We were settled in and hooked up to New York in about two hours.

At noon the next day there was a sizable women's demonstration against the United Nations and they insisted on seeing me, so I offered to meet their leaders. Two perspiring but well-dressed women were brought to my hotel suite. They gladly accepted some refreshments and visibly relaxed after the first few sips from their drinks. They explained that they were protesting the fact that the United Nations had occupied the hotel and barred it to civilians from the town. Their women's group met at the hotel regularly and now they could not even enter the lobby. I explained that the IAPF controlled the zone and that the United Nations had rooms at the hotel courtesy of the IAPF.

We chatted for a while and exchanged cards. These two women were Ligia Reid Cabral Bonetti and Luisa Mastrolili, both from powerful Dominican families. I soon discovered that they had nephews and their friends had children who were in my son Bhalinder's school in the United States. I became a frequent guest at the homes of these women and gained entry to high society, most of whose members were opposed to the UN presence. By the time these women left my hotel room, however, they had become good friends of the United Nations.

U Thant's final choice for his representative was José Antonio Mayobre, the articulate and brilliant economist, executive director of the UN Economic Commission of Latin America. I went to the airport to receive Mayobre and take him to the International Zone. As we approached the International Zone, we heard exchanges of fire and soon found ourselves in the middle of a small-scale battle between the forces of Wessín and Caamano. The cease-fire that had held shakily from the start was now broken by what looked like a military operation. We halted our car behind a house and I went around it to have a better look. Two or more of Wessín's tanks with what I could see was at least a platoon of infantry were attempting to push Caamano's troops across a prominent bend in the road that separated the International Zone from the part of the city under rebel control. The IAPF nearby did not appear to be taking any action to stop the fight. I went back to the car and, after reporting to Mayobre, said that it was not safe to remain in the area. The best way for us to stop the fighting was to reach our hotel to communicate with IAPF and OAS. As we drove away from the cover of the houses, Mayobre too saw Wessín's tanks and the continuing firefight. Mayobre and I later prepared a report on the fighting and the apparent lack of response on the part of the IAPF, which was permitting Wessín's force to expand their area of control. Mayobre informed the Secretary-General that he intended to meet with the parties to persuade them to call a cease-fire.

In a whirlwind effort, Mayobre met the Secretary-General of OAS and the representatives of the Dominican Red Cross, the International Red Cross, and the Pan American Sanitary Bureau, and they all agreed to call jointly for a cease-fire to evacuate the wounded and remove the dead. Thereafter, Mayobre and the representatives of the three organizations called on Caamano, who agreed to the cease-fire. Junta leader General Antonio Berreras Imbert, however, told them that he would have to consult the chiefs of the armed forces.

In New York U Thant had immediately presented Mayobre's report and his plans to the Security Council, which asked that the Secretary-General urge Mayobre to continue with his efforts for a cease-fire. The next day Mayobre obtained the assent of the junta. I quickly toured the cease-fire line and was glad to report to Mayobre that the cease-fire was holding and that the humanitarian organizations were busy in the old city, where the crowded hospitals lacked facilities and there were many dead awaiting burial.

The OAS Secretary-General and the special commission were greatly displeased by the arrival of the UN mission. Mayobre's report on the incident on the day of his arrival exposed the reality of the situation in the Dominican Republic. President Johnson had told the American public that he had ordered the marines to save American lives. By now, besides the Marines, a major part of the 82nd Airborne Division had arrived at San Isidro airbase and had cooperated with

9. Secretary-General Dag Hammarskjöld and the author in the Security Council, New York, 21 August 1960.

10. The author confers with Acting Secretary-General U Thant (*left*) and Under-Secretary for Special Political Affairs Ralph Bunche (*right*) in the Security Council, New York, 20 November 1961.

11. Colonel Caleff (*right*), IDF Liaison Officer, and the author visit the ADL in Jerusalem, 1965.

12. The author, on appointment as Commander UNEF I, February 1966.

Wessín's troops to secure the road to the city up to the eastern exit of Duarte Bridge. In the International Zone, American troops had coopted pro-junta civil police to ensure security and traffic control. Clearly, the Americans had acted less from concern to protect American civilians than from a desire to prevent a possible takeover by a procommunist group. Mayobre and his mission were always at odds with the Americans. I was never able to visit General Palmer's command post and was not welcome at the IAPF after General Alvim took over.

Mayobre by now had a solid political adviser, George Howard, an American; a Mexican-American information officer, Caeser Ortiz-Tinoco; and adequate support staff. My military staff included Lt. Col. Paul Mayer of Canada, Major Beneventura Cavalcanti of Brazil, who had served a year with me in New York in 1960-61, and Colonel Garcia Vivanca of Ecuador. It was one of the best teams I had in my UN service, professional, solid, frank, loyal, and daring to the extent that I sometimes had to rein them in. José Rolz-Benette, recently appointed under Secretary-General for special political affairs in New York, deserved credit for the manner in which he supported the mission. He was quick in keeping us informed of the developments in the United Nations and in responding to our requests.

Accompanied by at least one of my military colleagues, I was a frequent visitor to the Constitutionalists in the downtown area, which for some reason was called Ciudad Nueva. We always informed both sides of our itinerary. But while the Constitutionalists always held their fire, the IAPF on many occasions disregarded our presence whenever they chose to retaliate against snipers.

On one visit, Caamano admitted that armed civilians supporting the Constitutionalists were responsible for the sniper fire, but blamed these activities on IAPF efforts to expand its area of control and to seal Caamano's exits to the northern part of the city, where the population was sympathetic to his cause. Caamano's office in the Capello building in the northern part of Ciudad Nueva was under machine-gun fire. When I rose to leave, Caamano advised against it, as he felt that we would be in great danger. But my driver, Mayer, and I had to return to the hotel to report to Mayobre and assist in preparing his report to the Secretary-General, so we decided to leave.

As we were leaving, Caamano, who had always chided me for not being armed, offered Mayer and me handguns, but we declined. As we emerged from his building to enter our car, Caamano and some of his staff saw us off. An IAPF machine-gun post in a tower on the other bank of the river, on seeing a group come out of Caamano's office, was determined to take advantage of the target offered. Overlooking the fact that a UN flag car had arrived a half hour earlier and now waited on the street, it opened fire, spraying the street and the car. Caamano and his group dived for the door, shouting that we should follow, but Mayer and I took cover near the stone wall of the house. Our Dominican driver, who was about to open his door to enter the car, crouched where he stood. We paused for a couple of minutes and then ran to the car. The heavy-caliber bullets had destroyed the engine and smashed the glass but our driver was safe. We jumped into a jeep belonging to Caamano's forces and told Caamano's guard at his door to telephone our office to send another car to the IAPF check point. As we made our way back, Mayer took off his beret to mop his brow and noticed that a bullet had gone clean through the beret, leaving a gaping hole just a few millimeters above his head. We were lucky that we only lost a car.

On rejoining Mayobre we pieced together our report of the incident for New York. We had little doubt that the IAPF was responding to the menace of sniping. Added to this, Wessín was trying to impose his authority and Imbert had to demonstrate his power as the head of the National Government of Reconstruction. U Thant presented Mayobre's report to the Security Council, resulting in demands for strict compliance to the cease-fire and a debate on a possible expansion in the role of, and resources for, Mayobre's mission. Mayobre did not think these measures were necessary and the United States and some others on the council rejected the idea.

The number of Dominicans complaining of violations of human rights had increased and hundreds of requests had been made for information on captives and others who had disappeared. In collaboration with the Inter-American Human Rights Commission and local organizations, Mayobre launched a major effort to deal with these issues. Since Imbert's junta held some three thousand persons in a military transportation camp on the northern fringe of the city and others in forts around the country, Mayobre took a group of human rights observers to selected camps. We gave advanced notice of these visits to the press and always one or more of their cars followed the UN leader. Invariably, the fort commander would refuse entry. Mayobre would protest loudly, all in the presence of the press. These violations became the staple of the press as the situation quieted in the city. Thereafter, the UN mission used this technique routinely under different military observers with useful results. The frequency of reports of these incidents in the U.S. press persuaded the authorities to apply pressure on the junta. While there were only a few instances of human rights violations by Caamano, the reports also ensured improved conduct on his part, since he did not wish to be caught in this net.

Since I had begun my association with UN peacekeeping, having my sons with me during their holidays had become increasingly difficult. Ravi, my older son, was at Harvard. These were the 1960s, and young people's agendas those days, regardless of their home situations, were not family oriented. Ravi had his summer jobs, and he chose his own time for his visits, which were usually brief. My younger son, Bhalinder, was going to be fifteen and when I offered to arrange driving lessons for him, he willingly came to spend a month with me in Santo Domingo, where some school friends of his were also spending the summer. We often had a morning swim together, and while I went to work he played tennis and took driving lessons from a security officer who had volunteered to teach him. It was a good visit and I enjoyed it. One evening while we two were dining at a downtown restaurant, firing erupted. We came out to see what had happened. There were explosions and tracer bullets flying through the air. I brought my son back under cover. His observation was concise: "It is just like fireworks." I chose not to explain the reality of war and its horrors, which he had seen only on TV and cinema screens.

Mayobre was spending a good deal of his time attending conferences related to the Economic Commission of Latin America, and our work, though never dull, had slowed down. Intensive negotiations were under way on the formation of an interim government that would stay in place until elections could be held.

At first Silvester Antonio Guzman, a former minister of agriculture in the Bosch government, seemed a likely candidate to head the interim government. He was dropped in favor of Hector García Godoy, a former ambassador to the United States and foreign minister under Bosch. Throughout these negotiations, the death toll mounted and gross violations of human rights continued.

Juan Bosch had been allowed into the country and as a true patriot was busily engaged in facilitating an agreement. Ellsworth Bunker, acting in his dual capacity as a senior American diplomat and as delegate of the OAS, had settled into the penthouse at the Hotel Embajador and taken the lead at hammering out the agreement. An Act of Dominican Reconciliation was proposed that would set up a provisional government with García Godoy as president. An Institutional Act would provide the authority under which the provisional government would exercise its authority. The proposed legislation provided for general amnesty, the disarmament of the Constitutionalists and incorporation of the Constitutionalists' zone into a security zone, the integration of the Constitutionalists into the armed forces, the collection of arms from civilians, and finally, the withdrawal of the IAPF.

As the Dominican Republic moved toward resolving its political crisis, arrangements for the removal of the military leaders on both sides had to be made. This was to be accomplished—in a time-honored tradition of Latin America—by turning the leaders into diplomats and sending them overseas. In this case, the leaders were to be appointed as military attachés to various countries. The United States and its allies were willing to accept the pro-American officers for appointments to their countries, but the Constitutionalists presented a problem. Now the Western European democracies, mostly less conservative, offered to help. The British ambassador Ian Bell talked to me about Caamano, and the Canadians and others were also willing to consider helping the colonel. Caamano told me that he was willing to accept the British offer, but he wanted me to help him obtain American assurances that he would not be assassinated.

I arranged for Caamano to see Bunker. One of my officers drove Caamano to our hotel after dark, and he was brought to my room by the stairs, which were normally locked for security. After a drink,

I walked him up two floors for a meeting with Bunker. It was a fruitful meeting and Caamano felt reassured. After Caamano departed in a UN car, I drove to Ambassador Bell to give him the news that Her Majesty's Government would have a civil war hero as their guest.

More incidents of fighting did erupt, but generally the situation remained manageable. Early in January 1966 the senior echelon of military leadership from both sides left the country. I had taken a few days leave to return to New York when U Thant told me that since our mission was near its end, and because reduced peacekeeping operations had made it infeasible to activate the military adviser's job in New York, he had decided to appoint me commander of UNEF effective February 1966. He added with a laugh, "And don't come back." It was time for me to say my farewells.

15

Commander UNEF and the Six Day War

I had a couple of weeks to prepare for my move to Gaza. Bunche's primary concern, shared by U Thant, was to maintain the cease-fire along the area of UNEF's responsibility, which they hoped would lower the heat along Israel's borders with its neighboring Arab states. As the chief architect of the GAA of 1949 between Israel and its Arab neighbors, Bunche understood the delicacy of the situation along these borders very well. Besides the incendiary nature of the situation, U Thant and Bunche emphasized the importance of effecting further economies in UNEF. Since the declaration by the United States that it would no longer pay more than 25 per cent of their share of costs of the United Nations, on the Secretary-General's instructions the force had already made savings by reducing its strength. 1 was told to make further reductions without compromising on the overall efficiency of the force.

From Beirut, an RCAF Caribou, a duck-shaped Canadian transport aircraft, took me to Gaza. I was received by members of my senior staff: CAO Don Sullivan of the United States and chief of staff Colonel Lazar Musicki of Yugoslavia. Also present were Colonel Arvind Jatar, commander of the Indian Contingent, an old armor colleague, and Brig. Gen. Ibrahim Sharkawy, chief of staff, UAR liaison staff to UNEF. After brief introductions, a UN security officer drove me in the commander's Buick to my residence, next to the A mess of my earlier days.

I devoted the next few days to visiting troops and every UNEF post. Starting in the Gaza Strip, I spent the morning seeing posts and camps and lunching with the officers. After lunch, I went back to my office to deal with cables from New York and see my senior staff. Although my visits taught me a lot about UNEF's operations, I needed to understand better the political environment before I could formulate my suggestions for further UNEF reductions for the Secretary-General. With the assistance of Sharkawy, I met the members of the Egyptian administration in Gaza and Palestinian leaders, and then made my calls on the Egyptian high command in Cairo. The Indian embassy was a great help and the UN Information Center in Cairo further added to my contacts. Also, the embassies of countries with troops in Gaza not only offered hospitality but also enabled me to meet many other important diplomats and thus gain a broad view of current developments.

General Odd Bull's duties brought him to Gaza every few weeks, affording the two of us the opportunity to meet frequently. He invited me to Jerusalem and sent me his U.S.-lent C-41 airplane to fetch me. My time at his staff's briefing on events in the surrounding Arab states was well spent. I went on a personal visit to Damascus to meet India's ambassador Amrik Singh Mehta, a friend since college days. Amrik, a scion of a wealthy merchant family of old Rawalpindi (now in Pakistan), lived in a princely style and entertained generously. Although he gave the impression of a gentleman interested in antiques who enjoyed the company of the beautiful, rich, and famous, he was politically savvy and extremely well informed.

My visits to Beirut were usually related to my duties at UNEF. Besides being the home of a liaison office, the Lebanese capitol was UNEF's air transit point, and we opened a holiday camp there for all our troops each summer. I had no reason to go to Israel because UNEF had no troops there. Our political and diplomatic contacts there were through UNTSO and job-related contacts with IDF were through a liaison office at Tel Aviv. Similarly, I had no reason to visit Jordan.

By the end of March 1966 I had reached a better understanding of the situation in the area and came to the unhappy conclusion that the Arabs and Israelis were hurtling toward a serious crisis that, if not averted, could lead to a renewal of fighting. After seeing a measure of peace and quiet achieved along the armistice lines between Israel and its neighboring Arab states, the great powers and most of the world had switched their attention to other matters. The United Nations as an organization had yet to develop a response system for dealing with growing crises, and acted only when faced with emergencies. Attempts to warn of impending crises were considered alarmist and received with disdain in the office of the Secretary-General. Indeed, the entire international system was geared to dealing with incidents and restoring peace and quiet. The world had yet to learn that peacekeeping was only part of the process of peaceful conflict resolution and not a panacea.

Mired in problems and concerns within their own communities, the Arabs and the Israelis did not demand international attention. Besides the problem of inter-Arab relations, some Arab states hosted large numbers of Palestinian refugees and thus faced internal political and security concerns and had no wish to risk another war with Israel, preferring to keep the conflict at a declamatory level. The Israelis were able to deal on their own with Arab threats to their security and were assured of support from the United States, the West, and world Jewry. Satisfied with their gains for the present, they had no wish to negotiate with the Arabs the future of Palestinian refugees.

Palestinian refugees had become disappointed at the lack of progress in negotiations on their future, and their camps became breeding grounds for rebellion. The terrorists of the earlier decade reemerged as *fedayeen* (guerrillas), launching raids against Israeli targets. The IDF retaliated on a punishing scale. Blaming the Arab states for allowing raids from their territory, the IDF conducted punitive operations against the militaries of their neighboring states. This escalating cycle of violence led to the June 1967 Arab-Israeli war.

The Palestine Arabs' demand to join in the holy war against Israel had led to the creation of a Palestine Liberation Army (PLA), which included units recruited from the Palestinian population of surrounding Arab states. The PLA, a lightly armed force, was used primarily as a police force rather than as a fighting unit. These arrangements satisfied neither Palestinian leaders nor Palestinian aspirations. The radical Palestinian groups were convinced that the existing military gap between Arabs and Israel would further increase in favor of the latter. Therefore, it was better to have a military confrontation with Israel immediately rather than later.

By 1965 several Palestinian organizations had sprung up to conduct attacks against Israel, and one of these, al-Fatah, had gained prominence. The new Palestine leadership, recognizing the failure and probably the inability of Arab states to achieve the measure of unity that was a prerequisite to solving the Palestine problem, encouraged Palestinian guerrillas to plan operations inside Israel. However, Nasser was not ready for war and King Hussein had his own problems with the influx of Palestinian Arabs into the East Bank and with the administration of the West Bank. The king was anxious to avoid war and kept secret channels of communication open to Israel. The Lebanese had always been quiescent on Israel, except when driven by Arab politics and the Palestinian refugees in camps around Beirut and in the south. However, it was Syria, where a coup in February 1966 had brought the extremist Ba'ath Party to power, that adopted the doctrine of a "Popular War of Liberation" advocated by Palestinian *fedayeen*. Thereafter, the al-Fatah group in Syria known as Es-Saqa were given the backing of the Syrian army, including weapons, sabotage equipment, and training facilities.

Sensing that the Arab states seemed to regard the Palestinian refugees' problem as insoluble, Palestinian leaders chose confrontation with Israel to reawaken the world to their plight. The Palestinian leaders hoped to jeopardize international assistance to Israel and cause Israel to divert its resources to its defense. By accepting the challenge and retaliating, Israel would provoke a war with the Arabs. To this end, al-Fatah stepped up its raids against Israel in 1966.

Concerned over these developments, I felt that I should apprise U Thant and Bunche of my assessment of the situation. I realized that as commander of UNEF, any such communication to New York was beyond my mandate. I was also aware of the fact that my armistice lines were quieter than many of Israel's other borders with Arab states and that my mission was limited to the area of UNEF operations. After pondering the matter, I decided to write to U Thant anyway. My report did not bring reprobation, it was just ignored.

During my investigation into the organization and operations of the force, I soon concluded that we were already somewhat thin on the ground and had little response capability. The administrative and logistic support of the force called for remedial action. With few exceptions, the military personnel were rotated every six months and therefore it was the UN Field Service that provided continuity. More importantly, because of the constant movement of military personnel, only the civilian staff could be given budgetary responsibilities.

The number of raids into Israel by October, causing death and injury to Israeli soldiers. After a string of such raids across the border from Jordan, Israel carried out its largest military operation against Es Samu in Jordan since the 1956 war. The Security Council censured Israel and warned against retaliatory attacks.

Es Samu proved to be the turning point. The Jordanian army had not only kept apart from Palestinian fighters but also tried in vain to control cross-border raiding. Although secretly, Hussein had been the only friend the Israelis had among the Arabs. But the Israelis had destroyed the image of the invincibility of Jordan's Arab Legion and, much worse, they had humiliated Hussein. The Arab High Command was activated and an Egyptian general and his staff assumed command. Headquarters were established at Amman and plans for joint operations were revised.

Starting early in 1967, a series of incidents between Syria and Israel, mostly in the demilitarized zone (DMZ), led to exchanges of fire across the ADL. After three meetings of the Israeli–Syria Mixed Armistice Commission failed to reach agreement, General Odd Bull held separate meetings with the Syrians and the Israelis, but these too failed. On 7 April, the anniversary of the founding of the Ba'ath Party, President Atasi of Syria declared, "The battle is between us, on the one hand, and reaction, imperialism, and Zionism, on the other. It is a decisive battle of destiny. . . . The People's Liberation War will cleanse the entire Arab territory of Zionism, Imperialism, and their reactionaries." Syrian troops opened fire on Israeli tractors in the DMZ. Israel responded immediately with attacks involving seventy to eighty aircraft. Syrian air force MIG fighters dispatched to intercept Israeli aircraft were all reported shot down. The fighting on Israel's Syrian border caused a flare up along the Israel–Jordan front as well. U Thant informed the Security Council that the gap between the views of the parties had greatly widened and that both sides should exercise restraint.

The Arab League met and called on Egypt to move its troops into the Sinai and thereby reduce Israel's pressure on Syria. The tempo of *fedayeen* raids also picked up, inviting more retaliation by the IDF. After Nasser failed to move his troops into the Sinai, Amman Radio declared that "Nasser was hiding behind the skirts of UNEF." I recognized that this inflammatory statement was certain to provoke Egypt, but I was not sure how it would respond. I made a hurried trip to Cairo, which brought little evidence of any current or possible future activity.

Israel wanted to leave no doubt in the minds of the Arabs, the Syrians in particular, of its determination to deal firmly with threats from the *fedayeen*. The Arabs read these warnings as threats of war against Syria, with the intention of overthrowing its Ba'athist regime. The Syrians, Egyptians, and the Soviet Union complained to the Security Council that Israel was massing troops along the Syrian front. The Israelis agreed to an inspection by UNTSO, which found no evidence of unusual activity.

On 13 May a UNEF supply convoy reported units of the Egyptian army crossing the Suez Canal, and for the next two days I received reports of large-scale troop movements. On 14 May, Israeli independence day, there were the usual Palestinian demonstrations and the PLA was on alert. What most of the world and I did not know was that at a meeting on 13 May, Nasser's cabinet had decided to move troops into the Sinai for a major confrontation with Israel and to ask UNEF to vacate those areas along the international frontier.

On 16 May Sharkawy called to say that a courier with a special message for me was arriving from Cairo. He was flying to El Arish and would come by car from there. Sharkawy had no more information. It was not until almost 10 p.m. that Sharkawy telephoned to inform me that the courier had arrived and asked me to come to his office. Within ten minutes I was introduced to Brig. Gen. Eiz-El-Din Mokhtar of HQ Eastern Army operations staff, Ismalia. After a perfunctory greeting, Mokhtar handed me a letter from General Mohammed Fawzi, COS, UAR. General Fawzi stated that he had given instructions to a UAR force to be ready for action against Israel the moment its forces carried out any aggressive action against an Arab country. Because of this, UAR troops were required to concentrate in the Sinai. For their own security, UN troops in observation posts along their frontier should be withdrawn.

Stunned by the contents of the letter, I read it again. It indicated an end of consent for the UNEF mission, a requisite for its survival. If the request was complied with, it would sound the death knell of UNEF, with grave consequences for the region. UNEF withdrawal would be a shattering blow to the years of effort by the United Nations. It would also be a blow to me personally, because I knew that there was no need of my services at New York. Although he said it lightly, U Thant had told me not to come back.

I told Mokhtar that I had noted the contents of the letter and that I would immediately report to the Secretary-General for instructions. Mokhtar, not satisfied with my reply, said that as soon as Israel heard of the Egyptian request for the withdrawal of UNEF, the IDF would try to seize El Sabah and Sharm el Sheikh. Therefore, UNEF should immediately vacate these posts to avoid a clash with UAR troops, who had orders to occupy them that night.

I read the letter again, and there was no mention of El Sabah and Sharm el Sheikh. Mokhtar expressed his concerns at the inevitable clash between our troops if I did not act immediately. But I stood firm on my position. I added that as long as UAR troops did not use force against my troops there would be no clash.

It was an unhappy Mokhtar who left us to return to Ismalia. In anticipation of an important message, I had told my staff to stand by for a hurried meeting. As I rose to go to my office, Sharkawy, who had remained quiet throughout my meeting with Mokhtar, asked, "General, you have not given us your views on this letter. We have been friends for more than a year and you are known as a friend of Egypt. I want to know what you think."

I responded, "Ibrahim, have you all thought of the consequences of what you have asked me to do?"

With a broad smile he answered, "Sir, I will see you for lunch at the best restaurant in Tel Aviv in a few days."

For a moment I felt my face flush with trepidation as I thought of the inevitable disaster that faced Egypt's army and its people. I would meet with Sharkawy some six weeks later, but not in Tel Aviv. At my request, Moshe Dayan, the Israeli minister of defense, had arranged for me to meet Sharkawy at an Israeli POW camp near the Lebanese border, as I was on my way to Beirut and New York.

I rushed back to my office where Cynthia de Haan, my personal assistant, and my Swedish ADC, Lieutenant Steuch, were waiting for me. I called my senior staff and informed them of developments. Then I worked on my cable to New York and after showing it to my CAO and COS, asked Cynthia to go to the cable office, help encode it, and ensure that it was sent on highest priority: PRIORITY UNATIONS.

Both my senior staff agreed with me that the UNEF mandate was at an end. We had always kept a plan for withdrawal that was updated from time to time. Even at this stage I did not want the plan discussed beyond the contingent commanders' level. It was about 2 a.m. when I retired to my quarters.

I returned to my office at 8 a.m. and went to the operations room. The Egyptians had entered UNEF zones of operations all along the international frontier but there were no incidents between my troops and theirs. A cable from U Thant was delivered to me complimenting me on my stand with the Egyptians and advising that UNEF was to avoid incidents with the Egyptians. He had addressed a note to the Egyptian government seeking clarification of its intentions regarding the future of UNEF—whether its initial consent to UNEF's presence on Egyptian territory was to become so qualified and restricted as to make it impossible for UNEF to function effectively and thus necessitate its withdrawal. When I read these words, I concluded that the Egyptian response would be that UNEF should go. Don Sullivan agreed.

I spent the day dealing with Sharkawy over continuing Egyptian occupations of camps and posts, meeting contingent commanders, and discussing administrative and logistic support. There were UN relief workers and Egypt–Israel Mixed Armistice Commission personnel to take care of. There was also a handful of families of UNEF Field Service staff and a dozen or so female UNEF staff members. As the hours slipped by, my mind was focussed on questions relating to withdrawal, especially if hostilities were to break out.

The Yugoslav battalion informed me by telex that the Egyptians had refused clearance for RCAF supply flight to Yugoslav posts along the international frontier. Realizing that it would be difficult for Sharkawy to deal with the Egyptian air force at the El Arish base, I decided to fly there immediately to intercede. After two hours of negotiation, the Egyptian air force agreed to a one-time supply flight.

I flew back with the members of my staff who had accompanied me. As we approached Rafah, two Israeli fighter aircraft appeared and closed on the wing tips of my aircraft. They signalled my aircraft to follow them. Since UN aircraft used an international frequency, the IDF surely knew that I was on the plane. At this stage, the Israeli aircraft fired warning shots to insist that we follow them. My aircrew was in touch with their base and had received advice to act on my orders. When asked by my crew, I told them that I was not going to be highjacked by the Israelis, especially at this critical juncture, and therefore we must escape from the Israeli fighters and reach Gaza.

My crew took evasive action by diving to near ground level and then winging their way through sand dunes, maneuvers that the high-speed IDF fighters could not make. They decided to give up the chase and made for the Mediterranean. We returned to Gaza.

I said a silent prayer, for never had I been so near ignominy, a fate worse than death. I profusely thanked flying officers Simpson and Gagnon and the Canadian crew for their courage and loyalty. I put them up for awards and I was pleased to learn some months later that they had received the Queen's Commendation.

The incident made the headlines in the international news of that day; indeed, the Israeli attempt to highjack me seemed to have generated more news than the withdrawal of UNEF. General Yitzhak Rabin sent me a message of regret and Israel explained the action as a mistake due to a misunderstanding of the situation of UNEF as the Sinai was being overrun by Egyptian troops.

I spent the next day preparing for a variety of scenarios. First, all access to sea ports and airports might be denied to us, making it necessary to evacuate UNEF from the beaches. We had spent a lot of time practicing just such a contingency, based on the assumption that the U.S. Sixth Fleet would assist in an evacuation. Second, the host or troop countries might call for immediate withdrawal. In this case, the Egyptians were likely to agree to our air withdrawal from El

Arish and perhaps Port Said. Third, the Egyptians might allow us facilities at Port Said for sea lift and Cairo for air evacuation.

On 18 May, U Thant sent me a copy of the letter he had received from Mohamed Riad, Egypt's foreign minister, stating that Egypt had terminated its consent for the presence of UNEF on UAR territory and requesting the Secretary-General to take necessary steps for the withdrawal of the force. Early the next morning, I received formal orders from U Thant to make immediate arrangements for withdrawal.

I started withdrawal at 5 p.m. All posts were abandoned that night, with the troops returning first to platoon camps and then to company camps. That night the peace of the previous ten and a half years was shattered by exchanges of fire between Egyptian and Israeli troops.

The senior UN civilian staff and I had expected that a senior UN official from the Secretary-General's office would show up in Gaza. As it turned out, none other than U Thant journeyed to the Middle East. At the urging of some members of the Security Council, the Secretary-General decided to come to Cairo to persuade Nasser to agree to the return of UNEF to the armistice lines. U Thant finally reached Cairo on 23 May. When I was able to speak to him alone in his room, I told him that his visit was too late for the survival of UNEF.

U Thant's arrival in Cairo was preceded by Nasser's declaration of the closure of the Suez Canal and the Straits of Aqaba to Israel. The Israelis took this announcement as a casus belli, providing them with an international legal basis to go to war. But did Israeli intelligence not know the reality of the situation at Sharm el Sheikh, at the entrance to the straits? There, an Egyptian helicopter carrying Egyptian army engineer officers arrived to take over the UN water distillation plant. The Canadian engineer detachment, guarded by Swedish troops, told them that they had no orders to hand the plant over to the Egyptians. Thereupon, the Egyptians got back into the helicopter and took off, never to return while UNEF was present.

U Thant was justifiably upset over Nasser issuing his declaration while the SG was en route to Cairo, thereby reducing the value of what he hoped might be a historic journey. U Thant dined with me alone the first evening. He told me that he was expected to negotiate the return of UNEF and I emphasized that if for nothing else than maintaining prestige, the Egyptians were unlikely to accept redeployment. I said that perhaps it would have been possible to negotiate the future of UNEF on 17 or 18 May, but after U Thant's letter to the Egyptians on 18 May, seeking clarifications and mentioning withdrawal, it was too late. I suggested he try to arrange another observer mission or secure an expanded UNTSO. He said he had considered it, but he was obliged by the members of the Security Council to ask for reconsideration of the future of UNEF.

I accompanied U Thant to a lunch meeting with Mohamed Riad, and went over the main points of the situation, including matters related to UNEF withdrawal. Although a good friend of U Thant, Mohamed Riad stuck to the official line. That evening, Nasser called U Thant for a meeting and dinner, and the Secretary-General took me along. In discussing his cabinet meeting on 13 May, Nasser indicated that his military chiefs had persuaded him that Egyptian forces could defend their country. According to Nasser, Marshal Hakim Amer told him that if the Egyptian forces failed in their duty, "they deserved to die". It was then that Nasser reminded them that the military would have to deal with UNEF. When U Thant's suggested that UNEF should return to its posts, Nasser was firm in his refusal.

U Thant asked Nasser why he had declared the closure of the blockade at Sharm el Sheikh. Both Nasser and U Thant knew that UNEF was still in control of Sharm el Sheikh, and the mere threat of closure proved enough for Israel to act. Nasser replied that when he had heard that U Thant was coming to see him, he anticipated a request not to close the narrow waters. Therefore, to avoid refusing the Secretary-General's request, he did so in advance of his arrival. U Thant mused at this strange reply. Now, in a spirit of accommodation, Nasser agreed to establish a new observer mission in the Sinai.

U Thant returned to New York the next day. As expected, the Israelis rejected discussion of another UN mission. The media reported that Levi Eshkol was negotiating to form a national government that would include Moshe Dayan, who was known to favor war. As tensions built, two units of the Royal Canadian Navy, after completing exercises with NATO, lingered in the eastern Mediterranean. The Canadian position at New York, and as expressed by the Canadian embassy in Cairo, was opposed to the withdrawal of UNEF. Angered by the Canadian naval presence close to the Suez Canal, the Egyptians reacted by demanding the immediate withdrawal of the Canadian contingent.

On 30 May the Canadians left by their own air transport. With the exception of small Indian services units, UNEF was bereft of logistics troops. Several millions of dollars worth of stores were left behind to guard. I called the commanders of the Brazilian and Indian contingents and between us we rearranged logistic support. The Brazilian battalion would provide security and the Indians, reinforced by Field Service personnel, would take care of logistics. In addition, Indian troops would provide more military police and radio communications between each unit and UNEF headquarters. The Indian contingent was deployed from Port Said to the dunes overlooking Ashkelon.

On 1 June Israeli radio reported the formation of a national government and Moshe Dayan's assumption of the defense portfolio. In my mind the question was no longer if Israel would attack, but when. On the morning of 5 June, I received an answer. The IDF began its offensive against Gaza and Egypt. Waves of IDF aircraft attacked targets in Gaza. By midmorning Israeli artillery started to range at Egyptian anti-aircraft guns, which had suddenly appeared from behind our communications area in the vicinity of the Egyptian liaison office. Some shots fell on our building, causing casualties. I ordered all non-essential personnel to move to Camp Kroner and the B mess on the beaches. When my operations room was hit, I ordered its evacuation except for my operations staff and communications. Members of the Headquarters staff were running away from shelling down the main road from where all civilian traffic had vanished.

By the afternoon the Israelis had knocked out our communications to Geneva, but the link with Jerusalem survived. Later, a commando radio in Camp Kroner established contact with UNTSO and UNFICYP and I decided to shift my command post to that camp.

IDF armor thrust toward Rafah. The Israelis caught my supply convoy on the road and, mistaking it for a PLA unit, destroyed a good part of it and took many Indians prisoners. Later, they occupied Rafah camp, disarmed the soldiers, and held civil and military personnel prisoner. Bill Carvalho, the Indian Sikh battalion commander, an Anglo-Indian in the very image of a British officer, had to run through tank fire to reach an Israeli officer and explain that the IDF was firing at Indians who had taken cover in slit trenches and were not PLA. The Israeli looked at Carvalho with amazement but had the good sense to yell in his hand mike, in English for Carvalho's benefit, "These are Indians. Stop firing at the Indians."

Since my Buick was shattered, I climbed into a military police car for the drive to my villa. Steuch and Cynthia insisted on coming along in case I needed help to move to Camp Kroner. It was getting dark and the Israeli artillery was taking pot shots at the tail lights of the odd car plying the road. I decided that it was best to walk, and that the car should take cover until it was safe for the driver to return to his villa. It was not an easy walk, especially for Cynthia, who had never ceased to wear dresses and heels to the office. We had a quick supper and I packed my staff off. I was exhausted and fell asleep immediately.

The next morning I was comforted to see my staff well settled at Camp Kroner. I drove round to see that my troops and other UN personnel were reasonably comfortable. In my camp office, bad news awaited me. We had sustained a number of casualties but exactly how many was not yet clear. Captain Vijay Sachar, sent by the Indian commander in a radio jeep to contact the Sikh battalion, had hit a mine and was dead. Captain G.S. Sohal with the supply convoy was a prisoner. At least seven Indian soldiers were dead and several were wounded.

On 7 June the Israelis were mopping up in the Gaza Strip and radio news informed us that IDF was advancing deep into the Sinai, overcoming Egyptian resistance. Jordan too had joined in the fray and its troops had seized the Government House, where UNTSO headquarters was located. In Gaza we totaled our losses: eleven Indians were dead, thirteen were seriously wounded, and another thirty had minor injuries. One Brazilian had been killed. At Rafah, the IDF took all UN personnel prisoners and held them overnight in a field, forcing them to lie on their bellies. However, they did allow the UN hospital to cover our men with blankets. The next day, Israelis came in trucks and plundered the maintenance area. An inquiry later estimated the value of goods removed by Israelis at about $5 million, which the United States offered to compensate for by deducting it from the amount the United Nations owed it.

A citizen army trained and motivated to fight ferociously in the defense of its homeland, the IDF had shown itself a potent force. But it had also shown neglect of the international conventions of war. Surely, black and brown Brazilians, bearded Sikhs, and blonde Scandinavians do not look much like Palestinians.

The manhandling and disarming of UN personnel and the indignities they had to suffer would not be easily forgotten. Nor would the plunder of UN property, which was hauled east of the ADL. I could not get over my disappointment in the presence of such people in a society that I had always admired for their culture and high moral values.

On the third day of the war, learning from Sweden's embassy that Sweden had arranged evacuation of its contingent from Ashdod, I sought permission from New York to evacuate the entire force from that port. In the meantime, Colonel Ithzak Shany, IDF liaison officer to UNEF, arrived. It did not take him long to convince me that he was sent to help. He told me that Israel would not object to our use of Ashdod and that he would try to arrange transport to move our personnel and equipment. Later in the afternoon, General Dayan arrived by helicopter at the house of the former Egyptian governor and met the UN chiefs of missions. He offered his regrets at the losses suffered by Indian troops and others and then proceeded to agree to my requests. I was now able to go ahead with planning the departure of the troops from Ashdod, with the approval of New York. I was also able to evacuate the Indians wounded by a special charter plane from Tel Aviv to Cyprus, and have them sent from there to India. We had already cremated the Indian dead and arranged for their ashes to be taken to India.

With the troops gradually leaving, my remaining task was to close the mission, with the help of Sullivan and Carey Seward, who was sent by David Vaughan of the UN administration. By the end of June, my task was completed and, after my farewells to Rabin and Dayan, I returned to New York. Here, U Thant and Bunche were anxiously awaiting my return to help them prepare the report on the withdrawal of UNEF, which had raised considerable controversy, because it was seen as exposing Israel to the neighboring Arab armies. The Western media had heaped the blame on U Thant, who avoided placing the blame where it really belonged.

On my return to New York, I was only too aware that the Secretary-General preferred not to revive my old position of military adviser. As I was anxious to move on, I raised the question of my future with him. He said that I was needed to deal with UNEF issues and that he would decide my future depending on the possibility of another mission to the Middle East.

The most important task before me was to untangle my personal life. Although my wife and I shared an apartment and had tried to keep up appearances in public, we had led separate lives for most of my posting at New York. This arrangement endured because I was away a good deal. However, for quite a while we had grown weary of keeping up pretenses. Besides, the emotional cost to both of us and the financial cost of maintaining a divided family were great.

Usha was popular in society for her charm and wit. Educated at Waverly, Mussoorie, Uttar Pradesh, a convent boarding school, and having spent her vacations as a teenager during the Second World War in Bengal, where her father was constructing and maintaining airbases for the American air force and the China airlift, she was profoundly influenced by American culture. Although she was often taken for an Englishwoman, she was more American in her outlook. Ahead of her time, she was a born feminist. She felt at home in the United States and wished to remain there.

On my next visit to India, I asked my mother to agree to my separation and then divorce. The seamy side of the Indian divorce laws—which allowed for divorce only in cases of infidelity, madness, or venereal disease—had discouraged me from making an earlier attempt. I explained that New York state laws allowed for a more civilized divorce. I told her that I was getting on in age and that I wanted to remarry. Surprisingly, she said that my wife's family knew of our situation and would understand. However, I must comply with the traditional Hindu practice of supporting my wife for life, unless she were to remarry. (This practice was called 'alimony' by the New York state divorce laws.)

On my return to New York I started negotiating with my wife for a divorce. Meanwhile, a friend in New York offered me a business opportunity that I found hard to refuse. It would provide me with a dollar income with which to pay for the completion of my sons' education and my wife's alimony.

One afternoon, Lord Caradon, the British permanent representative to the United Nations, who as Hugh Foot had befriended me earlier in his career, came to see me. He said that the British had hoped that U Thant would replace the UN force commander in Cyprus. Before he spoke to Bunche, he wanted to consult me. He asked whether I was interested in the job. I thanked him and asked him to let the arrangements for my departure at the end of the year remain unchanged. I had done my duty to the United Nations and stayed longer than I had intended. I had made other commitments for employment that would allow me more flexibility to attend to my personal affairs in the United States and in India.

Evidently, he was disappointed. I refrained from telling him that I was seeking a divorce from my wife and did not want to go to another mission encumbered by such a problem. Besides, on completion of my divorce proceedings, I had arranged to marry Cynthia de Haan, an American. An Indian UN force commander, even a retired officer, taking a foreign and especially an American wife, would surely be creating problems for himself with the Indian Government at that time.

I had been about to start settling the long-neglected matter of my marital crisis when I was pulled out of Leh and sent to the United Nations in July 1960. I had attempted to return to the Indian Army after the war with China, but U Thant intervened. Again in 1965 I had spoken to my army chief, General 'Muchu' Chaudhari, about taking me back. He retorted, 'Where do I fit you in the army after your service in the UN? Do you want my job?' Now was the time to leave and pick up my personal affairs where I had left them ten years earlier. A product of the Indian Military Academy, I had put service before self, but the withdrawal of UNEF had drained me, and now I had serious doubts about the leadership at the United Nations.

Always kind and concerned for the welfare of his staff, U Thant offered to help me find an appointment with, perhaps, the UNDP in a country like Indonesia or Egypt. I thanked him and declined, informing him of my plans to join a private venture. With his usual wit, he said that being Brahmin born, I would never make a good businessman. I had heard this said often enough. But I explained that my future work primarily involved assisting an international corporation in meeting high-ranking officials and establishing business contacts.

I had always found it difficult to consult any of my friends, except for my mother, on my marital and related problems. I could perhaps have made my relations with my immediate colleagues somewhat easier by not always trying to cover up my disjointed family situation and its consequences. Now I had reached a point where I could not continue. I had to pull myself out of this mire and I could do this only by changing my professional life and joining a private-sector enterprise that would allow a certain freedom of action.

PART V

Educating for Peace

16

The Development of the International Peace Academy

In the spring of 1968, U Thant called me to his office to meet a couple of visitors. One was Norman Cousins, a friend of U Thant and editor of the *Saturday Review*. Cousins was currently chairman of the World Association of World Federalists, which promoted the notion of a world government, and a major supporter of the United Nations and the World Peace Through Law movement, which with the support of scores of senators and congressional members promoted efforts to resolve international conflicts by peaceful means, within the framework of international laws and institutions. Ruth Forbes Young, a philanthropist and activist in the effort to eliminate nuclear weapons, accompanied him. U Thant said that his visitors had some ideas for peacekeeping education. The Secretary-General thought that since the establishment of a UN Institute of Training and Research (UNITAR), sought by the Third World, had little support among the wealthy nations, perhaps non-governmental organizations could be of help in providing research and training for the United Nations. Turning to me, he added, "I told them that you were the one person on my staff who could help them and that they should catch you before you disappeared to make your money in business." Rising from his chair for his next appointment, he suggested to me, "Why don't you take them to your room and see what you can do."

In my office, Cousins asked Mrs. Young, "Ruth, Please tell the general what you said at the World Federalists assembly."

Ruth Forbes Young, in her early sixties, was elegantly dressed in pastel colors, with a large hat on her upswept hair. Speaking in an upper-class Boston accent, she explained what had led her to promote the development of a peacekeeping institute: "When the atom bomb was dropped on Hiroshima, I realized that something enormous had happened, something that had never happened before, and that the people should take responsibility for what to do about it."

After she had shared her views with Cousins, he had invited her to speak to the World Association of World Federalists. This assembly decided to establish a committee to study the kind of education other than military that was necessary for the development of a wholly new kind of international force appropriate for peacekeeping and peacemaking, and to develop a plan or alternate plans that might facilitate the creation of such a force. The committee asked Professor Arthur I. Waskow of the Institute of Public Policy, Washington, D.C., to examine whether it would be desirable and possible to create a center for the training of international peacekeepers. Waskow's 1967 study, *Towards a Peacekeepers Academy*, provided a clear vision for developing peacekeeping training. In its preamble, the paper stated, "One of the most effective ways of pursuing social change is for men to imagine some future they would like to live within, and then act in the present to create some part of that future, not merely to plead for its creation."

With a group of friends and Randolph Major, Jr., from the Experiment in International Living, Brattleboro, Vermont, Ruth Young formed an ad hoc committee to start work on development of an "International Peace Keeping Academy". Ruth had chosen this working title from Waskow's paper, where the term peacekeepers had been used in the biblical sense. She now invited me to join her committee and help make the concept a reality.

Ruth's concept for a peacekeeping training institution and mine coincided, so I happily agreed to join her committee. At that time I had no idea that this meeting was about to launch me in a new career. Shortly after I joined the committee, I was elected chairman.

As I became acquainted with Ruth and her husband, Arthur Young, I began to appreciate their unique qualities. Ruth was born into an old Boston family which had gained their wealth in shipping and the

China trade. Her father, Ralph Emerson Forbes, was the grandson of Ralph Waldo Emerson and her mother was Elise Cabot. Ruth's Uncle Cameron Forbes was the first governor-general of the Philippines and entertained figures from government and the military, including two presidents and General John J. Pershing. Ruth grew up in Milton, Massachusettes, and Naushan, a family-owned island off Cape Cod, into a spirited young woman who took to painting portraits and still lives. Her early social contacts made her neither shy of officials nor afraid of soldiers. It was this remarkable quality in her that I found refreshing at a time in the United States when the "Vietnam syndrome", with its strong aversion to all things military, was beginning to take hold.

Ruth had two sons, Michael and Cameron Paine, by her first husband, before she married Arthur Young, who in 1948 built the first helicopter to be certified for commercial use. Arthur was a philosopher, a mathematician, and an inventor with charm and wit. He had his own cause, his Institute for the Study of Consciousness, in Berkeley, California. But the two were great supporters of each other's interests.

Ruth had wisely recruited Randy Major, Jr. to manage the project and he had already contacted prominent peace scholars, among them members of the emerging peace research community. I was able to add some practitioners—by whom I mean people who had first-hand, practical experience of conflict resolution—to the list of contacts and we arranged a series of consultations in Europe, at Oslo and London. By this time it was clear that there was a need for peace education, but opinion differed among peace researchers, specialists in international affairs, and practitioners on the best way to provide this education.

The committee decided to change its name—to the International Peace Academy Committee—as some in the United Nations thought the original name implied a challenge to the ability of the world organization to meet the responsibility of training peacekeepers and questioned the ability of an NGO to assume this responsibility. The term *peace* had a wider connotation and was more acceptable. However, now we seemed to have upset political conservatives since the term had become associated with the Soviets, who had employed it to their advantage. (It may be noted, however, that conservative institutions subsequently used *peacekeeper* in a different, broader sense; a nuclear missile was even named "peacekeeper".)

In defining our philosophy, we agreed that the International Peace Academy (IPA) must make an explicit statement of what *peace* actually means. For us the term implied that whenever a conflict arose, those involved in efforts to resolve it must use peaceful means to achieve their objectives, and that the legitimate aspirations of individuals and groups for justice and human rights must be recognized and given full opportunity for expression and fulfilment, again by peaceful means.

The committee believed that the occurrence of violence in conflicts stemmed from the frustration of legitimate demands, especially the frustration by inflexible regimes of aspirations to nationhood or other forms of self-fulfilment by societies or groups. In order to prevent the breakdown of societies and the eruption of internal wars, experts had to be trained in the techniques of conflict moderation, conflict resolution, and the achievement of peaceful social change. (This need became even more pronounced some thirty years later.)

The academy, the committee decided, would turn to distinguished practitioners to develop creative skills that drew both from experience and analyses of past diplomatic ventures and from the intellectual work of the peace research community, including both its empirical and theoretical studies.

The academy would be a non-governmental organization and would seek private funding so as to avoid being tied to political strings. The academy would not be national or international but global. Its identity was defined by the moral value on which it was founded: the establishment of peace with justice. Its policy would be the promotion of systematic, scientific knowledge and skills concerning the means by which conflict resolution and change may be achieved without violence.

At a meeting in Vermont of the International Peace Academy Committee, more than fifty international consultants gathered for four days. This meeting substantially advanced both training concepts and international support. We agreed on two pilot training models. The first, a four-week program, focused on four areas: peace, conflict, and development theory; techniques of mediation, peacekeeping, and the promotion of human rights; peaceful social change; and development. The second, ten-day model, while covering the same agenda, concentrated on the skills required by mediators, peacekeepers, and human rights workers and development specialists. As anticipated, the first model was favored by scholars interested in theoretical aspects of the peaceful resolution of conflicts, while diplomats and military officers chose the second model for its emphasis on developing practical skills.

The Congo peacekeeping experience had convinced me that more than peacekeeping and peacemaking were required resolving conflicts peacefully. My exposure to many of the leading scholars of peace theory helped me to learn a new approach. However, it seemed that we were unable to relate theory to practice. We finally overcame this hurdle, partly by encouraging the career diplomats and military officers to learn peace theory and apply it to their practice of the peace profession, and partly by encouraging continuous dialogue between peace scholars and practitioners. Thereafter, the academy adopted a mixed model for its training programs, combining elementary peace theory with a major focus on professional skills.

In choosing a site for the experimental programs, I looked for a neutral or non-aligned host country with significant interest in strengthening the international process of peaceful conflict resolution. My final choice was Austria and its Diplomatic and Defense Academies in Vienna, which agreed to jointly sponsor seminars on the peaceful resolution of conflicts. Ambassador Kurt Waldheim, then permanent representative of Austria to the United Nations, assured me of his support.

In Vienna, we achieved some of our project goals. However, we were able to find neither a conceptual language nor an application of peace theory that were readily accessible to practitioners. Although we were on our way to creating a climate in which people of different cultures could reorient their thinking about peace and war issues, we were unable to develop related practical skills. There was more work ahead. In time, we made progress toward a better understanding of attitudes but did not succeed in furthering the professional skills that could foster peaceful social change. However, we did establish a greater awareness of the need for such skills and of the fact that peacebuilding was integral to the peace process.

A picture of the desired structure of the academy began to emerge. The academy should be broadly representative in terms of geography, political alliances, and ideologies. Young leaders of popular movements should be given an equal footing with officials to participate in the academy's programs. The academy's programs should be offered in different locations and its headquarters should be located at a neutral site near the United Nations. Lastly, the academy would be autonomous and have national and regional committees.

At this stage, the committee decided to organize the academy's staff. I agreed to become the president and chief executive officer, Philip Roupp was appointed vice-president, and Lauranne Pazhoor from Wales became secretary and later finance and administrative officer. The committee also opened its fund-raising drive, with Roupp and I taking turns speaking to foundations and other potential donors.

Working with the committee, Roupp and I also worked on the development of programs. Seed capital was vital and here Ruth Young proved to be invaluable. She not only led the way with her generous contributions but also rallied her friends and relations in support. Norman Cousins, busy as he was with editing the *Saturday Review*, found time to reach out to people he knew and meet me occasionally at breakfast to advise me.

To widen our base of support, we started work on area committees in New York, Philadelphia, Washington, D.C., Minneapolis, and California. These committees enabled the staff to reach out for support from the major foundations in these areas. Gradually, we became recipients of donations from the Rockefeller Brothers Fund, the Rockefeller Foundation, the McKnight Foundation, and the Weyerhaeuser Foundation. Members of area committees across the United States, although seldom seen in New York, were pillars of the nascent academy, and without their support the academy could not have been built.

Growing support from individuals and family foundations, for example Ira and Miriam Wallach, in turn attracted the interest of individuals from the major foundations. These included John Stremlau at the Rockefeller Foundation, individual members of the Rockefeller family, Enid Shoettle at the Ford Foundation, and James and Virginia McKnight Binger at the McKnight Foundation. With Roupp's help, we also secured the support of the Kettering Foundation. Our efforts to establish a broad base of individual support in the major cities was greatly facilitated by the help of Mildred Robbin Leet in New York, Priscilla Goldstien and Stanley and Martha Platt in Minneapolis, and Larry Dawson and Georgiana Stevens in San Franscisco. This group not only gave generously but also assisted in organizing programs and hosted many functions to make the work of the academy known in their communities.

My efforts to establish groups of supporters in other parts of the world also began to bear fruit. With the help of Hugh Hanning, a defense analyst and supporter of the United Nations, a committee was formed in the United Kingdom. Brigadier Michael Harbottle, former chief of staff UNFICYP, and his wife Eirwen, both of whom had lived through the crisis in Cyprus, joined the group. I asked Michael to work with me on a book I had planned on peacekeeping. With additional grants I was able to launch preparation of the *Peacekeepers Handbook*. While we engaged more than forty writers, I did a significant part of writing, only to be more than matched by Michael's contributions and editing. Michael's death in 1996, while he was still actively engaged in peace-related work, was a great loss not only to Eirwen and their family but also to the international peace professional community. I laud Eirwen for her valiant efforts in continuing Michael's work for "Generals for Peace".

Besides peacekeeping activities, we forged ahead with the development of mediation and negotiation-training programs. I turned for assistance to Arthur Lall, a former permanent representative of India to the United Nations in New York and Geneva. He was on the faculty of the School of International Affairs and Government at Columbia University, New York. His wife, Betty Lall, a former disarmament and arms control adviser to U.S. Vice-President Hubert Humphrey, was at New York University, where she taught labor relations. Brilliant academics and highly articulate practitioners of multilateral diplomacy, the couple were a valuable asset. Arthur organized our peacemaking program—with an emphasis on the practice of negotiations—and Betty helped to organize the even more complex program of peacebuilding. Both programs met difficult challenges. The academy's aim was to prepare a group of men and women drawn from across the globe for peace-related roles. The participants from the northern group generally favored the status quo, while participants from the developing world were seeking ammunition for change. The pro-Maoists and other advocates of the communist view that there were just wars (for changing the social order) and unjust wars (in defense of existing non-communist societies) drove us to be more active and strident. I found it interesting that in their personal lives such advocates pursued the lifestyle of the free market system. I decided to shelve peacebuilding as a separate program. For the time being, I also canceled the peacemaking program. I now devoted more time to consulting with other peace professionals in finding ways to reach acceptable and practical solutions. I was able to resume these programs five years later.

My association with the UN staff and diplomats proved most helpful. In seeking their assistance, I understood the restraints under which they worked and therefore did my best to avoid embarrassing them diplomatically. As such I was careful in selecting case studies for our programs. Accordingly, in our first model training programs, I excluded discussion of the India-Pakistan situation, the Arab–Israeli conflicts, and apartheid-related examples. It was the second or third day of the first program when Arab participants from Egypt, Jordan, and Saudi Arabia asked me why such an important case as the Arab–Israeli conflict had been ignored in our discussions. I informed them that their countries had sent them to the program on my assurance that no Israeli diplomat or military officer was to be invited and therefore I had invited only Israeli scholars. I was greatly relieved when the Arabs accepted these arrangements, even though all Israeli citizens were subject to military service and trained as reserves.

The workshops generated a series of reports, all of which avoided attributing particular comments to individual participants. I prepared a summary of each report for the leaders of the states involved, which was sent to them via their diplomatic pouches. I also hand-delivered a copy for the perusal of the UN Secretary-General. I was always pleased when a head of government, a foreign minister, or a senior-level official told me that the academy's summaries were useful. Essentially, the academy's work was directed toward preparing middle-ranking personnel to support their superiors and to be prepared, in time, to undertake such tasks. However, if our efforts to teach choices and tactics for negotiations proved useful to a party or parties to a conflict, it provided us added satisfaction. In time, I was able to devote more time to writing on ways to improve training for, and the conduct of, peacekeeping and negotiations.

The Yom Kippur War in 1973 between the Arabs and Israel led to a renewal of peacekeeping operations in the Middle East. This led the UN staff to be more actively involved in the work of the academy. Sir Brian Urquhart, then UN under Secretary-General for peace-keeping, joined the board of directors, and he and his staff gave invaluable help in many ways. Our training programs drew more participants and improved because of the greater diversity and more recent experience of the participants.

Once the academy was properly established, Ruth wanted to spend more time helping Arthur with his institute at Berkeley. I was eventually able to persuade James Binger, former chairman of Honeywell Corporation in Minneapolis, to replace Ruth as chairman of the academy's board of directors. An astute business executive and a popular polo player, he brought his leadership and management skills to our fledgling institution.

In 1985, after fifteen years with the academy and having just turned sixty-five, I turned my attention to the search for a successor. A few years earlier I had thought I found the right person in Canadian Brigadier Edward "Ted" Leslie. He had done a stint as COS, UNFICYP and on retirement from the army had contested for a seat in Canada's parliament, but lost. He joined me as vice-president. It was a matter of great regret to me when he died in New York. John Mroz, a graduate of the Fletcher School of Diplomacy and Law, Tufts University, Massachusetts, succeeded him. Mroz was ambitious, hard working, and smart. After five years with me, he established the East-West Institute in New York. He and his institute are both thriving. Retired British colonel Peter Harvey followed Mroz. Harvey had been equerry to Queen Elizabeth II. His devotion to religion led him to engage in social causes, including the promotion of peace. After a few years of invaluable service he decided to return home for personal reasons.

Still not having found a successor, I made the decision to step down after twenty years' service. The board, while understanding my wish to retire, was not thrilled at the idea of having to find a replacement. When faced with refusals by qualified candidates and demands for much higher wages than I was receiving, a number of board members tried to persuade me to remain. But I had no intention of changing my mind.

The academy's final choice as my successor was Olara Otunnu of Uganda. Academically brilliant, Otunnu was the first head of the UN permanent mission from Uganda on its independence. As a member of the Security Council, he established his reputation as a skillful diplomat. Later, as foreign minister of his native country, he played a major role in negotiating the end of Uganda's civil war. The rise of Yoweri Museveni to power and intertribal rivalries led Otunnu and his extended family to depart for Tanzania, Europe, and the United States.

I left the academy on 30 September 1989 and turned my thoughts to personal affairs and to establishing priorities for things that I had always wanted to do, but had little time for. Besides encouraging the study of techniques of conflict resolution, during my years at the IPA I had sought to facilitate off-the-record dialogue between conflicting parties to resolve their differences. I was keen to continue to play some role in conflict resolution in two areas in which I had served as a peacekeeper, the Middle East and Africa. I was also personally involved in the India-Pakistan conflict and felt the urgent need for its resolution.

In the next chapter, I recount an episode of personal diplomacy in the conflict between India and Pakistan that I undertook while still at the academy.

17

Personal Diplomacy

An Exploration in Opening Negotiations between India and Pakistan

At the end of the fighting between India and Pakistan in 1948, it was my hope that our two countries would resolve the question of Jammu and Kashmir. I always felt that having agreed to the Partition of India, which called for great sacrifice on the part of millions of Hindus and Muslims, our two nations should surely be able to negotiate a settlement on J&K.

On my posting to the United Nations, I was among the first to propose that the Secretary-General should ask Pakistan, as well as India, for logistics troops for the Congo peacekeeping operation. With Rajeshwar Dayal, Hammarskjöld's special representative in the Congo and recently India's high commissioner in Pakistan, I received full support in coordinating the two contingents into an effective support service that made a valuable contribution to the operation. I was fortunate to have an outstanding Pakistani officer, Major Eijaz Azim (later lieutenant general and ambassador to the United States), on my staff and to be friends with the Pakistani military adviser in New York. Later, in 1962, when the Security Council authorized a mission to end the war between the Netherlands and Indonesia in West Irian, Pakistan provided the main contingent for the security force. U Thant sent me to Pakistan to brief its army staff at Karachi. My visit proved useful to the Pakistanis and the UN. The commander of the force turned out to be my former classmate at the IMA, Brigadier Said-ud-din Khan. We made a great team.

As a matter of policy, and for good reason, I was not involved at the United Nations in matters relating to the India–Pakistan conflict. My presence caused suspicion among Pakistanis and, to say the least, gave them little joy. Zulfiqar Bhutto included me among the Indians supposedly influencing U Thant when Bhutto attacked the integrity of the Secretary-General at a Security Council meeting dealing with the India–Pakistan war of 1965. Bhutto was wrong in his allegations, for I was in the Dominican Republic at that time.

At the IPA, I dealt with Pakistan as I did with any other member of the world organization. When the crisis in East Pakistan emerged, I was discouraged by my friends at the United Nations and my American contacts in Washington, D.C., from becoming involved. I was at a seminar at Helsinki just before the 1971 war between India and Pakistan, and I was able to arrange to have participants from both countries discuss the conflict, but they were unenthusiastic to start a dialogue. It was only after the Bangladesh war that the IPA was able to assist the new nation by providing training for its officials to deal with humanitarian disasters. Later, the IPA helped Bangladesh initiate a training module for peacekeeping at its Staff College. It is satisfying to note that Bangladesh presently is a useful participant in UN peacekeeping operations.

President Mohammed Zia ul-Haq of Pakistan, in his capacity as the chairman of the Islamic Organization, was scheduled to address the General Assembly during the fall session of 1982. In 1946 Zia, then a lieutenant, was posted to my Jat squadron of 6th Lancers in Kohat. He had arrived with an adverse report for a regular commission. I learned that it was his commitment to faithful compliance to his religious practices, as well as his love for popular Indian music, that had annoyed his fellow British officers. Zia was a good officer and I recommended him for a regular commission. I had not seen him since my departure from Pakistan in September 1947. I decided to go to the assembly to listen to his address and, if possible, to greet him.

Zia had nothing dramatic to say; he referred to India's "grab of Kashmir contrary to the wishes of the people", as was made routinely by Pakistani speakers. It never ceased to amaze me how Pakistan leaders could call for the expression of free will by the Kashmiri people when they denied the same to their own as well as to their territories of the former princely states that they occupied. After the applause and his return to his delegation's seats, I joined the queue to greet him. When Zia saw me, he arose to wrap me in an embrace typical of Punjabi greetings. We met after thirty-six years during which the world around us had changed a great deal. So had our lives. He had acquired notoriety as a ruthless ruler and military dictator and I had become a peacekeeper.

Zia invited me to Pakistan as his guest and asked me to bring my wife. I promised to give him an answer soon. I would indeed enjoy visiting the land of my birth and meeting old friends. But my greater interest was to promote a dialogue between our two countries. My soundings of the governments of India and Pakistan led me to believe that, while there was little enthusiasm for any initiative by me, there were no objections. I decided to go ahead, and I arranged to see Prime Minister Indira Gandhi before going to Pakistan.

At a meeting with Mrs. Gandhi, I described the circumstances of my visit to Pakistan and asked if there was anything I could do to help promote better relations between our two countries. Her answer was, "Woh to bahut kattar hai" (He [Zia] is an extreme fundamentalist], implying that there was little flexibility in Zia's attitude toward India.

Indeed, Zia was always very religious, but I did not recall his ever expressing strong views on Islam or Pakistani independence when we two served on the old Indian frontier. Zia had not shown any zeal for the concept of Pakistan at that time. As he rose in the military hierarchy of Pakistan he had remained apolitical. In fact, Zulfiqar Bhutto had selected him as the chief of staff because of Zia's reliability.

Mrs. Gandhi was not too happy with my suggestion that Zia might not be the extremist he seemed, and she said, "What good did Zia do for Bhutto anyway when he had him strung up at the end of a rope." Obviously, she had been more comfortable dealing with Bhutto, who like Indira was educated in England, even though it was Bhutto who had demolished a democratically elected government in East Pakistan and launched the military to end the rebellion that followed.

Mrs. Gandhi had negotiated the Shimla Accord with Bhutto, after the Bangladesh war, and established a rapport with him. While she was popular with the Indian armed forces and enjoyed excellent working relations with the military because she was firm and decisive, she believed that the military belonged in the barracks, from where they might occasionally be summoned to help the civil power maintain law and order and to fight in the defense of their country. What did soldiers know about politics? Mrs. Gandhi, other Indian politicians, and Indian civil servants had kept the Indian armed forces under a tight rein. But now she and the Indian leaders had to deal with an "iron head" in Pakistan, a prospect that had little appeal for them.

She concluded our talk by saying that we had a good ambassador, Shankar Bajpai, in Islamabad and that when I saw him I should discuss available options. In any event, I was to let her know how my visit went. This exchange was fresh in my mind as my wife and I prepared to be the guests of the president of Pakistan.

This was Cynthia's first visit to Pakistan, whereas I was returning for the first time since my departure in 1947, except for a one-day visit to collect personal belongings and a two-day visit to Karachi in 1962 in connection with Pakistan's participation in the West Irian UN security force. We took an Indian Airline flight to Lahore. Zia had arranged a two-day stay for sightseeing, so on arrival we were driven to the State Guest House via the cantonments, the canal, and Lawrence Gardens, all very familiar to me. Our guest-house was none other than the residence of the British agent to the north Indian princely states, a place that had invoked mystery when I was younger.

The historic, sprawling city of Lahore, the seat of the past rulers of the Punjab and the provincial capital under British rule, had multiplied manifold with the influx of refugees from India and its new role as the seat of the most important province of Pakistan. The communal fighting before and after the Partition had led to a mass exodus of Hindus and Sikhs from Pakistan. The departure of the handsome, bearded Sikhs with turbans of many different hues, and of Hindu and Sikh women in their colorful shirts and baggy trousers (*salwar kameez*), faces uncovered and veils (*chunni*) wrapped around their necks or gracefully flowing behind them, had changed Lahore's face. Unveiled Pakistani women were scarce, as most were covered from head to foot in a shuttlecock-shaped dress that had slits (*burqa*) for the eyes. Lahore, like Pakistan's other cities, had become completely male dominated.

The following day, we drove along the Mall, past some old and many new stores and cinemas and stopped at the Dum Duma gun in front of the Lahore museum. The gun, built by the Afghans and captured by the British during their wars against these great central Asian warriors, was made famous by Rudyard Kipling in his story of Kim. I was born in the home of my maternal grandparents in a house at the end of Anarkali, adjacent to the Mall. The corner house provided easy access to the colorful and crowded shopping street, which was named after a great beauty of the Mughal period. It also opened onto a modern vista of a wide road and attractive stores.

After a quick look at Kim's gun and the surroundings, we drove along the lower Mall to visit the Government College and the Central Model School, the institutions where I was educated. Lahore was known as the "Garden City" and it truly was so, and looked even better than I remembered it. The trees, shrubs, lawns, and flowerbeds were well tended. The park at the end of the lower Mall remained a green gem encircled by a garland of lush trees.

In the afternoon Cynthia and I went to Multan Road to see my parents' villa. It was a disappointing experience. As we approached the area where I remembered our old house existed, my escort pulled up in front of a run-down home. He assured me that it was the correct address. I could see on the face of the officer the question of how a reputed Indian general, a guest of honor of their president and married to a rich American (all American wives of the native born are reputed to be rich), could once have lived in such a place.

The place looked nothing like the house that I had helped build while in college. Our old villa and the surrounding garden were now abandoned to refugees. I stopped where I stood, and had no desire to go further. The young escort officer, on alert, submachine gun in his hand, glanced at my face and could surely read my thoughts. I could not remember where I had read the words that came to my mind: "One man builds. Another man destroys." I said to my escort, "This is nothing like my old house. Let us go to the fort", where we were due next.

We rode up the lower Mall along the route that I used to cycle from our old house to my college. Once past Chauburji, the road traversed the civil lines. To the west and beyond the small bungalows lay the additional playing fields of my old college. I drilled there with the University Training Corps. Just beyond was a housing development, Krishan Nagar, where my maternal grandmother had built a townhouse. Shortly, we drove past my college and old school, continuing along the west side of the old walled city of Lahore until we reached Peshawar Gate and the nearby fort, built to guard the northern approach to the city. The motor road climbed a short distance between the fort gate and the entrance to the *gurdwara*—a Sikh holy shrine. The fort gate was high and wide enough for an elephant to pass through. This is where renegade Sikh soldiers were believed to have killed Kharak Singh, son of Maharaja Ranjit Singh, the founder of the Sikh state of the Punjab, by felling the heavy gateway on the elephant carrying the ruler.

The fort was clean and in good repair. I had frequently come here in my younger days. Both my paternal and maternal ancestors had close ties with Maharaja Ranjit Singh. This was where my ancestor Kanhaya Lal was brought as a destitute and where he left as an adopted son of one of the wealthiest of the Punjab. The fort had poignant meaning, too, for my mother's ancestor, Misar Beli Ram. Guarding the Koh-i-Noor and other treasures, he was murdered at the treasury in the fort. I was pleased to see a room set aside for pictures and mementos of the Sikh rulers, the last native-born rulers of this state before it was annexed by the British in the nineteenth century. The pictures included photographs of Maharaja Dalip Singh, grandson of Ranjit Singh and last of the line of Sikh princes. Fate had ordained that my father's family were to continue their loyal service to their prince and that Father and Mother's *beradari* (clans) would eventually unite through their marriage and remain close to Dalip Singh's daughter, Princess Bamba.

The following day a small prop-jet plane took us to Chaklala, the airport for Rawalpindi and Islamabad, Pakistan's new capital. Rawalpindi was one of the largest cities of the Punjab. I spent many happy vacations with my maternal grandparents and later with my parents in this town and I spent summers in the Murree hills nearby.

After the usual protocol reception, we were taken to the Holiday Inn at Islamabad. Rawalpindi had grown enormously and in every direction. The airport seemed to be a part of the city of Rawalpindi, and it took only a few minutes to reach the new capital. In my younger days the site of Islamabad was a scrub forest with wild game and a spring with delicious, cool water. Our family had a favorite picnic spot with a view of the toll gate some five miles away, at the bend on the road to Murree. Beyond lay the high Murree ridge, with its greenery and English-style houses that were visible on clear days. Now, houses and buildings replaced the trees and bushes. Islamabad is more attractive than Chandigarh, the new city of East Punjab, designed by Le Corbousier, and the seat of the governments of the Indian states of the Punjab and Haryana. Chandigarh, a marvel of architecture and design, was built on rich agricultural land in the plains, at the edge of the low hills that gently ascend to Kasauli, about six thousand feet high. Islamabad, equally well designed, is built on gradually rising hills that almost reach the lower slopes of the Murree hills, which are as high as Kasauli.

The hotel had received a number of calls from my old school and family friends. Apparently, my upcoming meeting with the president had been reported by the press. I arranged to meet some of my friends at the hotel.

After the painful experience of visiting my old home in Lahore I had no further desire to walk down my "memory lane". My ancestors, since the coming of the Aryans across the Indus to the land of five rivers, had inhabited these lands. They suffered invaders and survived. The Partition of India, for the first time, moved them out of their homes and made them strangers in their own country. My family suffered humiliation and the loss of members brutally killed in the name of religion. The wounds of the Partition of India, the sacrifice and suffering of my family for the price for freedom, were still raw under my scars.

At 5 p.m. Cynthia and I were brought to Zia's house, where the president waited for us on the verandah. After effusive greetings, he led Cynthia to his drawing room to be received by his wife, a daughter, and two sons. The daughter, about ten, was handicapped and greatly attached to her father. In turn, he showed great affection and tremendous understanding. Zia had kept his residence at the house designated for the chief of staff of the army. This house was located in the cantonment area for the general officer commander-in-chief of the Northern Command, which had been the largest British military command, responsible for west India, extending to the frontier with Afghanistan and Iran. The house's last British occupant was the much admired hero of the Second World War, General Sir Douglas Gracey. On Independence and the Partition of India he became the first commander-in-chief of Pakistan. When Zia said, "Welcome to our humble abode", in a traditional oriental greeting, I asked: "But why don't you move to the house built for the head of the government?"

He demurred, saying, "That house is for a civilian head of government. I am only a transitional head and I prefer to remain here. Besides," he added, "the other house was ominous", in an obvious reference to the fate of Bhutto. It was also a smart move for a military head of government to reside in the cantonment, showing his continuing allegiance to the military.

After tea and a polite exchange of news of our respective children, Begum Zia took Cynthia to show her the house and the *zenana*, the traditional living area of Muslim ladies of the house, who normally observed *purdah* (went veiled).

As soon as we were alone, Zia asked, "When did you start writing, sir? You never showed such talent in the old days."

Thinking that he was referring to my books *The Blue Beret* and *The Sinai Blunder*, I modestly remarked, "Oh well! After all, these books are on peacekeeping and that is what I have been doing for the last twenty-five years."

I added in a lighter vein, "I wrote a lot of reports on peacekeeping operations for the UN. Writing my books was not much different."

Zia intervened to say, "No! No! I am talking of your books on our part of the world . . . your more recent book, the *Fourth Round* on a possible war between India and Pakistan in 1984." Zia had mistakenly understood that I was writing under the guise of my son Ravi.

"You have got it wrong, Zia. It is Bachu, my son Ravi, who writes on India–Pakistan." Zia had seen my recently born son after my first wife had rejoined me in Kohat in the spring of 1947. We lived in a bungalow in the cantonment and Zia came to our Sunday lunches for the single Indian officers of the regiment.

Pausing for a moment, Zia smiled and said, "Fancy Bachu as an author on strategic issues. He was so small and cried a lot, as I was to learn that babies do at that age."

The conversation about Ravi's writing on a possible war segued into an exchange of views on relations between our two countries. Zia believed the thought of another war between India and Pakistan was preposterous. Compared to Pakistan, India was too large and had an enormous military establishment and a stronger economy. Pakistan had had to "give" after each of the three wars.

He defined two major issues between our two countries. We had to resolve the dispute over Jammu and Kashmir, and India had to accept the historical inevitability of Pakistan. The election of the Janata Party government of Morarji Desai, with its foreign minister Atal Behari Vajpayee of the Bharatiya Janata Party (BJP, or Indian people's party, popularly considered a Hindu nationalist party), had convinced Zia that peace between our countries was not only desirable but also possible. But Zia was not at all sure that Mrs. Gandhi's Congress government had warmed toward Pakistan. He had observed notable differences between Desai and Gandhi. When Morarji's coalition won the Indian election, Zia telephoned to congratulate Morarji and had a pleasant exchange with the prime minister. But when he called Mrs. Gandhi to congratulate her and wish her well on her return to office, her response was "bilkul sukha" (very dry).

I told Zia that Indira Gandhi was not known to indulge in small talk. Surely, Pakistani diplomats would know her well enough to have suggested that after preliminary greetings, Zia should move on to some substantive topic, other than the sensitive issue of relations between our countries. Zia insisted that he was courteous and effusive in his congratulations and had not expected a cold exchange. I suggested he should have an agenda in advance of a meeting with Mrs. Gandhi and cut out Punjabi and Lucknow-style pleasantries. Apparently this is exactly what he did at a subsequent meeting of Heads of State of the Commonwealth. Zia was generous enough to convey to me through an emissary on a visit to New York that my ideas had worked at this meeting. He had enjoyed his tête-à-tête with

Mrs. Gandhi, during which they discussed the future role of the Commonwealth on a somewhat intellectual plane.

Returning to Zia's comments on the two major points of conflict between our countries, I first addressed the subject of J&K, saying that we were both familiar with the history of the conflict. I said we should have fulfilled the six-month Stand Still Agreement negotiated by Mountbatten before independence and used the time to resume negotiations. After all, we had negotiated a division of the Punjab, our most precious asset. I emphasized that in basic terms we exchanged our ancestral homes. "Your family gave up Jullundur to East Punjab and mine gave up Gujranwala to West Punjab." Instead of negotiations on J&K, Pakistan sent in frontier tribes with the expectation that India would cave in.

I asked, "Did you know who were the first Indian troops to stop the raiders and then to drive them out of the Kashmir valley?"

He said that he knew it was 7th Light Cavalry and Sen's infantry brigade (formerly of the Baluch Regiment, allotted to Pakistan).

"That is correct," I said, "but the advance squadron of 7th Light Cavalry was none other than the Jats of Lancers, led by me: the very squadron in which you had served with me. And you know how we had dealt with the tribal thugs when we were together on the frontier." Zia just shook his head in dismay.

As for his second point, on the Indian acceptance of the historical inevitability of Pakistan, I said, "I know that none of us who left West Punjab in 1947 have any desire to return. You know we Punjabis are an adventurous and courageous people. Since ancient times our ancestors have lived through many invasions of India by land. Therefore, human disasters are a part of our history. We suffer as humans do, but we have the ability in our genes to resume life. There have been times when our new life was better than the old one. This is what has happened to most of us after Partition. India is making good progress. So why should any of us wish to return?"

Zia remarked, "Yes I can see that. But since India is so divisive and more of a continent than a nation, it helps the leaders to unify the country by having Pakistan as an enemy. Besides, you have your extremists who destroy mosques and are enemies of Islam."

Zia was referring to Hindutva, originally called Hindu Rashtra (warriors), members of the Rashtriya Swayamsevak Sangh (RSS), formed in 1925. Membership in RSS received a boost during the Hindu–Muslim riots before and during the Partition. The RSS is fundamentalist in its defense of Hindu culture. While BJP owes its origins to RSS, its focus is political and it has gradually grown independent of its origins. The Vishwa Hindu Parishad (VHP), which has ties to RSS, is made up of militant Hindus who in propagating their religion are determined to undo the conversion of Hindu temples into mosques by Muslim conquerors and to reconstruct Hindu shrines destroyed and replaced with mosques on the same sites.

I replied, "Indeed we do. Just as you have yours. Come on Zia, your population is one-eighth the size of India. East Bengal has already broken away as a separate independent state and you have problems governing your remaining provinces. I realize that you are relying on Islam to hold the country together, but Pakistan remains as diverse as the rest of the subcontinent. Surely there are politicians here too who ride the bandwagon of Kashmir and religion."

Zia replied, "Indeed religion provides the glue for us to build Pakistan. As you know, I am no religious zealot, but I believe in my faith and that it should hold true believers together. Given the diversity of our people, somewhat like your situation in India, religion is all that allows our people to remain united. I am only too aware of the desire of Islamic fundamentalists in Pakistan to become more militantly anti-Hindu. As president I have to be a politician and therefore I don't want to antagonize the religious leaders. At the same time I realize that while religion has a place in the world today, it is not the only way to remain united."

He paused a moment and then added, "You know, sir, we have more cause to be worried about your fundamentalists, like the RSS, and your extremist Sikhs." Zia's reference to Sikhs was especially relevant. By the sixteenth century the spread of Islam by the sword in India had given rise to organized bands of Hindus. They hid in the jungle, lived a Spartan life, and fought back to save Hindu lives. It was their tenth guru who declared these groups to be Sikhs, with their symbolic five Ks: kirpan, kara, kes, kangha, and kachcha (dagger, bangle, uncut and unshaved hair, comb, and shorts). In time, the Sikhs raised a special force, Akali Dal, which was fearless and ruthless in waging war.

"We both have stereotypes," I answered. "Indians worry about your religious zealots who declare that Islam will again prevail on the Indian subcontinent just as it did for five centuries before the British seized power, and your people fear that Indian hard-liners, after tearing away East Pakistan, will dismember what is left of Pakistan. We have to eliminate stereotypes, breakdown barriers, and establish better communications. We must take steps to remove the fear of attack by the other."

He looked me in the eye and spoke with feeling: "Sir, I assure you by all that is sacred to me, my faith, my country, my children, that I will not instigate another war with India. I said that to Morarji and Vajpayee and now that Congress is back in power I have communicated this to Mrs. Gandhi through your Ambassador Bajpai. Please tell Mrs. Gandhi that."

I had read of this very declaration by Zia in the press and heard it discussed in Delhi. No one believed it. Zia's image in India was exactly as Mrs. Gandhi had portrayed him. He was seen as a ruthless military dictator for hanging Bhutto. The Indians had little love for Bhutto but no one wished him to die by hanging for a questionable crime.

I had overstayed my visit and felt enough had been said at this meeting. Zia too decided we should call it a day and noted that we were going to see more of each other over the next few days and talked of my trip to Peshawar.

Zia had arranged for me to go to the frontier to see Afghan refugees and meet Lt. Gen. Fazli Haq, the governor of the province. I had met Fazli, a fellow armor officer, about a year earlier while we were both staying at the Cavalry & Guards Club in London. He was a typical forthright Pathan and I looked forward to seeing him. Cynthia and I drove to Peshawar on the Grand Trunk Road, romanticized by Rudyard Kipling in his writing. We crossed the Indus at Attock and drove through Nowshera. Pakistan's armor and artillery schools were here. On the entrance to the armor center sat a war trophy, a Russian made Indian tank.

I could have mentioned the war trophies seized by the Indian forces from Pakistani troops, but instead I remarked to the protocol officer accompanying us that I had never heard the music tape that he was playing in his car. He looked at me with a smile and announced, "It is

Indian film music . . . smuggled of course." I would not have known the difference, since I never listened to Indian film music by choice. I had only referred to the music as a conversation opener. However, I had read in the papers that India and Pakistan had banned imports of each other's films, music, publications, and so on. Our escort confided that Indian films and music were very popular in Pakistan. Whereas it was difficult to view Indian films, smuggled music was pirated and commonly available.

"Surely anyone caught would be in trouble," I said.

He laughed. "Trouble! No, sir. Everyone listens to these tapes. Even those who are supposed to monitor the ban. No, no . . . music is for everyone." It was fascinating to witness a human side to the problems between our two countries.

Shortly after our arrival, Cynthia and I set-off to see the Khyber Pass and visit refugees camps. Viewing the pass has always been a breathtaking experience for me. It is 35 miles long, the first 25 miles in Pakistan. Jamrud fort is at the entrance. A busy trucking road runs through the pass to Afghanistan, with heavy traffic in goods both ways. A railway line runs from Peshawar to Landi Kotal to supply Shagai fort, built by the British between the two world wars to control the independent-minded and tough Afridis, who populate the area. Alexander the Great, Tamburlane, Babur, and Nadir Shah all came through the pass. Cynthia and I viewed the pass from high ground near the road outside Shagai fort. As always in the past, nature and the history of the pass overwhelmed me. We had to move on to the see the refugees.

The camps were crowded but well organized. Although the Peshawar valley is well irrigated and abundant in food and fruit, the camps were outside the city on bare soil, for little natural grass abounds in the area. The international community was pouring in a lot of money. The refugees were well cared for and fed, and had all the amenities and social services that could possibly be provided under canvas. They, especially the children, looked clean, reasonably well dressed, and healthy. Now, I turned my attention to the politics of the camps and learned of the future of the refugees. A majority were Pashtuns. Divided by the Durand Line early in the nineteenth century, they lived on both sides of the border between Afghanistan and

Pakistan. Not being strangers in Pakistan, they lived in refugee camps or with members of their clan.

Relations between the United States and Pakistan, virtually frozen since the civil war in East Bengal, followed by war with India in 1971 and the emergence of Bangladesh from the ruins of East Pakistan, had begun to thaw as the United States turned more and more to Pakistan to inflict a humiliating defeat on the Soviet troops that were in Afghanistan to support the Najibullah regime. Indeed, Pakistan played a vital role in the war in Afghanistan but could not escape the limitations imposed by its ties to the Pashtuns and therefore the inherited conflicts with other Afghan tribal groups. This would become more apparent after the Soviets withdrew from Afghanistan and Pakistan found that it had little ability to broker a peace. When the civil war renewed, much of the country, including Kabul, would come under the control of the Taliban, a fundamentalist group sponsored by Pakistan.

Pakistani expectations that once the British and Hindus left, the frontier would see peace between Muslim brethren proved to be unfounded. Tribal behavior across the Durand Line did not change with the birth of Pakistan. And the rebellion in Afghanistan had further exacerbated internal conflict. During the Cold War there were scarce reports of lawlessness and internal disorder in the world press because both East and West exercised controls over the news of their allies to varying degrees. Nevertheless, increased smuggling of drugs from Afghanistan through Pakistan and to India could not be concealed from the public.

The war in Afghanistan was yet another area of disagreement between India and Pakistan. India supported a non-fundamentalist regime in Kabul, whereas Pakistan was committed to helping establish a fundamentalist Islamic group to ensure a friendly regime on its north-western frontier and extend its influence in central Asia. For these very reasons, India supported anti-fundamentalist groups. Since Pakistan was also committed to assisting the United States in the removal of Soviet troops and a communist regime from Afghanistan, Pakistan had chosen the winning side. In the Cold War context, India was again on the Soviet side, not an enviable position considering that its interests varied considerably from those of the Soviets.

13. At Ruth and Arthur Young's estate, Dowingtown, Pennsylvania. *From left to right:* the author, Ruth, Arthur, the author's grandson Evan, and the author's wife Cynthia.

14. Twenty-fifth anniversary of the International Peace Academy, December 1996. *From left to right: back row*—F.T. Liu, author, Andrea Loomis, Elisa Forbes Tripp, Nick Bancroft; *front row*—Elisabeth Lindenmayer, George Sherry, and guest.

15. Last gathering with mother. *From left to right:* Sodarshan, Rajeshwar, the author's mother, Indra, Hemwant, author.

16. The author's eightieth birthday celebration. *From left to right: seated*—author, Kai, Cynthia, Giai; *standing*—Ravi, Rachna, Evan, Anna-Lisa, Cathy, Kiran, Bhalinder.

Lt. Gen. Fazli Haq, the governor of the North West Frontier Province, had arranged a lunch in my honor to meet former Indian Armored Corps officers residing in the area. It was an only-for-men affair, so I went alone in an escorted limousine to the Government House. After a few minutes of exchanging formalities, Fazli led us into a large reception room where eleven serving and retired armor colleagues were already present. There was utter pandemonium for a few minutes, as we effusively greeted each other like former schoolchildren at a reunion. We quieted only when lunch was announced and we were led into a magnificent wood-paneled dining room.

This house had been the forward post of the "Great Game" between British imperial India and tsarist Russia, and of the replay between the West and the communist East. I was most interested to learn of Pakistan's role in the new game being played out there in the wild north-west. In his welcome, Fazli said, "Indar, all of us here wish to welcome you. We are especially pleased to receive you, as we consider you as one of us. We know of your service in J&K and surely you know what we have done since Partition. We all did what we had to. But what your old friends in Pakistan have appreciated and admired is that you have dealt with our people after the operations in J&K and in your work at the United Nations fairly, and with the same old affection that you always had for the land of your birth."

There was loud clapping and exclamations of "Bilkul theek hai!" ("Absolutely right!"). Fazli continued, "All of us want to talk to you. We know that you understand us and we trust that you will give us your honest answers."

Though I felt flattered at their compliments I realized that I was in for a grilling. I responded by first thanking Fazli for lunch and arranging for me to meet so many of my old colleagues. I concluded, "You know that I retired from the Indian Army and later from the United Nations. But, with my limited knowledge, I will try to do my best and will be glad to share my analysis."

As lunch was served, Fazli told us that we were to eat first and then resume our discussion. The pulao (saffron-colored rice with meats) and a variety of grilled meats and game were exquisitely prepared. It was quite a feast by any standard and we washed it down with soft beverages. As coffee was served, Fazli opened the discussion. In the main, we discussed the future of Pakistan and the plight of the Muslims in India.

I heard again and again the refrain that India was responsible for waging three wars against Pakistan (in 1947, 1965, and 1971) and was determined to destroy Pakistan. Their arguments were not new, and their methodical presentations sounded to me like reverse logic. I decided not to respond freely and frankly, as I had been able to do with Zia, because apart from Fazli my acquaintance with the others had only been brief. It would have been foolhardy for me to enter in a debate with these tough warriors on complex political issues. So, I sidetracked our discussion to the more parochial matter of India's traditional good relations with the Pathans who, like other trans-Indus tribes, straddle the line that divides Central Asia from what was once British India and is now Pakistan. I said that from what I knew of India, it remained a friend of the Pathans. There are Pathan traders, guards, and even moneylenders in Mumbai. This raised a laugh.

When it was time to leave, I thanked Fazli for lunch and the others for their welcome, and I reiterated what I had told Zia earlier, that India had no designs to destroy Pakistan. There was, I declared, a great need for people-to-people contact. As time went by, we had allowed our isolation from one another to increase. We had to rediscover each other and discuss our mutual concerns.

The next morning Cynthia and I returned to Islamabad. On our journey back we went by the Indus River Dam, a joint Indo-Pakistani project located some twenty miles up the river, where it breaks through the last of the Himalayas. Sponsored by the World Bank and negotiated by Eugene Black, the bank's president, the project is not only a marvel of modern hydraulic engineering but a great diplomatic achievement as well. The project has withstood major crises, including wars between India and Pakistan. My wife and I expressed our wish that the project continue to provide for the needs of millions of people of the subcontinent. We made a second stop at Taxila to see the Gandhara sculptors. While my parents were at Campbellpur and Rawalpindi, we went to see this museum several times, accompanying visiting relatives. Not far from here was the holy Sikh shrine of Punja Sahib, which bore the impression of the palm of Guru Gobind Singh on the rock face. Unlike the Lahore fort, the museum deserved more attention than it was getting and I mentioned this to the authorities on my return to the capital.

Back in Islamabad I had a few appointments to keep. I called on the director of the Institute of Strategic Studies and had lunch with Sahebzada Mohamed Yaqub Khan, the foreign minister, who was assisted by Shahriyar Khan, the foreign secretary. Yaqub had been at the IMA with me. Both were scions of Indian princely families. Nothing of substance was discussed at these two meetings. My visit to the vice chancellor and staff of Quaid e Azam University proved more interesting.

In between meetings with India's capable and popular Ambassador Shankar Bajpai, we had a happy reunion with Brigadier Mohammed Sadiq Awan and his wife Nafis. Sadiq, a cavalry officer, was, as liaison officer at Beirut, the only Pakistani in UNEF when I joined the peacekeeping force. We became instant friends.

During my remaining two days I sought more information that would give me a better grasp of two main issues of concern to me. First, what could possibly be done at the non-official level to counter the stereotypes that India and Pakistan held of each other and help prevent a renewal of conflict? Second, what could be done by non-governmental organizations to minimize the consequences of the war in Afghanistan, a conflict that bade ill not only for Pakistan in the long-term but also for India? The United Nations was engaged in intensive efforts to end the fighting in Afghanistan. However, the conditions prevalent in the country made any NGO effort not merely hazardous but impossible. The war had yet to reach a stage where the parties would see advantage in a respite in, if not an end to, the fighting. Meanwhile, NGOs should continue their relentless efforts to expedite medical, food, and other essential supplies to control death from injuries, sickness, and hunger.

In my conversation with Ambassador Bajpai I discussed various confidence-building measures between the two countries that could be considered. Bajpai indicated reluctance by the two countries to move forward. In my next meeting with Zia, I suggested a number of options, including: school, college, and regimental reunions; exchanges of media reporters; visits by sporting teams and artists; trade; and talks on the control of nuclear weapons development.

Zia's response to my first three suggestions was that there was no objection to such meetings and exchanges. But these could be held only when a cooperative atmosphere prevailed. On nuclear weapons, he pointed out that India had already exploded "the bomb" and now it expected Pakistan to agree to halt its research. This was unacceptable to Pakistan. As for trade, he said, "India is so far ahead of us. If we were to trade with India we would become reliant on it and India could cut off the supply at its own will. No, no. We can trade with India only when we have near parity in production."

I found it interesting that Zia responded to my suggestions without hesitation. Surely, these ideas had been discussed with India before and he had a clear conception of Pakistan's attitude on these issues. I wondered why on some other defense and security-related questions in my earlier meetings he had withheld comment and then picked up the thread of that conversation at one of our following meetings.

I wondered if Zia was truly a stereotypical military ruler, as autocratic as Indians saw him, or if he was advised or guided by another authority. It was common knowledge that Zia was the main proponent if not the architect of Pakistan's entry into the Great Game in Afghanistan. This policy aimed to extricate Pakistan from disasters that followed the civil war in East Bengal by restoring Pakistan's usefulness to the United States and its importance in west Asia. Since Pakistan's Inter-Services Intelligence (ISI) had gained control of the country's Afghan operations in 1973, it had steadily grown in importance in its homeland. It continues to exercise enough power to act independently. Certainly, by 1983 it had acquired great authority.

I am not suggesting that Zia was in any way taking instructions from ISI, but he understood by the early 1980s that he could no longer ignore this organization. Nor could he ignore the Annual Conference of the Corps Commanders or the Joint Staff Committee, which implemented the decisions of the Corps Commanders conference. During military rule, these two bodies were the de facto supreme authority in the land.

A conversation with Zia about Zulfiqar Bhutto remains vivid in my mind. In discussing those days, I asked Zia, "Why did you hang Bhutto in spite of appeals from world great leaders to spare his life?"

Zia was silent for a while. Then he looked me straight in the eyes, drew his right hand across his throat, and declared, "It was either him or me."

It was such a dramatic moment that I held my breath for a while, because I did not quite understand. It was only afterwards that I began to comprehend what he had tried to convey to me. It was a question of survival. The military had decided that Bhutto was to die. Zia was the face of the military and not its master. I seriously doubt that he could have exercised his so-called presidential authority to save Bhutto's life, and if he tried to do so he would have done so at his own peril. It was Bhutto's life or his own.

I left Zia, convinced that he was more of a pragmatist than a religious fanatic and that he was more than willing to negotiate with India. A final resolution of differences would not be easy but it was possible for the two countries to start a meaningful dialogue that could lead to step-by-step agreements on the road to normalcy. Certainly Zia and his bright military associates had concluded that the use of force had failed. The issue of Kashmir presented an immediate challenge to both countries. Since Pakistan had so far not achieved success in Kashmir, it was left with two options: negotiate with India or encourage a popular rebellion. Since India had enormous resources compared to Pakistan and was adept at dealing with internal wars, the latter would be a prolonged effort with no guarantee of success. Zia was willing to try the easier solution of negotiating with India.

Cynthia and I left Pakistan the next day with the images of our exciting days there racing through our minds. Zia's responsibilities were awesome. He had not sought the presidency of Pakistan. The position of COS Army had come to him by dint of hard and honest work. It was commonly known that Bhutto had promoted him over some others because he thought Zia would be more manageable. Evidently, Zia's military colleagues chose him for the presidency after they collectively decided to overthrow Bhutto's regime and assume authority. Zia was determined and tough, but that is how the army trained him.

Zia was commonly labeled a military dictator. I have known a number of dictators, civilian and military, and Zia did not fit that category. The life of democracy has been short in Pakistan. From its infancy, Pakistan has been ruled by a combination of landowners, the military, and the bureaucracy. This has been true whether Pakistan has been under civilian rule, as with the governments of Zulfiqar Bhutto and his daughter Benazir, or the military rule of Field Marshal Mohammed Ayub Khan or Zia ul-Haq. The fall of Benazir Bhutto in the last months of 1996 seems to have confirmed this reality, as did the removal of Nawaz Sharif as prime minister in 1999 by yet another military coup, led by General Pervez Musharraf. The United States is leading the way in seeking a return of democracy to Pakistan. But it will have to be a form of government that an artificially carved state can digest. I am left to wonder if the countries bordering India between the Indus and the Sutlej and east of the Ganges are part of a long history marked by a continual state of flux.

I never saw Zia again. On 17 August 1988, after watching a demonstration of new American military equipment, and accompanied by the U.S. ambassador, Raphael, and other U.S. officials, he took off in his air force plane for Islamabad. The plane blew up, leaving no survivors. The mystery surrounding Zia's death remains. In the absence of a definitve announcement by Pakistan or the United States, a number of theories have circulated. Was it a foreign plot? Did a domestic opposition group assassinate him? Or was it that he was no longer useful to Pakistan's military high command? Perhaps the Americans, who lost their ambassador to Pakistan in the explosion, have some knowledge of the matter; if so, they have not shared it.

18

Finding a Nest

At seventy years of age I was anxious to retire to spend more time with my family, do more writing, and draw on my years of experience in operational training to improve the education of peace-related professionals. Therefore, when I was offered a Visiting Distinguished Fellowship by Ambassador Samuel Lewis, president of the United States Institute of Peace (USIP), in Washington, D.C., I readily accepted. I joined USIP in January 1990 and was asked immediately to work with a small group led by Robert Oakley, former National Security Council staff member and ambassador to Pakistan, on the crisis in Somalia. I was also invited to be USIP's adviser on UN affairs. I left USIP in 1993, shortly after Lewis was invited to take over as the director of policy planning at the State Department.

During the 1990s, the number of peace operations dramatically increased, as did the level of interest in the United States in such operations. Until the end of the Cold War, the United States had played a limited role in peacekeeping. Partly, this was because of a tacit agreement between the two superpowers that neither would send its combat forces on UN missions; partly, perhaps, it reflected the fact that in the United States, the National Guard is responsible for assisting civil authority, whereas the armed services focus on fighting wars. Thus, the U.S. military found it difficult to reconcile this tradition with peacekeeping, where there is no enemy to fight. During the Cold War, the United States had contributed military observers, logistics, and air and sea transportation to peacekeeping missions. After the end of the Cold War, however, the U.S. armed forces showed greater interest in peacekeeping operations. The U.S. military establishment launched research programs into peacekeeping operations. The National Defense University in Washington, D.C., and the services' war colleges had followed developments in the United Nations and regional organizations, and began to include peace operations as an important subject. A number of universities policy institutes likewise added this subject to their work.

As the sole remaining super power, the United States faces numerous and conflicting demands on its military and police forces, and peace operations now tend to be accorded a relatively lower priority in Washington. Whereas in the early 1990s there was significant enthusiasm for participating in peace operations, today most U.S. commentators believe that the high-tech, well-trained, and well-equipped U.S. military is better suited for peace enforcement operations and other missions that call for forceful presence. Given this attitude, and in light of the reluctance of the Bush administration to intervene, it is likely that the other member states of the United Nations and regional organizations will have to shoulder a greater share of the burden of maintaining international peace and security.

As peace support operations (multifunctional operations involving diplomats, military forces, and humanitarian agencies) proliferated in the early 1990s, Ruth Young and I became convinced that to meet the increased demand for qualified personnel more institutes were required to develop and conduct training models to prepare personnel for this special area. After the shift in the priorities of the International Peace Academy in 1990, from training to research, Ruth decided on three approaches to meet the increasing demand for training peacekeepers: first, she sought the help of some of the fellow IPA directors, especially Robert O'Neill, a highly respected scholar in international strategic affairs, for IPA to retain some essential aspects of training; second, she encouraged me to seek wider involvement in developing peacekeeping training; three, she arranged for a close family friend, Sabrina (Andrea) Loomis-Watt, to represent her at IPA to keep herself better informed of its activities.

With Ruth's generosity, I was able to facilitate training programs at the United Nations Institute for Training and Research (UNITAR). When UNITAR moved to Geneva, Ruth and I looked for another suitable institute and turned to the Institute of World Affairs in

Washington, D.C., and Salisbury, Connecticut. In cooperation with its chairperson, Geraldine Kunstadter, and its president, Bradford Johnson (and on his retirement, Hrach Gregorian), an annual training seminar for UN diplomats on negotiations was established.

The increase in peacekeeping operations heightened interest in academia. This made it possible to conduct a model program at the School of International Affairs at the American University in Washington, D.C. Also, I was able to assist Ambassador Walter Stadtler and Professor David F. Davis of the Program for Peacekeeping at George Mason University's School of Public Policy in Fairfax, Virginia.

When Cynthia and I moved to Charlottesville, we were immediately impressed by the University of Virginia. The university community includes many serving and retired faculty of renown in international relations. The area is also home to former diplomats and retired military officers, who maintain their interest in defense and foreign affairs. On my arrival here, I was invited by Professor John Norton Moore to participate in his Center for National Security Law summer programs. This led to my association with the nearby Army Judge Advocate General's School programs.

My membership in Nadir—a small group led by Professor Inis Claude and the local chapter of the Committee on Foreign Relations—provides opportunities to exchange views and stay abreast of world affairs. I have received honorary affiliations with the university's South Asia Studies program, with the help of Professor Emeritus Walter Hauser. I have agreed to assist in the development of a Program on Leadership of Peacekeeping for the Institute for Global Policy Research under a distinguished director, Nathaniel W. Howell, ambassador to Kuwait during the Gulf War of 1991.

At the United States Institute of Peace, I had started writing a book entitled *UN Peacekeeping*, past, present, and future. I was able to complete the first draft by the end of 1996, which was then edited with the help of the Army Peacekeeping Institute in Carlisle, Pennsylvania. The book was published by the Pearson Peacekeeping Center in Clementsport, Nova Scotia, in 2000.

When I retired from the IPA, Ruth encouraged me to continue my peacekeeping-related work. Ruth, as an activist, never ceased her pursuit of her goals. While never strident in her conversation or public speaking, she conveyed the importance of her mission. Her clear enunciation of her ideas and the personal example she set in giving so generously to her cause allowed her to rouse others to action.

I count Ruth among the few people I have known who have had a profound influence on my life. The list of those people begins with my parents. Calm, hard working, upright, and a caring parent, my father has been my role model; he gave his life to medicine and the care of mankind. His long hours of work as a physician in general practice during my adult life afforded me few opportunities to get to know him better. Thus, it was my mother who managed and influenced the lives of their children. After Father died, within four years of the Partition of India, my mother assumed all parental responsibilities.

Another great influence on my life has been Mahatma Gandhi. It was a chance meeting with him, the most respected leader in India and a man of great prestige abroad, that made it possible for me to make the army my career. Like many people, Indians and other, I will always remain grateful for being blessed by him. Next to the *Bhagwad Gita*, his writing has inspired me more than any other and guided me in many a tough situation.

In my acceptance address for the UNESCO Peace Prize for Education in 1985 at Paris, it was natural for me to speak of Gandhi. I spoke of his dilemma at the start of the First World War. Although increasingly drawn to the principles of non-violence and eager to throw off the yoke of British imperialism, he urged Indians to join the British forces in large numbers. When he faced the same dilemma again, at the outbreak of the Second World War, Gandhi readily offered to help raise a large volunteer army in India. But after twenty-five years of little progress toward Independence in India, this time Gandhi called for granting of independence before he launched his recruiting campaign. We know the consequences.

The non-violence of Gandhi and others who shared his sentiments provided the strength to generate a response to the British, which Indians called *satyagraha*, or civil disobedience. This was, to be sure, a principled stand, but it was also a pragmatic one, for Gandhi recognized that the majority who responded to his call to take up passive resistance were too weak to succeed by violent means.

Between the two world wars Gandhi actively promoted the recruitment of larger numbers of Indians for the officer corps of the armed forces. His efforts, together with those of other national leaders, boosted the number of Indians in ranks equal to British officers and eventually led to the opening of the Indian Military Academy, of which I am a product. In discussions on Gandhi, when I refer to his philosophy and policy on defense matters, I get a muted response. It seems to me that most people are either ignorant of Gandhi's role as an activist politician or they are so taken with his non-violence that they don't wish to hear about the other side of Gandhi's actions.

U Thant, well versed in Buddhist philosophy yet a pragmatic diplomat, in discussing developing conflicts would often say, "There is conflict in the minds of men. There will be no peace until violence is eliminated." But the space scientist Werner von Braun, in a discussion with me on peacekeeping, said, "Ah, general! You must not completely eradicate violence in man, for there would have been no Columbus to discover America and no John Glenn to attempt to reach the moon. Mankind should strive to control violence and channel it for the betterment of our species and not to destroy it." I tend to follow the latter thought.

Other influences on my personal and professional life include Captain Francis Ingall, my first squadron commander when I joined 6th Lancers, who left an indelible impression on me of how an officer should conduct himself. General Douglas Russell, my divisional commander in the Italian campaign, taught me higher leadership. And Dag Hammarskjöld, with his remarkable devotion to keeping peace in our troubled world, opened new vistas to me, as he did to the international community as a whole.

Ruth, last but by no means least on my list of influences, was a lady of many parts. Always elegantly dressed, she was a charming hostess. Her strong moral values and work ethic, her sense of service to humanity, and her humane American values made her a model representative of her noble family and of a great nation. She was frugal and caring and was a tower of strength to the causes she espoused. She devoted her life to banning the use of atomic, biological, and chemical weapons, becoming an active member of the World Federalists and supporting the congressional World Peace through

Law movement in Washington, D.C. She supported Democrats who not only were concerned with improving American society but also had global interests. She expected the United States to be an active player in the development and promotion of peace in the world. She exemplified the belief in the equality of humanity, having little care for race, color, creed, or social class. Ruth belonged to my mother's generation, but she reminded me of my maternal grandmother, who spent her life trying to improve the lot of women in the Punjab through prayer and social reform. Back in my old country, surely Ruth would have earned the affectionate title of *mataji* long since. When she died on 5 March 1998 at the age of ninety-four at Berkeley, California, it seemed to mark the end of an era.

In the 1990s, IPA built on its earlier achievements and launched out in new directions under its new president, Olara Otunnu. His interests and experience lay more in the politics of war and peace than in peacekeeping as such. Accordingly, while maintaining IPA's traditional interest in the development of peacekeeping doctrine and training with the assistance of F.T. Liu, a highly experienced and respected former assistant secretary-general in the UN Department of Peacekeeping, Otunnu redirected IPA's overall efforts to the fields of conflict prevention and peace implementation. In this he was assisted greatly by his brilliant vice-president, Michael Doyle of Princeton University (appointed a UN assistant secretary-general and special adviser to Secretary-General Kofi Annan in 2001), and by Nigerian scholar Margaret Voight. Otunnu and Doyle attracted talented scholars who produced an impressive array of scholarly and policy-oriented publications.

Following Otunnu's appointment as UN under-secretary general for children and armed conflict, David Malone, a young ambassador on leave from the Canadian Foreign Service, became IPA's third president. Malone, a scholar of the UN Security Council, shared Otunnu's interest in the pathology of conflict and peacebuilding. Together with IPA vice-presidents Necla Tschirigi (a leading Turkish scholar and practitioner of peacebuilding) and John Hirsch (a former U.S. ambassador and distinguished Africanist), Malone organized IPA's efforts to focus on subjects such as Africa; transitional administration from the UN to the reconstituted state; conflict prevention; UN-

NATO relations; and peacebuilding. The IPA also produced cutting-edge work on multilateral sanctions, humanitarian intervention, and the economics of war and peace. Its multinational staff, wide geographical network of partners, particularly in the developing world, and a broad basis of financial support from foundations and governments are great assets.

While I have been greatly impressed by the new directions that the IPA has taken since my retirement, I have been a little disappointed (as was Ruth) to see that the emphasis on training has diminished. IPA peacekeeping programs were pathfinders, providing the basis of peacekeeping training adopted universally; now, however, IPA has almost ceased to play this function.

The discussions and publications sponsored by various peace-related institutions provide education about peacekeeping; they do not provide training in the sense of offering a course of instruction in the professional skills required by peacekeepers. The troop-contributing countries have improved basic training in peace operations for their personnel. The UN Staff College, Milan, Italy, is providing middle-level professional training. Other institutions, such as the Pearson Peacekeeping Centre in Canada, also offer training, but only to the level of contingent commanders. A modest beginning in developing training programs in peace operations for higher leadership was designed at the Institute of Global Policy Research of the University of Virginia, Charlottesville, Virginia, in 1999; it was revised by the Naval Justice School, Newport, Rhode Island, and will be conducted starting at the end of 2001. Much more needs to be done, however. Civil wars, like interstate wars, are chaotic. The side that triumphs in those wars is usually the one that can cope best with chaos. Peacekeepers thus must learn to manage chaos if they are to accomplish their mission effectively and cost-effectively. There are only two choices when it comes to learning the skills of managing chaos; one can do so the hard way, in the field, or one can do so through training.

Other than this one concern, I greatly admire the way in which the IPA has furthered its reputation for making significant contributions to international peace and security. The IPA is now in its thirty-first year, and its future seems secure. Rita Hauser, chair of IPA's board of directors, possesses great professional skills as a lawyer and diplomat. With the assistance of successive presidents, she has gathered a group of highly competent directors who give their best to support the staff. On a personal note, I greatly appreciate and am grateful for the many courtesies extended to me on my visits to the IPA by its leadership and staff.

The International Peace Academy will remain a continuing memorial to Ruth's vision of a peaceful world, one free of weapons of mass destruction. Happily, two members of her family—Elise Forbes Tripp and William N. Bancroft—have taken up Ruth's banner and are actively engaged in the affairs of the academy. They not only have inherited Ruth's devotion to promoting peace and serving humanity but also have proven credentials for continuing the development of the IPA in the coming century.

Addressing the Congress on the eve of his retirement, General Douglas MacArthur remarked famously, "Old soldiers never die, they just fade away." As a devotee of Ruth, however, I have chosen to ignore MacArthur's axiom.

Bibliography

PART I

Amini, Iradj (1994), *Maharaja and the Koh-i-Noor, Lotus Collection*, Delhi: Rolli Books.

Barr, Pat and Ray Desmond (1978), *Simla: A Hill Station in British India*, New York: Charles Scribner.

Basham, A.L. (1977), 'The Wonder That Was India', in *Evergreen Encyclopedia*, vol. 1. rpt. edn., New York: Macmillan.

Buck, Edward J. (1979), *Shimla Past and Present*, First published, 1904, Reprint, Delhi: Summit Publications.

Combined Inter-Services Historical Section (India and Pakistan); Dharam Pal and Bisheshwar Prasad, eds. (1957) *Official History of the Indian Armed Forces in the Second World War, 1939-45: Campaign in West Asia*, Delhi: Orient Longman.

Gardner, Brian (1971), *The East India Company*, New York: McCall.

Garett, H.L.O. and Abdul Hamid (1964), *A History of Government College, Lahore*, Lahore: Ripon Printing Press.

General Staff, Army Headquarters, India (1919) *Official Account of the Third Afghan War*, Calcutta: Central Publications Branch of the Government of India.

Ingall, Francis (1988), *The Last of the Bengal Lancers*, Novato, Calif.: Presidio Press.

Khilani, N.M. (1990), *The Rise of the Sikh Power in the Punjab*, Delhi: Independent Publishing Company.

Mackenzie, Compton (1948), *All Over the Place*, London: Chatto and Windus.

Majumdar, Romesh Chandra (1973), *An Advanced History of India*, London: Macmillan.

Schwartzburg, Joseph (1978), ed., *A Historical Atlas of South Asia*, Chicago and London: University of Chicago Press.

Singh, Khushwant (1977), *A History of the Sikhs*, vol. 2, Delhi: Oxford University Press.

Yeats-Brown, Francis Charles Claypon (1930), *Bengal Lancers*, London: V. Gollancz. Published in 1946 by Bantam Press, New York, as *The Lives of a Bengal Lancer*.

PART II

Ambrose, Stephen (1976), *The Supreme Commander: The War Years of General Dwight Eisenhower*, Garden City, N.Y.: Double Day.

Collins, Larry and Dominique Lepierre (1975), *Freedom at Midnight*, New York: Simon and Schuster.

Combined Inter-Services Historical Section (India and Pakistan); Dharam Pal and Bisheshwar Prasad, eds. (1957), *Official History of the Indian Armed Forces in the Second World War, 1939-45: Campaign in West Asia*, Delhi: Orient Longman.

Gandhi, M.K. (1957), *Gandhi: An Autobiography*, First published, 1930. Paperback edn., Boston: Beacon Press.

Gopal, Servapalli (1979), *Nehru: A Biography*, vols. 1 and 2, Delhi: Oxford University Press.

Hatch, Alden (1965), *The Mountbattens*, Chaps. 16-18, New York: Random House.

Moorehead, W.H. and Atul Chander Chatterjee (1958), *A Short History of India*, India: Orient Longman.

Nehru, Jawaharlal (1946), *The Discovery of India*, Calcutta: Signet Press.

Schmidt, Karl J. (1995), *An Atlas and Survey of South Asian History*, Armonk, N.Y.: M.E. Sharpe.

Spear, Percival (1955), *History of India*, vols. 1-3. Oxford: Oxford University Press.

PART III

Burns, E.L.M. (1969), *Between Arab and Israeli*, Beirut: Middle East Institute.

Dalvi, J.P., Brig., *The Himalayan Blunder*, Delhi: Orient Pocketbooks, n.d.

Dayan, Moshe (1966), *Diary of the Sinai Campaign*, Jerusalem and Haifa: Steimatzky's.

Kaul, B.M., Lt. Gen. (1967), *The Untold Story*, Chaps. 4-5, Bombay: Allied Publishers.

Maxwell, Neville (1970), *India's China War*, New York: Pantheon Books, Random House.

Sachar, Howard M. (1699), *The Emergence of the Middle East, 1914-1924*, New York: Alfred A. Knopf.

——— (1972), *Europe Leaves the Middle East, 1936-1954*, New York: Alfred A. Knopf.

Teveth, Sabatai (1973), *Moshe Dayan*, Boston: Houghton Mifflin.

PART IV

Bosch, Juan (1965), *The Unfinished Experiment*, New York: Fredrick A. Praeger.

Dayal, Rajeshwar (1976), *Mission for Hammarskjöld*, Princeton, N.J.: Princeton University Press.

Eban, Abba (1968), *My People: The Story of the Jews*, New York: Random House.

Fahmy, Ismail (1983), *Negotiating for Peace in the Middle East*, Canberra: American University Press, Egypt; London: Croom Helm.

Harbottle, Michael (1970), *The Impartial Soldier*, London: Oxford University Press.

Heikal, Mohamd (1973), *The Cairo Documents*, Garden City, N.Y.: Doubleday.

Kennedy, Robert (1993), *Thirteen Days: A Memoir of the Cuban Missile Crisis*, New York: Signet, New Library.

Lall, Arthur (1968), *The UN and the Middle East Crisis, 1967*, New York and London: Columbia University Press.

Lefever, Ernest W. (1965), *Crisis in the Congo*, Washington, D.C.: Brookings Institution.

O'Brien, Connor Cruise (1962), *To Katanga and Back*, London: Hutchinson.

Pearson, Lester (1973), *Memoirs 2*, Toronto: University of Toronto Press.

Rikhye, Indar Jit (1983), 'Hammarskjöld and Peacekeeping', in *Dag Hammarskjöld Revisited*, ed. Robert S. Jordan Durham, N.C.: Carolina Academic Press.

———— (1978), *The Sinai Blunder*, New Delhi: Oxford & IBH Publishing; London: Frank Cass.

———— (1993), *Military Advisor to the Secretary General (Hammarskjöld and U Thant), UN Peacekeeping Operation in the Congo*, London: C. Hurst; New York: St. Martin Press.

———— (1975), with John Volkmar, *The Middle East and New Realism*, New York: International Peace Academy.

Stenga, James A.A. (1968), *United Nations Force in Cyprus*, Columbus: Ohio State University Press.

Szulc, Ted (1965), *Dominican Diary*, New York: Delacorte Press.

PART V

Arif, Khalid Mohamed (1995), *Working with Zia: Pakistan's Power Politics 1977-1988*, Karachi: Oxford University Press.

Ayoob, Muhammed (1975), *India, Pakistan, Bangladesh: Search for a New Relationship*, New Delhi: Indian Council for World Affairs.

Baxter, Craig (1985), ed. *Zia's Pakistan: Politics and Stability in a Front Line States*, Boulder, Colo.: Westview Press.

Bose, Sujata and Ayesha Jalal (1998), *Modern South Asia: History, Culture, and Economy*, London and New York: Routledge Press.

Burki, Shahid Javed and Craig Baxter (1991), *Pakistan under the Military: Eleven Years of Zia-ul-Haq*, Boulder, Colo.: Westview Press.

Gandhi, M.K. (1957), *Gandhi: An Autobiography*. First published, 1930, paperback edn., Boston: Beacon Press.

International Peace Academy, International Committee (1970), *Report from Vienna: An Appraisal of the International Committee's 1970 Pilot Projects*, New York: International Peace Academy.

Jacob, J.F.R., Lt. Gen., PVSM (1997), *Surrender at Dacca: Birth of a Nation*, New Delhi: Manohar.

Malik, Tajammal Hussain, Gen. (1991), *The Story of My Struggle*, Lahore: Jang Press.

Waskow, Arthur I. (1967), *Towards a Peacekeepers Academy*, The Hague: Dr. Junk Publishers.

PEACEKEEPING IN GENERAL

Cordier, Andrew W. and Wilder Foote (1969), eds., *Public Papers of the Secretaries-General of the United Nations*, vol. 1, *Trygve Lie, 1946-1953*, New York: Columbia University Press.

Narasimhan, C.V. (1988), *United Nations: An Inside View*, New Delhi: Konark Publishers.

———— (1997), *United Nations: At Fifty*, New Delhi: Konark Publishers.

Norton Moore, John (1977), *The Arab-Israeli Conflict*, Princeton, N.J.: Princeton University Press.

Rikhye, Indar Jit (2000), *The Politics and Practice of Peacekeeping: Past, Present, and Future*, Clementsport, Canada: Lester B. Pearson Canadian International Peacekeeping Center.

———— (1984), *The Theory and Practice of Peacekeeping*, London: C. Hurst.

———— (1977), with Michael Harbottle and Bjorn Egge, *The Thin Blue Line*, New Haven, Conn., and London: Yale University Press.

United Nations (1996), *The Blue Helmets*, Third edn., New York: United Nations, Department of Public Information.

Urquhart, Brian (1972), *Hammarskjöld*, New York: Alfred A. Knopf.

———— (1987), *A Life in Peace and War*, New York: Harper & Row.

———— *Ralph Bunche, An American Life*, New York and London: W.W. Norton.

U Thant (1978), *View from the UN, The Memoirs of U Thant*, Garden City, N.Y.: Doubleday.

Wainhouse, David W. et al. (1966), *International Peace Observation*, Baltimore: John Hopkins University Press.

———— (1973), *International Peacekeeping at the Cross Roads*, Baltimore: John Hopkins University Press.

Index